Mock On!

Lax

brand
new
day

the highs
and lows
of starting
a small business

Lara Solomon creator of

Published by LaRoo Pty Ltd
Suite 1,
6, Powells Road,
Brookvale
NSW 2100 Australia
www.LaRoo.com.au

First published by LaRoo Pty Ltd, 2008

Text copyright © Lara Solomon 2008

The moral right of the author has been asserted

Cover design by Cobalt Creative www.cobaltcreative.com.au
Edited by Spin Drift Media, www.Spindriftmedia.com.au
Proofread by Vanessa Winter
Typeset by Inconceivable Enterprises www.inconceivableenterprises.com
Book name thought up by Jake Solomon www.suddenstatechange.com

Printed and bound in China

National Library of Australia
Cataloguing-in-Publication data:
Solomon, Lara, 1975-

Brand New Day : The Highs and Lows of Starting a Small business

1st ed.

ISBN: 9780980521504

1. New business enterprises--Australia--Planning. 2. Small business--Australia--Planning. 3. New products--Australia.

Dewey Number: 658.11410994

This book is dedicated in loving memory to my Dad, without his ongoing support, love and challenging me in my business, my dreams would have been far harder to realise.

My Dad's favourite quote
"all effort is in vain, strive unremittingly"
Leslie Solomon

What's it all about?

The day I finally decided to go into business for myself, my life changed completely. I had dreamed about it since I was a little girl … *Brand New Day* is a true story (names have been changed) in diary format of my journey from starting a business from nothing, launching an unknown product and brand into the market and making it a success!

The idea for Mocks came to me when I was on my honeymoon in Thailand in 2003. There I saw socks for mobiles being sold. The quality was very poor, the designs were unappealing, but overall the concept worked. What appealed to me about the sock idea was that one size fitted all mobiles, so the range would only have to include different designs, not different sizes. They were also really light and easy to send, but this wasn't something I'd really appreciate until later.

My diary starts at the beginning of 2004 when I was still working as a marketing manager for a US company based in Sydney. I left at the end of February 2004 to pursue my dream. My diary tells it how it was starting a business from scratch with a teeny, tiny budget and a lot of hard work. My aim was to write a completely honest story, with both the good and not so good, so anyone going into business, thinking about it or already in it can read it, get ideas and feel inspired to reach their dream.

2004
January 2004

I've had a long think over Christmas, and I have decided that I need to break out of corporate life, and my current role of Marketing Manager for an electrical appliances company. I love the marketing, but I just can't face working for someone else any more; it is too restrictive. I have my own ideas of what to do and how to do it. Working for someone just doesn't give me the autonomy and responsibility to do that.

I am job hunting with a passion this month. I'm trying to find a part-time role to go to from here. It would be great to leave at the end of March, but that's only three months away. Meanwhile I need to start looking into business ideas and get everything set up to leave. Mr Johns (my husband) has said he will support me, but I've had to agree to go back to a paid job if I haven't paid myself from my business within a year of leaving my job. I really have to make this work. I really believe that hard work, will power and passion will go a long way for me. Mr Johns says he's pretty sure he married me because of my determination to make things happen ...

A few different ideas – like socks for mobiles, websites, a new store, a game and special shower caps for covering food – are bobbing around in my head at the moment. I want to investigate them all simultaneously. I think the socks for mobiles will be a goer. They personalise mobile phones and protect them from getting scratched, and will really appeal to teenagers. When I saw a similar product sold in the markets in Thailand last year I thought people would be interested. I love the one I bought, as does everyone I've shown it to. I'll need to improve on the designs, packaging and quality of the product, plus think of a brand name, but I love all that marketing stuff so it will be fun. I need to think about the size of the socks. Hilariously, some of the mobile socks I saw in Thailand were actually babies' socks with the heel sewn in. That didn't look good! I can improve on that ... baby socks are definitively the way to go, but without the heel.

I still need to persuade the backers, which I think at the moment

2

means Mum and Dad. I can't see the bank lending me anything, and Mr Johns isn't keen. Business plan writing, here I come.

Monday 19th January 2004

I had a disappointing day at work today. Not surprisingly, the so-called monthly sales and marketing meeting at work was cancelled, yet again by my boss. I know that we are busy, but I think it is really important that we are all on the same page and know what is going on, which was the point of the meeting. My feeling is that teamwork within the business really isn't working at all when members of the team aren't willing to attend meetings. When I have my business going I will make sure I stick by what I say, otherwise I really think there is no point.

Tuesday 27th January 2004

Things are getting very hard at work. I will have to keep a record of the time I am in the office, in case I need it. I got told off for having a sick day last Friday because it was before the long weekend. I was told I need a doctor's note – where is the trust?

Thursday 29th January 2004

I had another run-in today with the boss. She is awful at facing conflict; she will only tell me off on the phone, not in person. When she was out today she called me on the phone regarding a meeting I didn't attend. I didn't think it was relevant for me to attend, and I did tell the organisers. I probably should have let her know too, but I didn't think it was a big deal. I am getting frustrated as I really want to be spending my time on my own idea, only two months to go until I plan to leave, but I'm not sure I can last …

Business bank account balance: no account yet
Mood: ☹

February 2004

Monday 2nd February 2004

I came into work today to find a note on my desk saying that I had a formal warning. It was for a number of very silly things, like leaving to go to the doctor last Friday, it was a good thing I had got a doctor's note; I'd had a feeling it was going to be a problem. I had to

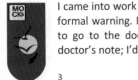

meet with her today to discuss it, it did not go well. I couldn't believe that my boss said she'd prefer me to go to the doctor during the day rather than at the end of the day, even if it means being out for three hours rather than one! I handed in my notice at the end, which made her very cross, but that's OK. It's done now. I just need to concentrate on getting through the next four weeks, and then I can focus completely on my business. I hadn't planned to hand in my notice today, but to be honest, I have completely had enough of being here.

Mr Johns agreed I'd done the right thing – I think he's fed up with me moaning to him about how much I hate my job. He still doesn't think my business will really take off; he imagines I'll spend my days watching daytime TV ... I don't think that one year is going to be a problem; I will have my business running by then, I am sure. My manager in my first job told me I was very tenacious. It might also help that my star sign is Taurus, but I am not sure I believe that; maybe it's more related to my age – 28 years old.

Tuesday 10th February 2004

I spoke to a graphic design friend, Gina today about the designs for my company logo. I've found it really hard to find a business name that works and that is available as a website, but finally I have decided on LaRoo as the company name – a combination of Lara and roo from kangaroo because we are in Australia. It was Mr Johns' idea, and a good one. I love the idea of reinforcing that my company is Australian, even though I am originally from the UK. It makes me laugh that Mr Johns sees himself as an Aussie now, even though he's from the UK as well. I find it funny writing "Mr Johns" when he's my husband, but I think it separates him from the business in my mind.

Unfortunately for the website, I've had to go with a .com.au as the .com was taken. It's a bit annoying, but I guess it reinforces the Australian company angle.

I am so glad I have Gina onboard to help me. When I met her last year in one of my previous roles we got on so well, then when she started her own design agency it seemed like the perfect match. I will really enjoy working with Gina, especially as she is going to do the logo for me as a favour, and then I will pay her for the Mock designs – I just love friends ...

Monday 16th February 2004

I have been busy searching on a fantastic global sourcing website – alibaba.com – for a supplier to make the mobile socks for me. I searched under baby socks today, which I think are around the right size for mobiles. There were something like 150 different suppliers, so quite a long list to go through to find what I need.

Monday 23rd February 2004

Only a week left at work. I am so excited, I can't wait to finish. I have got the home office all set up with a computer, printer and broadband internet. I have managed to get a waitressing job at a chocolate cafe in Manly. I go for a trial on Sunday; if it is good the hours will work well: 6.30am to 3pm three days a week. I'll have the afternoons free to work on my business. I figure that working on my business for two days should be enough for now, and will keep Mr Johns happy as I would be contributing to the household.

The business plan is all written. I just need to finalise a few things, such as the supplier, my exact approach to get stores selling the socks and sales forecast for the year.

Business bank account balance: no account yet
Mood: ☺

March 2004

Monday 1st March 2004

The first day of my new adventure ... I went to Kirribilli markets on Saturday. It was busy, but people just aren't buying the Zippy purses - purses made solely from zips. I still have around 300 in stock from the 400 I initially bought when I saw them in Thailand on our honeymoon last year. It seemed like a great idea at the time, and the market research was really positive, but now in the real world, people struggle to understand why you need a purse made of zips. I explain that it is a design feature, but they find it hard to grasp. I use mine a lot, but despite my grand plans, I can already see that this isn't going to be the product that I can make a living from – I just won't sell enough. I think my mobile socks are going to be huge. Everyone has a mobile phone, but not everyone wants a purse made of zips!

I had my first full day of work at the chocolate place. The people are lovely; the only problem is that I can eat whatever I like when I'm working, today I had waffles with melted chocolate and strawberries, yum. This job isn't really good for my figure ... seeing as I am such a chocoholic.

I organised a PO Box today at the post office in Manly, where I live. I think it is more professional than using just my home address, although I will put both on my business cards. I say "suite", though as it sounds so much more businesslike than "unit".

Wednesday 3rd March 2004

I am still excited about my business ideas. I had another day at the chocolate place today, and I am in there again tomorrow, I am enjoying meeting different people, and it is a fun place to work, plus I get on really well with the manager. I rather enjoyed spending yesterday at home just doing my own thing. I don't find it hard to work from home at all – I love it!

I finally managed to configure Outlook to get my Hotmail emails. It was quite a challenge and took a while. I guess that working on my own I'll have to do it all. Luckily, Mr Johns is good with PCs, so that helps. I worked out the profit and loss statement for the socks today, and I have finished the business plan. I just need to check that it all makes sense. I have worked out that I need to borrow around $12,000 to buy the socks. I want to put the plan to Mum and Dad to get them to lend me the cash. I think it is better to be formal about money. It works better for me, then I don't forget anything.

I have also been in contact with a few recruitment agencies looking for temp work. The chocolate place doesn't pay well – $10 an hour for the first two weeks, then it increases to $12 – I could get paid a lot more doing temp work.

Wednesday 10th March 2004

I've had a busy few days signing on at recruitment agencies. It takes so long, and usually they can't find you anything, but I guess it is just one of those things. I met up with Gina the designer last Friday and we discussed the sock designs and what I was looking for, so that we can get the designs going. I also saw the first logo designs. They are coming along, but are just not quite right yet. The logo is a tricky one; it needs to be used in print, Web and TV, sewn and basically re-created as easily as possible, so it has to be simple.

I am still trying to get the Zippy purses out there. I called the David Jones and Myer department stores today, but no luck. I couldn't get hold of the buyers, so I sent them information. Since the Zippy purses haven't worked I have decided I don't want to put all my eggs in one basket, so now I have four different projects on the go: mobile phone socks, shower caps for food containers, a shoe store for large sizes and a game. I will see which one develops first and I will focus on that one.

Today I called up a friend from a place I used to work to ask a favour. I wanted some market data for one of my projects. It is great that I have previously worked in the fast-moving consumer goods industry, so I know what I am looking for and where to find it. Knowing the size of the market and the opportunity really helps when I'm working out the sales and what to expect in regards to the business plan.

I chatted to Gina today about the sock designs, and we discussed branding. I know that eventually I will want to sell the brand, so it needs to have a different name to my company. I want to hang onto the company name. After much brainstorming, I decided on the brand name Mocks. Mocks is a combination of "mobile" and "socks". It fits well, and could apply to mobile phones or to mobile items in general, like digital cameras, iPods, make-up, keys and more. So now I need a logo for Mocks as well. It has to appeal to the target audience, which I have determined, by asking people, to be predominantly teens to start with. I will use the logo on the actual sock as well as in advertising and on the website. I want something that stands out really well, but also fits with the brand personality.

Friday 12th March 2004

I finished the Mocks business plan today and emailed it over to Dad and Mum, who live in France, for feedback. I am sure it won't be a problem borrowing the cash. I found it was a good exercise to write the plan, since there were a few things I realised I had overlooked. I also wrote a list of questions for the accountants I'm interviewing next week. I have five lined up for interview; I want to find someone I can work with long term, hence the list of questions. Interviewing them is rather formal, but I know it will help me decide who to choose. I think that an accountant is a very important part of my business, and I need to make sure that I get the right one. I don't want to be changing every year.

I started a new ideas folder this week, so that I capture everything that comes up, and it will help spark off other new ideas.

I finished up at the chocolate place today, although I enjoyed it I found that eating as much chocolate as I wanted was not doing my figure any good! Plus the temp work seems to be coming in now.

Tuesday 16th March 2004

I interviewed three accountants today; I like the one based in Manly best so far. One guy I saw was so stuck in the 1980s it was ridiculous, from the furniture to the people in the office. I know I shouldn't judge a book by its cover, but they really didn't look with it. Also I went to Weight Watchers today, in that never-ending battle of weight loss, although this time it will be different. Third time lucky on the program! I managed to lose 500g this week. I'm quite pleased with that for my fourth week.

I'm doing some work for Mr Johns' hockey club. I have put myself in charge of sponsorship, only because no-one else wanted to do it. I have written a number of proposals to ask for money or equipment and sent them out; I am hoping that I will learn a lot from it since I haven't really done this before.

I spent yesterday in the library researching various projects. They have a great selection of trade magazines, so I got lots of useful info. To make it easier to estimate sales, I was trying to find out about the size of the mobile accessories market and the mobile market in general: how old mobile users are and how many there are in each age group. I'm not very good at estimating sales; I tend to get *very* carried away. I remember when I was doing the first business plan for the Zippy purses, my first year of sales on the first set of financials was $4 million – needless to say I didn't achieve it! Better to aim high is what I say, but I need to be a bit realistic ...

I have found a company in western Sydney that owns a sock factory in China. They are going to make some samples of Mocks for me, so I can see what the quality is like. I think that they could be good as a supplier, because they have fluent English and they are based here, rather than overseas.

Friday 19th March 2004

I had an interview today for a part-time marketing job, two days a week. It sounds good, but the guy was a bit vague, and I am concerned that it might turn out to be a lot more hours than I really want, but I will wait and see if he wants me first. My other concern is that it could require a lot of energy to get it going, as they haven't done much yet. I know how excited and how passionate I get about ideas, and I am worried it might distract me from focusing my energy on Mocks.

I did some reception work this afternoon. Reception is a great temp job. Normally it is dead quiet and they don't have any extra work even when I ask for it, so I can get on with what I want to do and they don't mind as long as I look busy. I guess that I need to watch for that when I have employees, and keep them busy.

I finished the Mocks questionnaire yesterday. I want to get it out and see what people actually think of the designs and the whole concept. I really need to talk to at least 100 teens. I think will go round the shopping mall. It's the largest one on the Northern Beaches in Sydney, so there should be a few teens hanging out there! I will see who I can find.

I emailed lastminute.com.au yesterday to talk to them about listing Zippy purses on their website. I hope they take them – fingers crossed. I need to sell them off, as I could really use the money.

Wednesday 24th March 2004

It's been busy, busy so far this week. I had two days' work at Streets ice-cream in the marketing department. It was well paid, but kind of strange, since I was reporting to a girl that used to work with me, and who reported to me then. It was all fine; it was nice to be working with someone I know and who knows me.

I had a meeting this morning with a buyer for the biggest newsagency in Manly. It's my favourite newsagency – I'm in there every week and I really think they'd work. I showed her the purses, but she just wasn't keen. To be honest I am not sure if I should keep pushing the purses. I am going to give myself until Friday to decide, I can't keep going on forever, especially with next to no positive feedback. I am hoping that the Mocks will go much better. I also called the David Jones department store again today and left another message. I find it frustrating that they can't at least call to say "thanks but no thanks".

I saw a law firm on Monday for an introductory meeting. I want to get lawyers sorted out before I get properly underway so that I know who to go to if I have a problem.

I've put together the Mocks presentation for retail stores, ready to send to buyers. I'm still waiting on the sample from the factory, but at least I can get the ball rolling. I have already identified through my business plan which stores I want to target and I have their contact details.

Friday 26th March 2004

I had lunch with Gina today. Great designs are coming together for the Mocks logo and the actual socks – very exciting! It's pretty amazing to see the ideas happening, and it won't be long until I can get the actual product. It's lovely chatting to Gina. Her business is doing so well – after such a short time, they already have some huge clients – plus she is so supportive.

I had an interview for another part-time job today, at a scrapbooking store. It was supposed to be to work on the shop floor, but after chatting it turned into me doing marketing for her. The pay is $20 per hour, so I'll see how it goes. It's a small business; my only concern with it is that she doesn't understand marketing.

I really have to get a Pantone book of colour swatches. I need to know the actual colour reference so I can tell the printers and manufacturers exactly which colours to use, and they can make the colours in the designs exactly as I want them. The books are *so* expensive – $300. Pantone advises that they are replaced every year. I don't think that will be happening; I will just look after it really well.

Wednesday 31st March 2004

I had a good results day today. Firstly I have arranged an appointment with Strathfield Car Radio, a chain of around 70 stores that sell car and music accessories. Secondly I got the email address for Steve, a buyer for Fone Zone, a big chain of 100 mobile phone stores, so I sent him the presentation. I am really excited to actually be talking to a buyer. I hope that they love the Mocks; I am sure they will. I also feel a bit nervous, as I don't feel that I am very good at negotiating, and they might start haggling on price. Steve sounded really friendly on the phone. It's great; I finally feel that the wheels are in motion!

I accepted the job at the scrapbooking store this week. It starts tomorrow, and it should be interesting, something quite different. I turned down the marketing role I went for a couple of weeks ago. It's nice to be in demand. I have Gina's team working on the Mocks front label for the packaging. I need to make sure we can say what we need to from a legal point of view. I've also been working on a stronger sales plan, after finishing reading a book about increasing sales. I don't really have that much experience in sales. I think that a lot of it is just getting out there – but lack of experience does make me feel slightly nervous.

Business bank account balance: no account yet
Mood: ☺ ☺

April 2004
Monday 5th April 2004

I found the name of a potential mobile phone store distributor for Mocks late last week. It would be so much easier for me to use a distributor. It depends on how much they would charge, but it would certainly save me a lot of time and effort. I am finding that a lot of mobile chain stores buy from them, and to get into those stores I would need to go through the distributor. I will see what happens.

I set up a FedEx account over the weekend. It will be useful if I have to send packages back and forth to China. Although I know it's not the cheapest way to send items, it's a cost of doing business …

Now I'm keeping two different to do lists in my diary: one for LaRoo and one for scrapbooking. It could get confusing otherwise.

I sent off my business cards for printing today – very exciting … I can't wait to start handing them out. I will probably have to send Mum and Dad about 100, just for them!

Tuesday 13th April 2004

I just got back yesterday from the Easter long weekend – a six-hour drive inland to stay with a friend, but it was a lot of fun.

I did two days' work at the scrapbooking place last week so I didn't have a whole lot of time to work on Mocks. I had a good conversation with Tom, the Dick Smith Electronics buyer, on Thursday about Mocks, but I had to leave messages for everyone else. Dick Smith would be a great chain to get into since they sell mobile phones, digital cameras and MP3 players.

I decided that I need a backup option for the sock manufacturing in case I don't go with the company in western Sydney, so today I organised samples from a supplier in China – Mr Gao. I am expecting them this week, I found him on the sourcing website Alibaba.com; I hope they turn out well.

I am still investigating two of my other ideas, so I am splitting my time up a lot, but I think the Mocks idea will work. The buyer at Harvey Norman electronics has agreed to a meeting about Mocks, I just need to arrange a date. Great news.

Tuesday 20th April 2004

I haven't had any feedback from Tom at Dick Smith yet, but that isn't necessarily bad. He was very friendly, and at least he talks to me. I also sent information on Mocks last week to two other chains: Big W department store – they'd be good because they sell prepaid mobiles as well as books, DVDs, clothes and practically everything else, and they get a lot of traffic in their stores; and Digicall, which has 60 Vodafone mobile stores. I called today to follow up, but no answer; I left a message. I'm never sure how long to leave calling back. Leave it too long and they've forgotten about you; make it too soon and they haven't had time to read the info. I think it's a fine line.

I love having the PO Box in Manly; it gives me a reason to get out for fresh air every day. It's only a ten-minute walk, but it's good to get out and about. Not that I really need an excuse, but if I know I have to do it I structure it into my day.

I finished a one pager on Mocks today. I wanted to have an A4 page with all the critical information on it so I could leave it with buyers when I see them. It will make it easier for them to remember everything. I just need to finalise the price list now. Each design is going to be the same price – I've already decided that, but the actual price is a bit trickier. I think that they should retail for $7.50, based on what else is out there in the market, so I will start at that price point and work backwards.

I also decided today that I really need a fax machine. Even though I thought that the age of faxes was dying, it seems that people still like to fax, small retailers especially. I put a bid on one today on eBay.

Wednesday 21st April 2004
Hurray! I have a meeting set up on 3rd May with the Harvey Norman buyer ... Big win!

Friday 23rd April 2004
I went and opened a business bank account today with St George. It has a special offer with six months' free banking, and I have to say I was sucked in. I haven't banked with them before, but their business section seems good, and to be honest most of the banks offer pretty much the same deals – well, it looks that way to me. I paid in $10 to start my account off; the next money paid in has to be from sales.

I managed to fit in a one-hour walk today. I have been trying to get out every day this week, but I get so involved in work, I don't always get around to it. Sometimes I am just so engrossed that time flies – I love that!

Tuesday 27th April 2004
I won the fax machine on eBay: $52 ... Mr Johns thinks I am crazy, but as usual I am not listening to him. I have a *hugely huge* meeting on Thursday with Steve, the buyer for Fone Zone. I am really excited. This will be my first face-to-face meeting with a mobile chain store buyer, and could be the start of Mocks. I am flying to Brisbane for the afternoon; it's only an hour each way from Sydney.

Thursday 29th April 2004
I just got back from the airport and my meeting with Steve. It went well, I think. Steve was really nice, about my age, and very open to new ideas, I am pretty sure he liked them; I left him with a sample. Steve mentioned that he thought that Mocks could retail for $9.95 rather than the $7.50 I initially had in mind. Although I don't want to charge consumers more, in reality I can't force stores to charge a certain price. If I know that the stores will sell them for $9.95, I can factor that into my selling price. I tried to persuade him to take the

Mocks, or even just do a trial in a few stores. I need to follow him up next week once he has had time to think about it.

Business bank account balance: $10
Mood: ☺ ☺ ☺

May 2004
Monday 3rd May 2004
I sent a thankyou note and some chocolates to Steve. I think it is important that he knows that I appreciate him giving up his time to talk to me, even if he doesn't take Mocks. Chocolates are always good to put people in the right mood!

I'm really pleased that lastminute.com.au decided to take the Zippy purses. I invoiced them today for the first time for what they have sold. They are selling a few, and every bit helps. Once they are all sold, that will be it; I'm definitely not reordering.

My Dad recommended a new online foreign exchange place to me today – ozforex.com.au. It seems like a great process; I can book the transfer online and transfer the funds to OzForex, which then pays the recipient. It will be much easier than organising it through the bank, especially since once the Mocks take off I will need to pay my suppliers in US dollars, rather than Australian dollars.

The fax machine arrived today, my eBay purchase. Only one problem: it doesn't work. I will have to arrange a refund. The guy seemed fine on the phone, so it shouldn't be a problem, but still rather annoying.

Thursday 6th May 2004
I've had a crazy week. I worked at the scrapbooking store yesterday and got through quite a bit, but I find it hard to promote someone else's business when I really want to be working on my own. I am still calling and following up stores about Mocks. I was supposed to have a meeting with the Harvey Norman buyer this afternoon, but it got cancelled. I am hoping I can reschedule it, since they would be a good retailer to get into. I was disappointed that the meeting was cancelled. I hope he's not fobbing me off.

I have organised a social at the local Thai restaurant to raise funds for Mr Johns' hockey club. It will give everyone a chance to get to know each other. I think it's kind of fun arranging these dos, but I couldn't do it as a full-time job.

Tonight I went to a talk on neurolinguistic programming. I love learning, especially about developing positive thinking and how to build better relationships with others. It was a good refresher for me from the weekend course I did last year. I really should practise it more. At the talk I won a free workshop day, except I can't go due to my birthday party. I visualised winning and it happened. The whole visualising something will happen really works for me, not every time, but probably six to seven times out of 10, and when it happens, I always find it very weird ...

Thursday 13th May 2004

A *huge* day today. I had meetings with Ken at Strathfield and John at Digicall, a very *big* deal! Both the buyers were nice. Ken was interested and seemed enthusiastic; I left some samples and he wants to show people and get back to me. John was much more enthusiastic; he really liked them and wanted to know about merchandising. He is keen to take them, but wants to me develop a display stand for them to be used in stores, which is a good idea, it means that Mocks will be more likely to be merchandised on the counter, therefore more people will see them. Woohoo!

I called Steve at Fone Zone, there is still no answer about putting Mocks into stores. He hasn't shown them to the sales guys for feedback, so I will have to call back next week. I left another message for Tom at Dick Smith. All this chasing sure takes time. I did some marketing consulting work for a sandwich store today. The scrapbook store owner referred him to me – I must be doing something right.

I had a meeting with the company in western Sydney that has a factory in China. They are going to make a sample, but the price will be higher than going directly to the factory. I think I will see what the sample is like and go from there. I keep finding that so much of starting this business is complete trial and error.

Tonight I went to the Yellow Pages Business Idea Grants entry night to find out about entering and what is expected. The prizes are cash, which would be very useful, plus the exposure would be good. It was at Randwick Race course in Sydney, all rather formal. There were about 200 people there, and I didn't really get to talk to many of them. The presenters ran through the entry criteria and what they were looking for. I am definitely going to enter; it looks like the application form will take a while, though. I chatted to the winner from last year. I didn't really understand her concept, as it hasn't been built yet, and she didn't want to tell us much. She kept mentioning non-disclosure agreements. It sounds like she got anyone and everyone involved in her business to sign them so that no-one could spill the beans … It's probably a good idea; I will add it to my growing to-do list. The grant sounds appropriate for me, as it is all about innovation in small businesses and giving you the money to develop your innovation further. I think a Mock is an innovation.

Wednesday 19th May 2004

I spent the weekend in Launceston with Mr Johns, staying with friends, which was lovely, although very cold! I just got back today. I have to say I like managing my own time, just working when it works for me. It's much more my scene, especially as I like working in the evenings. Although, I have had to put an "open/closed" sign on the office door, so that Mr Johns knows when I am working, otherwise he just pops in for a chat – very distracting.

Friday was hectic. I had meetings with plastic companies about getting the display stand made for Digicall. The guys at Warringah Plastics seemed best. It's a plastics company based in Sydney that already makes display stands for various companies, so they were very switched on to what I want. I wrote a quite detailed brief so that we were all clear about what was happening, I have realised over the past few months that most people in small business don't do that; they keep it more verbal. I find that writing the brief clarifies things in my head, apart from the fact it makes it easier for the supplier. Definitely something I want to keep up. Needless to say

I took non-disclosures for both companies to sign. I can't be too careful, as the Yellow Pages Business Idea Grant winner mentioned.

Monday 24th May 2004

I had a busy end to the week last week. I had to catch up on my scrapbooking hours, so I went to several playgroups to promote scrapbooking. I also had a meeting with a guy from a mobile accessory distribution company. It currently distributes mobile accessories to several of the mobile phone retail chains, so could potentially distribute Mocks for me. The guy didn't seem to think that Mocks would work, but is going to get back to me on a price, so I'll see. I find that guys in particular find the whole Mock concept hard to understand, and really don't think it will go anywhere. Sometimes I feel that I am pushing a heavy truck backwards up a hill! But I *know* they will sell. I just *know* it; I have *no* doubt in my mind, and if they don't believe in the product then I don't really want them selling it.

I did more calling to follow up Dick Smith and Strathfield. It gets frustrating. I just can't believe the time it takes to make a decision … surely it's not that hard?

Warringah Plastics are making me a dummy display stand, so I can see if it's what I want. It also means I can then get artwork done and present it to John at Digicall. The stand is a good idea. The Mocks are pretty small in their bags, so this will make them stand out on the shelf. I can put branding and an explanation about Mocks on the stand, which will help customers when they are buying them in store.

I have found another potential distributor for Mocks, and once I have the quote from the first company I can compare the pricing. I have applied for bar codes for the packaging. Each Mock design will need its own bar code, there's an annual fee for barcodes unfortunately. I'm glad I've had experience marketing supermarket brands, so I know that each product needs a bar code if it's going to be sold into the large stores, to be scanned at the checkout. I could start without bar codes, but it would limit who I can sell to and I'd just have to go back and add them later, so it wouldn't save me any money.

It's funny, when I started working on Mocks I wrote down a list of everything in the business plan that I needed to do based on my experience, but I am finding that as a smaller company, I can sometimes do things a bit differently. It's definitely hard working with the mobile phone retail chains. With the supermarkets I worked with before, there were set head office rules for each department, so I knew what to expect, whereas mobile store chains seem to vary with the buyer.

Friday 28th May 2004

I got the sample from the sock company in western Sydney this week, and I have decided that it is way too expensive compared with what I can get direct from China, and the quality is really no better. The company I have found in China seems just as good. I put together an action plan for Mocks for this week. There is still a lot to do to get ready to launch in August!

I have been in touch with magazines this week about advertising – it is unlikely that I will advertise because, to be honest, I just can't afford it. It shocked me to find out that one page in a teen magazine is $10,000. I am getting to know to the best person to contact by talking to the magazines. Hopefully I can organise some PR with them, such as product giveaways – which are free, apart from the product. I know the monthly magazines all work three months in advance for each issue, so I need to get onto it now to get into August/September issues.

I had another job interview today for a part-time role. I need something a bit more basic to do while I am starting up, as I just don't have the energy and enthusiasm to focus on another business. This role was just admin tasks, but I don't think that I am really keen on it. I'll see.

Total stores: 0
Business bank account balance: $1,237 (from Zippy purse sales and $1,000 of my own money)

Mood: ☺

June 2004
Friday 4th June 2004

I had a meeting with Tom at Digicall this week. He loves the display stand with six hooks because it is so simple; it will sit on the counter and isn't too tall. He just wants to see it with the artwork so he can sign it off. Great news. Looks like that's one chain down, only the rest to conquer! I am still following up the two distributors regarding pricing. They are hard to get hold of. I am guessing that they are inundated with requests for distribution and it's not a high priority for them.

I love thinking up new business ideas. My ideas notebook is definitely getting fuller. Unfortunately I just don't have time to work on them all. One new idea that I think might work is a trivia game to play on the go. I put together a presentation, emailed it off to buyers at department stores, and am following it up. I know it's going to take a while to hear from them. I personally think it's a great idea, but I don't want to get it made until I have definite interest, as it would just cost too much. At least with the Mocks I can show them a physical sample and the designs on paper, and it doesn't cost much.

I am still waiting on my bar code numbers to be delivered. Hopefully they'll come through soon, as I need them for the artwork on the Mocks packaging.

I have started to look at the option of doing my own distribution. The distributors are so slow at getting back to me that it doesn't really bode well for the business relationship. This will mean that I need a courier company to pick up the parcels from me and send them to stores. The Mocks are cheap and light, so I need to get one which is inexpensive and ideally on a prepaid rate so I know how much I am going to spend and can work it into the price of the Mocks.

I had my favourite top stolen off the clothes line today – very, very annoying. Apparently no-one in the unit block saw anything, which I find very hard to believe, but it led me to thinking that I really need pegs that have a security device fitted so an alarm goes off if people try to remove your washing without deactivating the peg. Sounds like a good idea to me, but also one filled with flaws, such as the fact that a really windy day or rain could damage the alarm in the pegs, or if no-one is listening out it wouldn't really do much. It's an appealing idea in principle, I think, but it needs more work!

Monday 7th June 2004

I finally bought a Pantone book today to give me the colour references. Gina says I could just ask to use her agency's book each time I need it, but that is causing me delays, so after much deliberation I spent the $300.

I have written a funky Mocks press release booklet. It is mobile phone shaped, the front and back are laminated and the middle pages have the information on them. I plan to send them out to the magazines later this week. It's very different from just a plain page, but I want it to stand out and be memorable.

I spent time today updating the business plan and financials. A lot of it is guesstimates, therefore I need to keep revisiting it to check that it still makes sense. Sometimes I look at the plan and wonder how I will achieve it all, but then I think that it's just going to take a while! I will have lots of to-do lists to get me to the goals. Bit by bit I can chip away.

Sunday 13th June 2004

I've just got back from Avalon markets on the Northern Beaches in Sydney, selling the Zippy purses. Not a huge number of sales. Interest yes, but sales no. I have found that this does seem to be the case with markets; people are browsing and not really buying. They think it is nice to wander round and browse. However, it is good to get the feedback. A lot of people don't really understand why the purse has so many zips – the fact that it is a design feature seems to pass them by. I do tell them that it means that you can open the top, bottom or middle of the purse, which means that items don't fall to the bottom.

The Pantone book arrived this week from the US, it turned out that online was the cheapest place to buy it. I have been busy using it to decide on colours for the Mocks designs I want made in China, I have set up a product sheet with the picture, name, model number, bar code and colours on it so that each time I fill in the same information for each design and don't forget anything, plus it will make it easier when I come to reorder.

I have got another job this week, working one day a week just doing admin at a speed reading place. It will require less brainwork, so I can use all my energy on my business.

I spoke to Dad today. He and Mum have agreed to lend me the $12,900 I need for the first order of Mocks, and transferred it over to me today. Dad thought my business plan was good. We discussed it quite a bit, as he wanted to make sure that I had looked at all the options. I'm not too worried about borrowing the money from them. If this doesn't work, which it will, I could repay that amount in a year if I went and got another job. It's lovely to know that they believe in me enough to lend it to me.

Friday 18th June 2004

I worked my first day at the new admin job this week. Quite an odd place; they seem to be exceptionally disorganised, but maybe it is just how it looks to me. The girl I am taking over from trained me; it is going to be a very easy job.

I got the final design of the Mocks stand; it looks great. I think it explains really well what I want. I sent over the design to Digicall and Fone Zone, so hopefully they will give me some feedback and we can go forward. I am also looking at lanyards as a potential product extension; as they can be attached to mobiles and the mobile can be worn hanging from the strap, they're definitely in the same kind of accessory arena. I have had some samples sent to me, but am just not sure of the potential here in the market. They sell really cheaply in some stores, and I don't know if they are really a fashion accessory or just something useful. More research is required.

I have been looking at getting an accounting package to use, to do invoicing etc. I was looking at MYOB, but then I entered a competition and won a copy of QuickBooks – saving a *huge* amount of cash. I seem to win a lot; my theory is that not many small businesses enter these competitions. So far this year I have won two copies of Microsoft Office Small Business and this QuickBooks program, not bad ... I found a QuickBooks trainer, Ella, through the QuickBooks website. She came over and trained me today for two hours, and is coming back next week to cover more with me. I haven't done any accounts work since university and that wasn't invoicing, so it's good I pick things up quickly. It is really pretty straightforward, but it's important to do it right, as otherwise it could cause me grief at tax time. Speaking of tax time, it is not far away - June 30.

Part of the Fone Zone ordering process is that as a supplier I have to be able to accept and process files by Electronic Data Interchange (EDI). I met Global Exchange today and found out about what they can do. They have worked with Woolworths and Coles supermarkets as well as for smaller companies like my teeny, tiny one. The software will save me so much time; it means that the orders are imported into QuickBooks and turned into invoices at the touch of a button, rather than me typing them all out. The software I need is going to cost about $3,500, so obviously I won't be investing in it until Fone Zone is a definite, but at least I now know that I can do it, so it means that I can satisfy their requirements. Now I just need the order!

I bought a new fax machine today from a store for $99. Luckily I got a refund on the other one I bought on eBay. This one is pretty basic, but will do everything I need.

I have decided to use Toll couriers for my deliveries. The rep came and spoke to me, and they offer a prepaid service, which is perfect for what I need. The bags come in different sizes, and it is the same price for each bag of a certain size regardless of where I am sending them. It makes it easy for me to know how much the costs are, and will make budgeting much easier for me, if I know the average number of orders and the average number of Mocks per order. I can fit 100 Mocks in the 1kg bag and it is still under 1kg in weight ... I love that Mocks are so little and light. If I get into any other products I will not be going with big and heavy!

Tuesday 22nd June 2004

I had a *thrilling* morning today – *not*! I went to a morning of EAN bar code training from 9am until 1pm, and talk about boring. It was awful; the information was helpful, but could have been covered in a fraction of the time, like 30 minutes. I got the impression that pretty much everyone is the room was as thrilled to be there as I was. All I can say is thank goodness I don't have a job where I need to know lots and lots about barcoding – I'd be asleep in five minutes.

I flew down to Melbourne on the weekend with Mr Johns. He was there for business so we stayed at the Park Hyatt – my favourite hotel. They have a TV in the bathroom, so I lay in a fantastic bubble bath watching TV. I felt like a real lady of leisure ... I squeezed in a meeting with a guy about my project where I could potentially use special shower caps as food covers. It is a good product that works. There is already a company doing this, but they are about to close the division, as at $5 million it isn't a big enough market for them in Australia, but it would be fine for me. He can do what I want, but the minimum order quantities are huge, so I am not sure if a) the product interests me enough to take it further or b) if I see enough potential in the market. At least I have the information now to make a decision. To be honest, this is an idea that Mum and Dad love and would use, but I myself do not really get excited by it. I want to be passionate about my product, as it comes through to everyone I meet, and will make selling it much easier for me.

Friday 25th June 2004

I spent today at St Ives shopping centre in Sydney, selling the scrapbooking bits and promoting scrapbooking. I had a stand there, and in some ways it was useful for me, as I could evaluate it as an activity for my business. It was a pretty quiet day, but I sold enough to cover the cost of the stand, and gave out a lot of information on the shop, so it was successful, I think, but my boss wasn't quite so positive. She seems to want instant results, but she doesn't seem to understand that you need to build awareness for the product/brand first, and to do that you need to spend money. I think I will leave soon, as it is frustrating working in a place where what you are trying to do is not really understood.

I spoke to a patent lawyer this week, to see if Mocks can be patented. The answer was no, since there are already mobile phone socks, such as the ones I saw in Thailand, out in the market, but at least now I know. Previously when I have mentioned Mocks to people like my friends, designers and family, they have always said, "You should patent that". I guess that they are trying to help, and I'd love to patent the idea, but it is just not possible. I know that I can be headstrong and like to do things my way, but I do take their comments onboard. It's the repetition that gets to me sometimes.

I had a good workout last night with my friend Katherine and her boyfriend. I so need to do exercise, I never really want to do it, but I feel so much better afterwards. Thank goodness her boyfriend is a personal trainer.

Wednesday 30th June 2004

The last day of the financial year. It's been a busy few days, what with work and following up buyers. Rather annoyingly, the buyer at Digicall has changed, which means I now have to build the relationship all over again. Today I called the new guy, Josh. He is not convinced that Mocks will work. He sees it as a fad product that will leave him with lots of excess stock in the years to come. I couldn't say anything to persuade him otherwise, so I will just have to keep in contact and prove him wrong.

I set up a goods and services tax (GST) account today with the bank. It's free, and seems like a good idea. I am registered for GST, and I will save any GST I should be paying to the tax man in the bank account ready to pay the tax office at a later date; well, that's what I am going to try to do.

I started designing the Mocks website yesterday in Microsoft

FrontPage. It's very basic, but it will do until I can afford to get a proper one done. It's a pain to edit, as it is supposed to be "what you see is what you get" but it so isn't. When I put each page up on the internet it doesn't look the same as when I designed it. It's very frustrating. I hope the cash starts to roll in soon, so that it doesn't have to be up for long.

I got the details of potential mobile phone store distributors in New Zealand for Mocks. I want to achieve a lot in a short space of time, so I need to think big. There are only 4 million people in New Zealand versus 20 million in Oz, so it is never going to be a huge market. The way I see it is that I am really doing people a favour in providing them with a Mock. It's a public service, some would say. ☺

Total stores: 0
Business bank account balance: $14,419 (includes a loan from Dad of $12,900)
Mood: ☺ ☺

July 2004
Monday 5th July 2004
And so the new financial year starts – this is going to be the year that it all comes together and Mocks take off!

Today I have ordered some lollies that have the Mocks logo on them and are in the Mocks colours. The plan is to send them out to people when they order from the website. To order, customers will have to print off the order form, fill it in and send it in. I can also use the lollies to promote Mocks to buyers; it is something different. I am also looking at getting some Mocks-branded button badges made. I think it will really help increase brand awareness as people ask their friends "What are Mocks?" I can encourage people to write in for a free one; my target audience of teens love freebies.

I got my Yellow Pages Business Idea Grant application finished last week, so fingers crossed I will get it. I could really use the cash …

I have designed my own with compliments slips. I think it's a nice touch and they are so easy to print out. I have decided that all my invoices to customers will be on pink paper, for a few reasons: a) pink is my favourite colour, b) it will make them stand out in my office, as instantly recognisable as an invoice and c) they will be easy for customers, when I call I can say "Please pay the pink one".

My original press releases are taking *forever* to cut out because they're phone shaped, and there are eight phones for each release. I think that they look great, but there are so many steps involved, it's fortunate I only have 40 releases to do. I am getting Mr Johns to help while we are watching TV, but I wouldn't say he is an overly enthusiastic volunteer!

Thursday 8th July 2004

I am still trying to get an answer from Steve at Fone Zone, I know these guys are busy, but today I was told he is away until Monday. It's really frustrating when I just want an answer … grrr.

I have a new job, which I started yesterday, working at Dell. It's just in the customer service team, pretty easy and regular hours. I have given up all the other jobs. The hours were so unreliable at the admin place. A couple of mornings I turned up at 9am and no-one was there, so I sat on the doorstep for 30 minutes, plus I often finished early, which meant that I got paid less since I was paid at an hourly rate. Anyway, that's over now. The Dell job finishes at 4pm, and pays better, for only two days per week.

I was expecting to get the Mocks samples today via FedEx, but no joy. Hopefully tomorrow … so exciting – I can't wait!

Monday 12th July 2004

Great news today. Steve at Fone Zone got feedback from his sales team and is going to go with the Mocks. Hurray. A *huge* win. Yippee … I just need to get the EDI stuff set up now.

I have to work out my minimum order quantity for the small independent mobile stores that are run by the owners, so that at least I break even. At the moment I think I will just to get them to order 10 Mocks as a minimum. They need to try them and see how well they sell – which is going to be great, of course.

I'm still following up Josh at Digicall, but no joy there, and the other chains I am looking at are also hard to pin down. I haven't managed to rearrange that meeting with the Harvey Norman buyer yet either.

Friday 16th July 2004

The Dell job is proving to be very cruisy. I think next week I will be able to take in some of my work to do when there are no calls. They don't mind – fantastic!

Finally the press releases are finished. I am going to send them on Monday – hurray. I talked to Sandra, a friend of my friend Nora. Her business is product placement for TV shows, so she is going to try to get Mocks onto *Neighbours* and *Home and Away* – how cool. I've been watching *Neighbours* and *Home and Away* for years, so to see my product on them would be Mocktastic! These shows are the perfect audience for Mocks; it would really increase awareness for Mocks.

I finally had a meeting with Josh at Digicall yesterday. I made up a folder of all the designs and took the stand, samples and presentation I've done. He still wasn't overly enthused. He showed no interest in the product or the designs or what I am planning to do. He still seems to think the Mocks won't sell and is not willing to take a risk. I am not really sure what else I can do to persuade him.

I have finally got the meeting rearranged with the Harvey Norman buyer for Monday – I can't wait.

Monday 19th July 2004

The meeting went well with Fred at Harvey Norman. Well, that is to say he was interested in the product; however, I would need a sales team on the road to service every store because they use a franchise model. Each store is owned by a different owner and I'd need to have salespeople to go into each store and stock it up with Mocks. There are over 100 stores across Australia and they don't do the stocking themselves, which is a little bit of a problem since at the moment it is just me.

Friday 23rd July 2004

I followed up Sportsgirl teen clothing store and General Pants, skate/surf clothing store, today for the Zippy purses. I was hoping to get in to see the buyers. I think that they would sell really well in those stores – just the right amount of funkiness. I hope the buyers agree with me.

Still no Mocks samples ... they were supposed to be here by now.

Monday 26th July 2004

Woohoo! The samples arrived today. Very, very exciting ... I love them! There were just three of each design, and they all look great. The designs were the ones done by Gina and her team and researched by me at the shopping mall. There is Rabbit, Monkey, Aussie Flag, Ladybirds, Sea, Devil, Bear, Barcode, Flower, Animal Skin, Candy Stripes and Bubbles. The colours have come out really well; I am really pleased.

I have a new plan today. I am going to start targeting the small independent mobile stores that I can go and visit in Sydney. The Mocks should be here next month, so I can visit the stores and take orders, then deliver the order when they arrive. I got a list of stores from the Yellow Pages, and I'll start at the top ...

I got some cool jars for the Mocks lollies from Ikea, so I sent those out to all the buyers that I have seen so far. I want to keep Mocks top of mind with them.

The EDI software that I need to take orders from Fone Zone is now under development. I know it is a big punt for me to take at $3,500 when they are only committing to seven stores stocking them, but I am positive that Mocks are going to sell well. I know if I can say Fone Zone is taking Mocks and they are selling well for them, other chains will want to come onboard.

Friday 30th July 2004

Wow, another month gone. Time is going so fast. I went on an export course through the local business centre yesterday and picked up some tips on exporting, so I need to follow up the New Zealand distributors again and see if they are keen.

Great news, I got the list from Fone Zone of the seven stores that are going to take Mocks, three in Queensland and four in New South Wales – my first big chain.

I have been on the phone like crazy the last two days calling all the local mobile stores, and then emailing them some information. I have to do *a lot* of explaining. No-one gets it the first time, which I guess is to be expected, but it can get a little repetitive for me! I think Mocks are one of those products where people need to see the product to fully understand it.

I have to send the payment to China for the Mocks I ordered: $12,000 – a huge amount. Well it seems huge to me, but if it doesn't work out then the 24,000 Mocks will be a hell of a lot of Christmas and birthday presents for my friends!

Mocks sold this month: 0
Total stores: 0 officially, but 7 if you count Fone Zone, even though there are no Mocks in there yet!
Business bank account balance: $6,649
Mood: ☺ ☺

August 2004

Monday 2nd August 2004

According to the planned timings, the Mocks should leave China on 12th August and be here on 17th August. Not long now.

I looked in the bank account today and it's doing OK – I have $6,634, which is rather nice, but I do have to buy the stands, and all the mailing is adding up, but at least I don't need to pay myself yet. I still have six months.

Thursday 5th August 2004

I needed inspiration today, so I wrote this on the whiteboard:

POSITIVE THINKING = RESULTS

THINK BIG, ACT BIG, MAKE THINGS HAPPEN

I have to say it's hard doing all this cold-calling, having to be all bright and chirpy all the time. I am calling around 50 to 100 stores per day, and it does get repetitive.

I need to organise stands for Fone Zone now. They want to put them on their slat wall rather than on the counter, so the current stands will need a bit of modification. I'll have to pay for the stands for the stores, but I think that the Mocks will look much better on stands, rather than just on hooks on the wall, plus it gives consumers and store staff information on Mocks and will make them stand out on the wall.

I am still following up the department stores Target and Big W as well as mobile outlets like Retravision and Allphones, plus Australia Post and lots more... it all takes a while.

Friday 6th August 2004

I had a meeting with the marketing person at Leading Edge Telecoms, a buying group for 100 independent mobile phone stores, and she has agreed to take Mocks! It's great, although not a definite order as yet, head office decides what the stores in the group can buy. It basically just adds Mocks to the list of products. I will still need to get each store onboard separately, as each one is a small independent store, but at least now I can approach them all.

Wednesday 11th August 2004

I worked two days at Dell this week. It's so hard to fit everything in; I am rushing around like a loony. I know some of my friends would be asking "And how is that different from usual?" I've had four appointments this week with independent stores. It's good to meet the owners face to face. They are interested because it is my business, and most are keen to support someone starting out.

31

I am going to start doing Mocks orders on consignment, to try to get trials going, as it's very hard to get the small independent mobile phone stores to buy a product if they don't believe in it – no-one wants to be the first. Great news is that my local mobile store in Manly has agreed to take them.

I have downloaded a list of Melbourne stores from the Yellow Pages and I am going to start on those next week. Seeing as Melbourne is the next biggest city after Sydney, I thought that would be a good way to work.

I followed up the factory in China, to check that they are still on track for delivery. I don't want to promise a date to people and not be able to deliver.

Friday 13th August 2004
Unlucky for some, but not for me. I got another order today from a mobile phone store in Chatswood – hurray!

Most of the stores are owned by men, who don't respond to Mocks as positively as women do, so it requires a lot of explanation. They don't really see the point of the product, since it is not something they would use. Then they try to haggle me down on the price. I find it so hard that they try to beat me down. The usual line is that they can buy a leather case for 50 cents and sell it for $20, so why pay $3.50 for each Mock when it only sells for $9.95? I can understand their point, so I explain about the marketing and promotion that I will be putting behind the brand, but it is a big barrier for them. I have found that there does tend to be less haggling with women, although I have only met a handful.

Monday 16th August 2004
It's official, the Mocks have left China, so 24,000 are winging their way to me as I speak, and 24 boxes will be arriving in the spare room. That is one little problem, not really enough room; never mind, there is always the hall!

I had a thought today that maybe university campus shops would be good; they have the right kind of customers. I'll add it to my to-do list for tomorrow.

Friday 20th August 2004

I did a credit check on Fone Zone yesterday. It seems rather silly considering how big they are, but I need to make sure that I run my business right from the start. Unfortunately I had to agree to their terms, which is 30 days from month end, so if they order on September 1st they won't pay until the end of October. I guess after the first two months it will be fine, but everyone else is going on fourteen-day terms. I don't want to wait forever.

I got another store onboard on Tuesday, a small mobile phone store in St Ives shopping centre, a good hangout for teens. The manager was pretty young, and seemed cool, which is why it was an easier sale, he was more open to the idea. Another store agreed to order next week. I hope they come good on it.

I had to do my business activity statement (BAS) on tax for the government this week, yuk! There is a bit of tax paperwork, but at least I am getting a refund every month as I am only spending at the moment.

I need to start working on the next Mocks range. I have been saying that I will bring out a new range every three months, the idea being that there are 12 in the range, and people will buy one every week for 12 weeks and then a new range comes out with 12 to choose from, so they will buy one every week for 12 weeks etc. In reality I don't think it will work quite as well as this, but I do need to get ready. It will take a while to get the right range, especially as I need to find a designer. I can't really afford to use Gina's agency again. Much as they are great, it would send me broke.

I've been investigating UK opportunities today. I need to put that on the agenda. I could sell a lot there because there are so many people, and the exchange rate is great. Plus there are similarities in trends between Australia and the UK.

Tuesday 24th August 2004

An IT guy came and installed the EDI software for me today. I am sure it must have seemed strange to him to come to someone's flat and install it in the spare room. It seems to be pretty straightforward, so let the orders roll in …

I started calling the video chain stores this week. I thought since they sell recharge cards for mobiles the Mocks would go well. I've got the buyer's details now for the chains' head offices. I've also bought a map of Sydney so that I can mark the location of each store selling Mocks, then I can put it up on the wall. Kinda cool, I thought. I will be able to see the number of stores growing.

Thursday 26th August 2004

M Day – Mocks day. The Mocks are here! I had a bit of a dilemma when they arrived, as the courier wouldn't take them past the front gate. I had to carry all 24 boxes, each weighing seven kilos, up to our flat on the first floor with no lift – definitely a good workout. It was pretty amazing to see the result of nearly six months' work. There are a lot of Mocks! It doesn't really seem real, and makes me feel a bit nervous that I have to sell them all, but I have to think positive! This is so going to work. I just know it.

I collected the display stands from Warringah Plastics and then I set off delivering the Mocks and stands to the stores. It felt kind of strange, but good. I was really nervous about seeing people's reactions to the stands and the Mocks themselves. It was all positive but mostly the store staff members were fairly nonplussed, which I guess they would be – it's not a huge deal to them. I delivered to four stores today, and I have three tomorrow, plus I need to put together the seven Fone Zone orders tomorrow morning ready for the courier.

Monday 30th August 2004

I am now working my way through calling all the independent mobile phone stores in Australia – state by state. It is going to take a while, but how else am I going to be able to get the national distribution I want?

I sent the press release to all the TV stations today and the local radio stations. I will follow up next week. I'm still following up Josh at Digicall ...

Mocks sold this month: 586
Total stores: 17
Business bank account balance: $1,840
Mood: ☺ ☺ ☺ ☺ ☺

September 2004
Friday 3rd September 2004
Friday again, another busy week. I'm still following up press releases that I sent out to the magazines. Mostly I've had a pretty positive response, although I do wonder if they just say it will be in the mag to get rid of you. Cynical, I know. One editor I spoke to said yes, they would be featuring it, but did the company think that they would really sell? I replied that it was my company and yes, I did think that they would really sell. He started back-pedalling with a vengeance, saying he would be struck by lightning as he left work, and that he had never spoken directly to anyone from the companies supplying products before. It was very amusing.

I've managed to organise a few giveaways in *Girlfriend* mag, which is a very cheap way to get brand exposure. I think that PR is great way to build a new brand. The mags love anything quirky and unusual, so the Mocks are going down a treat. Most of the magazines ask for about $500 of product, valued at the recommended selling price, so it doesn't cost me too much.

This week I worked out my targets for this month and ongoing to the end of year in terms of store numbers and sales in units. I think for me it is so important to have targets otherwise I won't focus on what is important in driving my business and I'll end up spending most of my time on the creative aspect of Mocks, such as new Mock designs, rather than cold-calling.

Thursday 9th September 2004
Bondi markets were on last Sunday. It was rather disappointing in terms of Mocks sales, especially as I had to be there for 6am. Luckily

35

Mr Johns came with me for company. There were fewer people visiting the markets than last time and fewer sales, but it is still all about raising awareness for the Mocks, getting out there and seeing what the people on the street think. I am not sure if this is the right place to go; the other stalls tend to be trendy clothes and accessories. Now, I'd say Mocks are trendy ...

I spent a lot of time on the road this week. I went out to Bankstown in western Sydney – it took me over 1.5 hours! It's definitely good to get out and see different parts of the city, and store owners really appreciate meeting me and putting a face to the name, but it eats up the day. I probably should have sent the Mocks by courier, but I wanted to meet the store owner face to face.

I went on a negotiation skills course on Wednesday – another freebie as part of Small Business September. I'd have thought that these courses would be jam-packed, but not many people seem to know about them. This one was full of people who had been in business for about 10 years. I felt like the baby of the group, having been in business for three whole weeks. I learnt all about establishing the lowest position that I am willing to go to in the negotiation. I think that this will be of great assistance. It was good to talk through the issues, and I hope that a lot of it comes with confidence, both in what I'm selling and with the people I'm selling to.

I only worked one day at Dell this week, which was great. I can't wait to be able to afford to leave and do LaRoo full-time.

Steve at Fone Zone gave me details of the sales for August by each store. It's good to see how sales are going at the consumer level, since I can't get any market data otherwise. This will be especially useful when Mocks are sold in every Fone Zone store. It will give a true indication of the market's perception. In terms of the numbers, I wasn't really sure what to expect. Steve was pleased; he said the numbers were good for a new product. What counts is that he's happy. I don't want him to throw them out of stores before they have really started to sell!

Sunday 19th September 2004

I went to two gift tradeshows today: one at Darling Harbour in the city and one at Olympic Park at Homebush. Going to a tradeshow might be the way to get into the gift market if I can't find a distributor to represent me in this area. The Darling Harbour show was by far the best – it is also the most expensive, and the quality of products was far higher. I spoke to a few stallholders and was told that yes, you do cover your costs – $4,000-ish over the four days – so I think it would be worth it. I would be able to take orders at the fair and get contact details, so could be a good way to get into the gift stores. I also picked up some details on distributors I would be happy to have represent me, having seen what they currently sell, so I will contact them next week.

The rest of the week I spent phoning round and following up stores, trying to get orders, or just cold-calling, really not the most fun part of running my business.

Tuesday 21st September 2004

I had to look glam today, as the photographer from the local paper, the *Manly Daily*, came round to take the picture to go with an article they wrote – one of my press releases worked. I asked if she could airbrush out any fat, but apparently not! Hopefully the shots will turn out well, she was standing on the top step of our ladder to get the look she wanted, and I had to thrust my Mock into the camera.

Thursday 23rd September 2004

I went on two fantastic courses yesterday and today, both *free*. It doesn't get any better than that. Yesterday was all about exporting. It expanded on the course I went to recently, telling me what I need to look out for and about the government assistance that is available. Today's course was on budgeting, where it seems I am currently doing OK, but there are a few areas where I can stretch money out a bit more. Credit cards are definitely a key tip with cashflow; if I pay on credit card I can pay it all off much later. Often it is good to go to these events to hear other people's stories. One woman used a debt collecting agency because she hated doing any of the chasing up; another man used to phone up and tell them he was coming over to collect the money and then put the phone down and go! I always seem to pick up a new trick or two, or a different way of looking at problems and challenges.

Exporting is definitely an area I want to look at: going into the US and UK with Mocks in 2005. There is definite potential in these two markets; they are so much bigger than Australia. It will mean a trip over there – what a hardship! I need to look into it further to assess the actual potential before going. Doing my homework was very firmly pushed on the course.

Today I heard back from the gift distributors who sell to independent gift stores. They don't seem to be overly keen. As usual I am dealing with men, who generally don't understand Mocks and can't see the value of them. They weren't nasty about it, but just said that they weren't interested, or already had too many items on their books. Never mind, I will have to do it myself until the opportunity presents itself to go with a distributor.

Monday 27th September 2004
There is more publicity out today, an article in the *St Ives Village Magazine* – good PR for Mocks and the local stores. I know the editor, so he is going to plug the store selling them in another article, which is great news for all of us. I met the *Chik* teen magazine advertising girl on Friday. She was very nice and eager to help me, which is great. She is really behind Mocks and had thought of lots of ways that they could help me to promote them at little or no cost, offering me free publicity. She loved the designs and the whole concept – it was great having a meeting with someone who is enthusiastic. Otherwise today I have just been doing lots of following up of people, stores and opportunities.

Thursday 30th September 2004
I went to the Last Thursday Club today, with Sandra, my product placement friend. Sandra has been telling me about this networking group for a while, and the great speakers that they have, but as it's only on once a month we have only just managed to get to one. The evening was pretty interesting. There were people from all different

areas. I did a little bit of networking, but it was hard, as I could so easily get stuck with someone with whom I really had nothing to talk about. Chatting to Sandra was great. She has lots of ideas and is willing to help me get Mocks promoted. Unfortunately she couldn't get Mocks onto *Home And Away* or *Neighbours*; although the shows loved the product they couldn't see a way to include it. Instead, the stars are using the Mocks, which is still good for the brand.

Mocks sold this month: 552
Total stores: 40 (hurray!)
Original target: 40
Business bank account balance: $5,003 (finally, money from Mock sales!)
Mood: ☺ ☺

October 2004
Friday 1st October 2004
A big day on the road today driving from Sydney to Canberra. I couldn't be a full-time sales rep, that is for sure. I spent from 8am until 7.30pm driving and seeing stores today, and it was pouring down with rain all day – yuk! It was a positive day store-wise: I got three more stores, I had made appointments first, which really helps, and I had a good old chat with everyone. That is the nice bit about visiting stores, chatting once they have agreed to take Mocks. It builds up rapport, which hopefully leads to more orders. I'm glad I didn't have to drive back from Canberra today. I met Mr Johns there to stay for the weekend.

Tuesday 5th October 2004
I have decided to give up my part-time job at Dell now, after pressure from them to do the full amount of hours, rather than leaving early, which I often do. I can't wait. It will be great. I get stressed when I know that I have to go to work for two days because I don't have that time to make calls etc.

The bank account is not looking too healthy today after paying lots of bills. I had to call up my EDI supplier and ask if I could pay the bill at the end of October rather than now. Luckily they agreed. Now I need a fantastic month to get $3,800 in; it is something to aim for. I chatted to a designer friend and she only had $4 in the bank, so with $30 I actually feel a bit richer! I find it hard to get the cashflow going, so I've decided to reduce my credit terms from 14 days to seven days. It was one of the suggestions from the budgeting course last month.

Thursday 7th October 2004

I decided that I need to have a "National Sock Day", after researching on the internet, it seems that I can just make one up, which I find amazing. My idea is that the day will help promote Mocks. I called a charity today about my idea of a charity Mock with their design or logo on for "National Sock Day", but they were not overly keen. Considering that there is practically no involvement required from them and they get $1 from each Mock I sell, I find this very strange. I will have to move onto the next one on the list. One positive aspect about my part-time job was that I managed to research charities on the net. I want to find one that will fit really well with my target audience, and one that I personally want to give cash to.

Tuesday 12th October 2004

Today I spoke to Inspire, a national organisation that raises money to help teens with problems, they were very positive about the charity Mock. We're having a meeting tomorrow.

I had to chase stores for payment today. I read that the best time to call is Monday or Tuesday between 9.30am and 10.30am. I can't say I like doing it, but it has to be done otherwise I won't be here long. I can't wait until I make my millions – which is so going to happen! Then I can pay someone to do this for me.

A strange day today. The week feels long with no part-time job to go to, but I am getting lots done. I am beginning to establish a routine. There are certain jobs to do every day, like checking the mail at the post office, banking cheques, checking my bank account online in the hope that someone has mistakenly paid in lots of money ... I write a to-do list do in my diary every day and tick it off as I go. This is working really well for me. I also diarise anything I need to do, like calling someone, without having to remember it all.

Thursday 14th October 2004

I had to pay my business credit card bill today. I have two credit cards – a business one and a personal one – to help me track what I spend better. I only had half the money to pay the bill in the bank account so I will have to pay what I can afford now and then incur a bit of interest for the rest. Luckily the rate is pretty low. Having a credit card is working really well at the moment. It gives me some extra cash to pay urgent bills.

I had a meeting with Inspire yesterday. I proposed to them that we make a Reach Out! branded Mock and give $1 from each one we sell to Reach Out!, which helps teens in crisis. I think the meeting went well. There were lots of ideas and enthusiasm. I'll find out tomorrow. This will be a great project with them onboard, since they already have good brand recognition with teens.

Today I went to Bonnyrigg in western Sydney. It was another 1.5-hour trip to take 300 Mocks to a store – I love those big orders! They only bought 24 Mocks the first time. If only all the stores could do that. It was good to catch up with the owner and get feedback on how sales are going, but it may have been better use of my time to courier them.

I met the team from *Girlfriend* magazine on the way back, which was great. Again, they were very positive about the Mocks and had lots of good ideas. Next week I should hear the outcome as to whether they want to use Mocks as a covermount on the front of the magazine.

I'm still updating my website every few days with extra stores. Communication is very important for the brand, especially as I am directing everyone to the site for their nearest store. I love adding an extra store to my chart on the wall. I'm getting very into charts and keeping track of how well I am doing. It's important for me to realise how far I've have come.

Saturday 16th October 2004

A school fair today. I thought this would be worthwhile as it is the right target audience in a good area, and it was only from 2pm till 7pm. I went with my brother Will, who is over from the UK, staying for a few months. We sold 10 Mocks, which was very disappointing. We got probably four or five girls saying that they had seen the Mocks in a magazine, and two ran over saying something like "cool, these are the Mocks I was telling you about", which was fantastic. Then there was all the girlie screaming going on, saying that they are so cute, and these girls were wearing the latest clothes – it was Mocktastic! I wished that I had the camera to take pics, as they took the Mocks straight out of the packet and put them on their phones. However, there were not enough teens coming up to make us enough sales.

I didn't manage to do my walk today or yesterday, which isn't good. I have my walk on my to-do list every day now to get it done.

I heard from Inspire, and they are onboard – fantastic. I will need to get the press releases done and out next week to make the January issues of the monthly mags, in time to publicise National Sock Day.

It's Maitland market tomorrow. It's it is a two-hour drive away, but I heard from a bloke I met at Bondi that it is great. I'll see.

Monday 18th October 2004

Maitland was OK. It's a very big market – 600 stalls – but not as many people as I expected. I was rather disappointed in selling only 16 Mocks, I know it's a new concept, but still ... I will give it another go at the next one in two weeks.

Will started selling Mocks today at the English language school where he works in Manly. The mobile phone store in Manly had sold out of the designs that the students wanted, so he sold four Mocks to students today. Not bad considering I only sold 16 yesterday, and had to travel 200km to do it. I've made a note to go and see the Manly store. If his Mocks sales keep up I'll be trying to persuade Will to postpone his return to the UK. I started planning for next year today, which is going to be a big one. I don't think I'll make my million next year; it's really part of a five-year plan. I applied for a stall at the Big Day Out, the annual one-day music festival today. It's expensive, but filled with my target demographic – mmmmmmmmmmmm Mocks sales, here I come ...

Last week in October 2004
I'm feeling a lack in enthusiasm this week, but I think it must just be an end of the month feeling, as other people I know are also experiencing it. I find this is one of the hardest parts about working on my own, trying to keep up my enthusiasm and motivation when I don't feel like it. At least I've done lots of planning for next year and now understand my product development process, plus I have documented processes, so it was not a completely wasted week. On weeks like this I always seem to gain momentum towards the end of the week, hence Friday night at 7pm saw me firing on all cylinders – then, typically, I had a dinner with Mr Johns arranged, so I had to leave it. I can easily do work in the evening rather than watching TV, but it's definitely hard balancing work and life when working from home.

Mocks sold this month: 1,066
Total stores: 68
Original target: 55 (then I increased it to 70, so I'm 2 off the target)
Business bank account balance: $1,742
Mood: ☺ ☹

November 2004
Tuesday 2nd November 2004
It's the Melbourne Cup horse race today – I decided to have the afternoon off at the races, as it says in all those business books I read, I have to balance my life. I met a friend at her house near the races in western Sydney and I went to nearby Richmond on the way, to see a store. I had a productive meeting. They agreed to stock 48 Mocks and took the large stand. The owner was English so we had a good chat about "Poms" sticking together. He is part of a buying group of 15 stores and will put a good word in for me in the other stores. He is such a nice guy. I love visits where people offer to promote Mocks to other stores. He asked the same question of "So

how are they selling in other stores?" and I hate lying, but I needed to sound positive, so I raved about the store that reordered 300 after an initial order of 24. I mean, it wasn't lying; it's just that in reality none of the other stores have reordered as yet, but I know that they sell, because of Fone Zone's results. I still find sales hard.

Wednesday 3rd November 2004

I got the proposal from *Girlfriend* magazine today. It sounded fantastic when I read it through once, and then I thought no, it can't be this good, so I went back for a second look and made a list of what I need to ask to be clarified. I still feel sometimes that it's amazing that people believe in Mocks and me so easily. The offer from *Girlfriend* will enable me to launch Mocks on a big scale into Australia, and will probably increase awareness by up to 5% with the target audience, at a guess.

I ordered my Mocks T-shirts today, plain white with a large Mocks logo on the front and the website address on the back. I can't wait to see everyone in them at Homebake, a yearly music festival where I've organised a stand to sell Mocks. It will be huge.

Thursday 4th November 2004

A busy day today. I went to a store where the owner had asked to me fill up the current stands and put in the new stand. However, when I arrived there was no stand there, so it meant I spent two hours delivering – a real waste of time. In future I'll probe further, and maybe phone the store ahead to check. It's hard when the owner has three stores. I should have double-checked with the owner about exactly what he wanted. I will know for next time.

I spoke to the team at *Girlfriend* today. I should hear the outcome on Tuesday, but I might have to order the Mocks they need for the giveaway beforehand, as time is ticking away. They obviously really want me onboard and have now agreed to include all the design work for the ads for free, so that's even better. It's great dealing with people who really want Mocks, rather than me having to practically beg!

I had to take photos of girls with Mocks today, which was funny. Luckily Will could get some volunteers from the English language school he's working at. We took them to the beach and got them to pose with their phones wearing a Mock, this is for the *Girl Power* tween magazine. I should get the layout tomorrow, and hopefully it will look good.

Great news today: my first New Zealand order. It turns out someone saw advertising for *Girlfriend* magazine, which also sells in New Zealand, and then ordered Mocks from lastminute.com.au. I'm going to use this as leverage with the New Zealand distributor. I have to use everything I've got to persuade people.

Friday 5th November 2004

As usual I am leaving things to the last minute. There's a market on tomorrow from 10am to 10pm and I still have to do lots of sewing to make the stall table covers. It always feels like I have lots of time and then it just disappears ... I had more orders from Fone Zone today. I keep trying to persuade him to increase the orders to include more designs than the initial four he took. He did agree to add two more designs, which will add to sales. ☺

Monday 8th November 2004

I had a big weekend going to markets, both on Saturday and Sunday, I'm really trying to increase the Mocks brand awareness and get some cash flowing. It was good to hear that quite a few of the girls at the markets had heard of Mocks, mostly through *Girlfriend* magazine. I think the publicity is starting to work. It was worth the 40 stamps to post out the releases! Night-time was the best time for sales at the markets, when the right demographic was out and about. Although interestingly on Saturday morning one old lady bought a Mock. She produced her phone in a homemade Mock-type case, and was glad to get a new one that she didn't have to make!

Annoyingly, late on Saturday evening a girl stole the model phone that I use to show the Mocks off. This was particularly annoying as it doesn't actually work. It's funny because she actually asked me if the phone worked when she was looking at the Mock, to which I replied no – so why steal it? When I go to Homebake next month I need to make sure that I keep a really close eye on people. I found markets are a great place to hear comments such as ideas for designs straight from the customers' mouths, unprompted, and to get an idea of the awareness for Mocks. It's important to stay in contact with my consumers. If I don't understand how they think, what they like and what they buy, I won't get the insights that inspire new products and designs. One girl I met had bought two Mocks and changes them depending on what she feels like, proving my idea that users mix and match Mocks with their mood and/or outfit – hurray, my theory works!

Today was busy, busy. I was so tired after two days full-time at the markets that I was cross last night with Mr Johns. All the business books talk about looking after yourself, and I always thought that I did, but this weekend proved otherwise. One very big argument about nothing, getting upset then I slept for 10 hours. I had to go to the gym today to prove that I am looking after myself. I know it is important … I hate it when I think that all is going along fine then it all suddenly falls apart at the seams.

Friday 19th November 2004
The joys of workmen. There are workmen drilling into the road right outside my window. Way too noisy for my liking.

It has been an up and down week. It feels really long. Yesterday I felt like I just wasn't getting anywhere. The number of stores is increasing, but reordering is not happening in large numbers. I am also concerned about the liability of ordering more stock when I don't really have the cash to pay for it now. I spoke to Dad. It's good to have someone to discuss issues with; not being able to bounce around ideas is a difficult aspect of working on my own. Dad agreed with my ideas for solutions, and reassured me that he wouldn't have invested if he didn't think it was a promising business venture. Funnily enough after I spoke to Dad three orders came in on the fax, all reorders, and then a new store called me and ordered. I guess it is all the hard work finally starting to pay off.

I went to a presentation about the Leading Edge Telecoms National Conference yesterday, to show support for the group as a supplier. It was interesting to hear about the conference. It sounds like a great opportunity to mix with both store buyers and other suppliers, but it is in Auckland and the minimum cost to be there is $5,000, which is rather out of my reach, especially as I have decided not to invest any more funds in the business at the moment. I sat unintentionally next to the Microsoft supplier, who said they would probably get the $20,000 package, which will give them three trade stands. I suggested that he could give me one as they surely didn't need three. He thought about it for a second and said no! Oh well, if you don't ask you don't get and he wasn't offended. The buyer I know is going to see if she can get me a shared spot, so I'll see.

I had a lovely email today from my new supplier, Jackie, in China. After I explained about me just starting and hence the small orders, he said that he understood and hopefully soon I will be one of the biggest importers into Australia – so do I! I just hope that his samples turn out OK, as my other supplier is being very slow and it looks like I will have to pay for the Mocks to be sent airfreight again, instead of sea freight until he pulls his finger out – it's so hard not being in control of the whole process.

I met the advertising people from *TV Hits* magazine. They are very keen on Mocks, and so we may try to do a deal. I want to get Fone Zone onboard to help cover costs so I'll see what happens there. I got quotes for my website revamp this week. It looks like it is going to be within my budget of $5,000, but I will need to wait until January to see the response of the small ads and PR before I can commit fully. Maybe I should give it a go myself over Christmas and see what I can do to jazz it up a little, but my time is probably better spent elsewhere. I know I need to see my time as valuable, rather than free, as in the near future I will have to start paying myself, but it is hard to do when it is just me.

The next few weeks in the run-up to Christmas are really going to be crunch time for my Mocks. Will they be able to engage people enough to get them to buy? Plus my new store targets still need to be met. I just need to keep pushing along.

Wednesday 24th November 2004

I have 96 stores to date, so I have easily, with time to spare, achieved this month's target, but it is definitely quietening down for me now. I now need those reorders. Fone Zone are reordering, but not the smaller stores. Time for another ring around. Phoning is the most effective way to get orders, I have found so far. The email newsletters that I have been sending out have probably been read by only half the stores; I've put read receipts on them. When I am on the phone, I'm harder to avoid! Although it can be very hard to get hold of the right person, I have written targets in my diary for calls each day this week to motivate myself to get out there and do it. I can't really explain why I feel so driven to achieve my goals, but I just know the Mocks are going to sell, and most of the feedback from stores is positive, so it definitely gives me more energy to keep going.

I went to a breakfast networking meeting this morning. It was pretty informative and inspirational – good people. It is on every week, and I will have to think about whether it is something that I want to continue with, as it costs money and every bit is adding up at the moment. I need to do a big business plan review at Christmas and work out more realistic figures for 2005, based on store numbers and selling rates.

I keep getting the same message repeated to me this week at the networking place, in the books I'm reading and from friends: you have to believe it to make it happen, otherwise it won't happen. I can't work out if I believe strongly enough. I don't think that I am clearly enough focused on my goals. I need to have them written out in front of me and look at them often to get them to sink in. It's hard when I'm working in the lounge while my brother stays, and Mr Johns isn't keen on paper stuck up – it is hard enough to get him to agree to let me put my calendar on the wall!

Friday 26th November 2004

Mocks are teetering on an edge today, the edge of a century ... 99

stores. I wanted to get one more so that I can crack open the champers and celebrate the home run. I've been doing lots of positive thinking and visualising, but to no avail as yet. It is 4.08pm so a fax could still come through, I hope.

I did a big cashflow review today and last night. I'm looking at how I can find the additional money I need for paying bills and myself. I had a few new ideas. I think I will have to be naughty and delay payment on some big bills until the new year, and just hope that they don't get around to chasing up around Christmas. Either that or I can pretend to be away!

I am still trying to get the payment from a mobile store that gave me a cheque that bounced. When I went in on Wednesday with it they said that they didn't have enough cash in the till to pay me $100, and could I come back tomorrow. Well, I phoned yesterday and was told that they couldn't pay me in cash; it would have to be cheque or bank deposit, so I opted for bank deposit. Today, still no money, so tomorrow I am going in with Mr Johns to collect my stock. It has been over eleven weeks and that is just not good enough. For $100 it is so not worth the hassle of dealing with them. I also get the feeling that they think that they can mess me about because I am a girl. Well, they have got another thing coming. It is disappointing that they are being so difficult over such a small amount, and I know for a fact that they have sold some Mocks, so they have practically made the money they need to give me.

Saturday 27th November 2004
I went in and collected the Mocks today from the store that hadn't paid. I was very polite and just explained that as they hadn't paid their bill for three months that I was collecting all the Mocks. They still said that they would pay, but I said it was too late, and it was too inconvenient for me. They gave me the board and I walked out. Done. I felt a bit shaky afterwards, but it's done. I can do it; I can defend my brand and my business.

Monday 29th November 2004
It's the beginning of the week and I am not quite sure where to

start. I think that I need to plan the week. I have a few prospective meetings, which is great, but I need to start to work on the New Zealand distribution plan, as I had another four New Zealand orders from the online store lastminute.com.au this morning. I just hope the distributors in New Zealand liked the samples I sent them. My giant Mocks arrive tomorrow and the Mocks T-shirts arrive today, and I need to get everything ready for Homebake. It should be an exciting week. The giant Mocks are basically people-sized socks, big enough for someone to jump around in like in a sack race. That should get people's attention.

It has been a very big afternoon. An email from Steve at Fone Zone warned me he was sending through a large order for lots of stores. Then later in the day I got the order – 100 stores' worth of Mocks! This now means that Mocks have 100% distribution in Fone Zone. Great news, after only three months in stores they have the confidence to put them in all stores for the run-up to Christmas. Now I just need to pack them all …

Tuesday 30th November 2004

Well, seven hours later and finally 100 courier bags are packed with Mocks and labelled, with invoices and delivery notes printed. It's great having a huge order, but a nightmare to fill. It makes me think *I need a helper*.

I heard from the Yellow Pages Business Idea Grants today. Unfortunately, I wasn't a winner; still, it was good practice to put together the application, and the launch event was good for meeting people.

I am not counting the extra Fone Zone stores in this month's total, as stock won't be with them until the 1st December. What a great start and end to a month. I hope that the Mocks just fly out of the store doors.

Mocks sold this month: 2,336
Total stores: 99 (Mocktastic month!)
Original target: 70 (before October blew it out of the water)
Business bank account balance: $1,101

Mood: ☺ ☺ ☺ ☺

December 2004
Sunday 5th December 2004

What a week. I had ordered a banner to use at Homebake, but the banner guy let me down. He used the excuse that he was a new business, to which I replied that so was I, and I had given him eight weeks' notice. I really don't think that is the way to run a business. (Reading all these business books and going on courses can sometimes make me feel like a bit of an expert, although obviously I'm not really, I've only been doing this five minutes.) Plus there was apparently a problem with the embroidery of the designs for the giant Mocks that I was getting made in China, but I didn't find out until lunchtime on Friday. I then had to run round like a headless chicken to buy material to sew my own giant Mock, and organise a giant foam phone for it to go on, then rush out to Homebake in the city and check out the site and pick up the tickets. It was all go.

After all the running around, Homebake yesterday was fantastic. It was a long day, but I was busy for most of it. My friend Carla and I sold 118 Mocks in total, and we even had our own PR machine going – a guy called Dave who loved them so much he kept going and handing out flyers and sending people to our stall. The stand worked perfectly, and really stood out from the others, as it was the only really branded stand – very simple, just white tablecloths with the Mocks logo, plus we wore matching T-shirts. We had a lot of repeat business, where friends brought back friends, and we even promoted the Mocks as stubby holders for beer drinkers. Carla was great. She chatted, flirted and teased the customers as well as being basically being out and out cheeky, which worked really well! We even managed to persuade one drunk guy to buy two Aussie Flag Mocks to use as socks for his baby son. Brand/product awareness for the Mocks is still very low, with only two people all day having seen them before, and one girl said it was because she worked in a store that sold them. The number of Mocks sold covered the cost of the day and made a couple of hundred dollars in profit, so it was definitely worth it.

I have decided to go ahead with a new website. The website design company have said that I can pay in instalments, so it will be easier for me. I think with the increase in publicity I need to have somewhere good to send people. The site should go live at the beginning of January.

Friday 10th December 2004

The day after the LaRoo Christmas Party. It was a great party. I had about 15 people come along, all friends. We had a chat, a few drinks and I even sold some Mocks. I had a stand set up, as I knew that lots of them still hadn't bought any, and it's a good way to pay for the party grub … Mr Johns thought it very cheeky, but no-one minded, either that or they are used to my cheek. There were two awards, one for best salesman of the year, which went to my brother Will, for his outstanding sales at markets and at the school he taught at. The second award went to Mr Johns, the Mocks support person of the year. It was fun, and we did the cheesy photos of handshakes while receiving the awards. I had lots of emails today saying how much people enjoyed it. Next year will be even bigger and better, hopefully from a new global HQ.

Tuesday 14th December 2004

I am now back in my own office – the spare room. Will has finally moved out and the flat is very empty. After I had to work in the front room for six months, I really appreciate having my own space to be able to come in, shut the door and work. I have a massive desk now, as Mr Johns found me a new one from some office fitters that he knows, and I've set up my Mocks stock better, as well as being more organised. I even bought myself a new wrist rest today – a koala whose eyes pop out of his head when you rest on it; it makes me laugh.

I joined a gym last week after deciding that I really was not getting enough exercise. I'm planning to go every day during the day to a) break up the day, b) relieve stress and c) get fit/lose weight. So far I have been every weekday since I joined, so I am doing well, and I am feeling much better for it – hurray. Now I just need to cut out those little Nutella sandwich snacks and I will be onto a winner.

I got another order for 300 Mocks today from the store that ordered 300 only two months ago, plus yesterday I got an order for 500. It's going well, but I could still do with more orders, as according to my cashflow plan I will be out of money again by the end of the month. That is what stresses me out the most, looking at the cashflow forecast in the QuickBooks accounting package and noticing that I still need more money to break even and I still haven't paid myself. I absolutely have to pay myself in January, and I will put in the bills into QuickBooks for weekly pay so that it is harder to avoid it.

The *Girlfriend* promotion is nearly in place. The promotional materials are looking great. I really think it will be huge and will launch Mocks into the limelight.

I still haven't got the information from the Australian distributors I saw at the gift tradeshow. They don't seem to be overly keen. It has been two weeks now since I last heard from them. Maybe they thought that they would just get the work, but I still want all those i's dotted and t's crossed to make sure I am doing the right thing. They inquired about a bulk order for one of their customers who want their logo on a Mock, which would be great, but they are saying that it would have to go through them and I need to do a great price as it would be great exposure. I asked which company and what exposure so I could evaluate it and I haven't heard since. If I wait until January when Mocks are bigger after the *Girlfriend* promotion, hopefully people will be knocking on my door rather than me having to hammer harder and harder on theirs.

I am feeling pretty confident at the moment that the promotion will go well. I even had a panic today that I might run out of stock! Wouldn't that be nice.

Fone Zone orders are still going well. Some stores are selling 20 a week – wow! My other stores are also starting to reorder. I got a call today from a new store I approached months ago; they placed an order, which confirms that all my hard work paid off. It goes to show that I should never say die.

Mocks sold this month: 3,494
Total stores: 189
Original target: 120 (before Fone Zone came onboard, then the target increased to 200)
Business bank account balance: $2,629
Mood: ☺ ☺

2005
January 2005

2005, is going to be a fantastic year, I just know it, with the covermount and the advertising I've set up I am sure that Mocks sales will go through the roof. Last year was a lot of hard work, and I know that isn't going to stop, but at least most of the cold calling is over. I envisage that this year I can spend more time building the brand awareness and making sure that people know about Mocks. Plus I will probably be able to hire some help this year – which means less stress and I can achieve more, and I will prove to Mr Johns that the business is viable. I am really excited about it all. The new website went live on Christmas Eve, I am really glad it is ready for all the advertising and promotions I have planned this year. It is a million times better than the one I built.

Monday 3rd January 2005
The February issue of *Girlfriend* magazine went on sale today, the one with the free Mock on 45,000 copies.

Tuesday 4th January 2005
The order of Mocks with the new designs leaves China by airfreight today – 3,600 Mocks ...

Friday 7th January 2005
I just got back from five days of camping at the beach to find 400 emails from girls about Mocks. *Woohoo!* It took me *eight* hours to answer them all. At least people are visiting the website and are interested. I can't believe it. It is so exciting ... Mocks are really taking off.

Monday 10th January 2005
I spent three hours packing Mocks today. It is great to have all those orders, but also a bit crazy with everything I need to do!

Today I went into the mobile store in Manly (where I live) to top up their Mocks. They like me to do it and it's good for me because I get feedback on what is happening in the retail world, as well as which

Mocks are selling. The Aussie Flag design always does well in this store, probably because of all the tourists to Manly.

I got in touch with a call centre today, as a potential way to sell Mocks. People could call up and order them and pay for them over the phone. I still don't have an online shopping website as yet, and the only other option for customers is to fill in the order form and mail it in, so this could be a good alternative. I have a meeting set up for Thursday.

I finally bought a laminator today, and I love it. It was a pain having to borrow one every time I needed to laminate. This will be so much easier!

Friday 14th January 2005
I met up with the guy from the call centre yesterday. It definitely looks like a viable option. I need to run the numbers a bit more, but initially it's looking good.

I have spent one to two hours per day packing orders this week for stores. It is great that stores are ordering. It is still so exciting when orders arrive on the fax machine. Hopefully that feeling doesn't wear off.

I prepared the shareholders' report this month for the last quarter, even though I'm the only shareholder. I gave Mr Johns a copy and Mum and Dad, as they lent me the cash to start up and so have a vested interest in the business.

It's not long now until I go to the Big Day Out event. There will be live bands playing all day, 11am to midnight. I am hoping that the target audience is right. They might be a little bit older than teens.

I have been great on the exercise this week. I've done a class every day - I have been keeping those endorphins flowing.

Thursday 20th January 2005

Busy, busy. I had a meeting with Austrade today to discuss getting accepted onto the New Exporter Development Program. I thought it would be hard, but it actually wasn't too bad. I just took along what I've got for stores already, like the order form and also the PR folder I have, and they were impressed. Apparently lots of people go along with nothing and aren't even willing to go overseas to visit the places they want to export to! So it looks like I will be accepted onto the program, even though Mocks are not made in Australia – because they are designed in Australia and the company is Australian.

Great news, the guys at *TV Hits* magazine have agreed to wear Mocks T-shirts to the Big Day Out, just because they love Mocks! I need to drop off the T-shirts to them this week. Plus the Austrade guy is going to the Big Day Out with his wife, and says that she will wear a Mocks T-shirt – spreading the word, it's great.

I have been spending time the past few days chasing up people for money. It is so annoying when they don't pay on time. I know that my payment terms are short at seven days, but people know that when they sign up.

I am finally onto calling the Western Australia section of the Yellow Pages. It is taking forever, but it is having results ... store owners are interested, and want to get a sample.

Tuesday 25th January

Yesterday was exciting. I went and saw a potential office for the business. It is way too crowded in the spare room. I have to take everything out and rearrange it every week to have enough room for me in there! At the moment I have my desk with the computer and fax on it and enough room for my chair, but the rest of the room is just boxes of Mocks. It is a real squash. I am also going to need to take on someone to help with the packing soon, as I just don't have the time to do everything. Plus Mr Johns is getting rather annoyed with the 20,000 Mocks lining the hallway!

Wednesday 26th January 2005

I spent today at the Big Day Out music festival. It was such a long day; we got there about 9am and finished up at 11pm. My friend Nora came along to help me. The Reach Out! Mocks didn't get delivered in time, despite my constant calls to the shipping company. They kept saying that it was bumped off the plane in China due excess passenger luggage. The first time maybe I could believe this, but three times – it seems very unlikely. It is really frustrating dealing with people like that, when I think that they are lying to me. This is the first time I have used this company, and it will be the last.

The Reach Out! volunteers did a great job bouncing about in the giant Mocks in front of the stand. It would have been such hard work, but they bounced about handing out flyers in return for their entry ticket. Not really such a bad gig.

Sales today were disappointing. The event was so huge that lots of people didn't realise that the market bit was there until very late in the evening. We sold 70 Mocks over the day, which just covered the cost of the stand, but really I wanted it to be bigger than that. We did get some photos of people with their Mocks to put up on the website; people loved it when we did this after the Homebake festival.

Mocks sold this month: 4,008
Total stores: 199
Original target: 250
Business bank account balance: $6,188
Mood: ☺ ☺ ☹

February 2005
Tuesday 1st February 2005

I checked out another office today in Brookvale. I liked it, particularly because it is only five minutes' drive from home, but I could see that it wouldn't really be very practical. It is on two levels, which means the desks would have to be upstairs, but there isn't really enough room for all that I think I am going to need, nor is there any parking, and it seemed like a bit of a dodgy area to be alone in at night.

My brother Will came round and helped today. He did two hours of Mock packing, and three hours last Friday. If orders keep coming in as they are, there is definitely going to a full-time role there by the time the office move happens, which is probably May.

I had a lunch meeting with teenage magazine *Chik* yesterday, they are only 10 minutes' walk from our unit in Manly, so handy. It's really worthwhile to build relationships with the people at the magazines, as I then get much more exposure for Mocks. The girls there seem to love them, so I am hoping that we can work together on some giveaways and promotions.

I applied to have a show at Australian Fashion Week in Sydney. I'm still waiting to hear back. I don't really see why I can't be involved; Mocks are accessories and they are fashionable. It would be a great for brand awareness – they are still very unusual. Fingers crossed they say yes.

I have decided to try the call centre as a way for consumers to order Mocks. It is all set up. They have given me a phone number for people to call, and it will cost them the same as a local call. The call centre will take the details and process the payment, and then I will send out the Mocks. I added the phone number to the website today; fingers crossed sales will go well.

Thursday 3rd February 2005
I went to the Australian Businesswomen's Network Member Goals Group briefing evening last night. It was interesting; I like the idea of having a weekly meeting with a group of women who can hold me accountable for what I'm doing. Working on my own I find it hard to not procrastinate about jobs, especially when I'm not overly keen on doing them! I signed up with a group who live near me, but I'm not sure what they will be like as we are all at different stages in our businesses. One girl works for a large bank, so is employed, another runs a coaching business. They are all dealing in the service industry, rather than with products, I will see how it goes. The first meeting is next Tuesday.

Friday 4th February 2005

I am still looking at offices. Today's places were fine for me, but horrible for anyone that worked for me, as there were only small windows on one side and as soon as you divide up the office, everyone else is in the dark with no view.

Monday 7th February 2005

I think I have found the office! The one I saw today is really nice, with floor-to-ceiling windows on two sides. It is 55 square metres, which seems huge compared to the spare room. It's in a complex so security is pretty good, which I need if I am going to be there late at night. There are two car spots and a cafe in the building, it's modern and the rent is pretty reasonable, especially if I haggle with them.

Thursday 10th February 2005

I met a sales rep from a freight company called UTI today, it looks like they would be a good freight company to use to import the Mocks from China, and they have an office in Shanghai, which makes it much easier for me and the sock manufacturers. I just need to get a quote on their rates and I'll be away.

I had the first Goals Group meeting this week. It was OK, not fantastic. I don't think that anyone really understood what I do. I explained the issues around importing goods and then finding retailers, but they really struggled. I did explain it clearly, but their ideas were not really ones that I could use, which makes me think they didn't understand, or I didn't explain properly. Maybe it comes with time, but at the moment I don't really feel that I got much out of the session.

I did some bank reconciliations today, oh joy! I had to get the BAS bits ready for Ella. She is doing them for me now, as I have been having a few issues with them, and I had to redo the last three, when I realised that I had made a mistake! I don't mind doing the accounts when it goes right, but when it doesn't it is so time consuming and frustrating. I need to look at getting a laser printer as well soon. The inkjet is so slow … especially when Fone Zone sends in lots of orders.

I am off to Tokyo tomorrow. In January Mr Johns started a new job in the company he works for, setting up the Tokyo business from an operations standpoint. With the new role he will be away for a week then back for a week. I actually kind of like it as it gives me time to get on and work in my business. Plus there are bonuses like this trip. I have a meeting set up with Austrade in Tokyo on Monday, which will be interesting, as Mr Johns has commented that the Mocks would go well there. I will see what they think about selling Mocks in Japan.

Tuesday 15th February 2005

The meeting with Austrade yesterday was amusing. I got so lost getting there that I was an hour late. Really not a good look, but most of the roads aren't marked a) on the map and b) on the street, which makes it hard for a visitor, as does the fact that I only know a few words of Japanese: thank you and excuse me … I ended up going up to people, saying excuse me and then pointing on the map to where I wanted to go. Needless to say there was much confusion, but people were very friendly and helpful, even through most of them didn't have a clue as to what I was talking about! Luckily I met a girl who spoke English and knew where the Australian embassy was, so I finally made it. After all that, the Austrade girl told me that she didn't think the Mocks were of high enough quality to be sold in Japan, as people like high-quality western goods. She also told me I would be copied within six months, so I would need to go in hard. Japan is an expensive city, and to launch a product in a country where I don't speak the language and don't have the funds to give it the push it needs, I think that is something I should wait to do.

I've been going over the numbers on the new office. I have decided to make an offer on the one I like in Brookvale. They can only say no if they don't like what I offer, but it has been empty for a year, so I would think they would be pleased to rent it out.

Friday 18th February 2005

We have agreed on the lease terms for the office. Initially they wanted $350 per week with three months' bond and we have agreed on $300 per week plus GST, two months' bond, one-year lease with a one-year option to renew, plus I get the first month rent free. Seems like a good bargain to me, compared with what else is around. I signed the lease and I get the keys on May 1st, but this way I can pay the bond over the next two months, and it is better for my cashflow ... It's kinda scary, but this is the way forward to grow the business. Plus I can't stay in the spare room forever, even if it would have been nice to stay working in my PJs.

I had a meeting with *Girlfriend* magazine on Wednesday to review the covermount. They were really pleased. Apparently it was the biggest selling issue of *Girlfriend* ever. Wow! So now we just need to sort out the advertising and promotion that we are doing to follow it up. I love dealing with the *Girlfriend* team. They are so lovely, always enthusiastic and wanting to know what I have been doing; it's just great. I feel that they really care, which I think is probably unusual. They must deal with lots of advertisers, and yet I feel that they really go out of their way for me.

The call centre is not working out that well. The people there don't seem to understand the concept of taking an order. I have had confused calls every day this week from consumers and the call centre. One lady was kept on the phone for 13 minutes and still her order wasn't taken. I have trained the call centre staff and given them handouts to explain it all.

Monday 21st February 2005

I had my first breakfast catch-up with Alex today. I met Alex at a networking event last month, and even though she lives about 1.5 hours away from me, we are going to meet every fortnight, at a halfway point. We have formed our own goals group, because I decided to leave the other one. I told them in a nice way that I didn't think it was really going to work for me, and they were fine with that. She is just starting her business and has lots of good ideas, but just needs to get it off the ground. I think that this could work really well, and it is social interaction.

Wednesday 23rd February 2005

I went and saw a movie at Moonlight Cinema tonight with the Reach Out! team. They were sponsoring the event, so we went round and sold Mocks to the crowd. We sold about 30, which was not too bad, and it raises brand awareness. I stayed and watched the movie. I found the event bizarre, as I didn't know anyone except for Sophie from Reach Out! and she was meeting up with her friends. I always find that a kind of situation awkward. I am quite a social person, but I like to know everyone. I don't like to be on the outside of a group. I ended up talking to one of the other Reach Out! team members, and it was a pretty successful night. They all seem to be impressed with what I have done in my business, but I still don't feel like it is that much, and am not overly confident about it. It's hard to explain. I still feel like I am trying hard to get there, but I am not there, no matter what people say to me about how amazing my achievements are. Maybe it is something that will come with time and running my business for longer – then I will be able to accept compliments better and not feel so unsure about myself. I think I will just know from what I see around me when I have made it.

Friday 25th February 2005

I had a meeting today with the *Smash Hits* magazine advertising guy, we met at a restaurant in Manly for coffee, but he was 30 minutes late – I couldn't believe it. It wouldn't have been so bad if I'd been meeting with him at home, as I could have worked while I waited. Like I had nothing better to do … It was just out and out rude. I nearly left after 20 minutes and then he called to say he was nearly there. Some people!

The Mocks marketing plan for 2005 is coming along. I need to get it finalised in the next week, so that I know what is happening for the next 10 months.

I have an exciting day coming up on Monday. I am off to New Zealand for the day to see a mobile phone store distributor. They are really interested, so this could be huge! I decided against staying over, as it will just cost more and there isn't really anything I want to do or see in Auckland, so in and out is fine. I think I have about six hours there.

Mocks sold this month: 3,112
Total stores: 214
Original target: 1,000 by the end of 2005
Business bank account balance: $5,353
Mood: ☺ ☺

March 2005

Tuesday 1st March 2005

I had a big day today ... I paid myself $2,000. This means that I have met the terms of the deal I had with Mr Johns – paying myself in the first year or finishing up and getting a "proper" job. Luckily for me we didn't set an amount I had to pay myself. I think $2,000 is a lot. I could have just done $10!

Yesterday was *huge* as well. I got to New Zealand, where I rather threw the guy at customs. When he asked how long I was staying and I said six hours, he really didn't know what visa to give me ... in the end he gave me a six-month visa, which I said should just cover it. I met two really nice guys from the distributor Cellnet, which sells products to mobile phone stores. They loved Mocks; they loved the designs and what I was doing with them. They placed an order right away for 5,000 Mocks! My biggest order yet. I can't believe it ... very, very exciting. Of course in the meeting I tried to play it cool. I had champagne in the lounge at the airport to celebrate ... Sales are really getting going now; soon I will be exporting to the UK. Watch out world, here Mocks come.

Monday 7th March 2005

Needless to say the rest of last week was not quite as exciting as Monday. I went on a thrilling "Understanding Awards" course about staffing and paying people correctly. Necessary, but oh so boring. It did make me realise that when I was waitressing I was actually being underpaid – how cheeky! At least now I will know that I am paying people right so that they can't complain, plus I can answer any questions about the award, and the rates of pay give me a good indication of what to pay people.

Today I met with Silvia, a personal trainer. My 30th birthday is only just over two months away, and I am not going to look fat! I so need to get the weight off. I thought if I train with her once or twice a week and monitor my diet leading up to my birthday it will get me slim.

The next range of designs is now ready to have samples made. I have made up the design pages, ready to send to China. I think that these designs are a bit more sophisticated than the last lot. The market research on them was interesting, so we will see if they perform the way the research indicates they will. This time I have included quite a few designs that Mockis, the consumers who love Mocks, sent in. They tested really well with the research, so they made the cut – as simple as that. And how good is that going to be for Mocks, girls telling their friends that they designed that Mock? That has got to be good for sales …

Tuesday 8th March 2005

I had a stand this morning at the UNIFEM breakfast, which was a fundraiser for International Women's Day. Sales were not huge. The audience was women aged 30 plus with professional careers, I don't think that they really saw the appeal of Mocks, but then again maybe they thought that the designs are too young. My stand was next to another girl, whom I hit it off with right away. We will definitely keep in touch because we might be able to help each other in the future. Her business was funky underwear for brides. Nothing like Mocks, but it was really interesting to talk to her about the challenges she's faced in her business.

Friday 11th March 2005

I have organised a "design a Mock" competition in *Girlfriend* magazine. Hopefully we will get lots of entries, and the one that is voted best by readers will be made and sold in stores. It's a really good way to get the readers involved; they love interaction with the brand.

I wrote the press release for the new range. I really have to send it out next week, but I need the samples and the photos first.

I reassessed the call centre sales today. They have been very small, around 10 per week; it is not worth the hassle. There are still problems with taking orders, and the number of calls I am getting about problems has not decreased much. I have decided to call it quits on this idea. At least I gave it a go.

Friday 18th March 2005
It has been another quietly busy week. I'm still calling around stores following up to see if they are interested in stocking Mocks. It is hard to get hold of the right person; it normally means lots of calls for a no.

I am still updating the website weekly with new content on the home page, and I also want to look at getting a game incorporated into the website to make it more fun and interactive. I was thinking that you could have Mocks that you have to catch on your phone falling from the sky, so it would be a bit like Tetris … I need to find out about costs.

I went on another exciting course this week, about recruitment and termination this time. Again, they're important topics, just not very thrilling. It is useful to know the best practices for hiring new people, and what to put in writing, like having a contract and a letter of offer.

I have been busy packing up the 5,000 Mocks for the New Zealand order. I will send it out next week. It takes a while to count that many because they ordered a few different designs. I have bags and bags of Mocks in the front room, waiting to go. I want to make sure I count them right; it is so easy to make mistakes.

I met up with Jane, who used to work for me in my last full-time role. She is so not happy there, so it looks like she will come over and work for me full-time when I move into the office. It will be good to be working with someone I know and trust. She is going to start doing some Mock packing in the evenings to help me out from Monday, since my brother is no longer here and available as free labour.

Friday 25th March 2005

An exciting week this week. Lots of potential sales coming together. I had an inquiry from *T3* technology magazine for 15,000 specially designed Mocks to be given away on the cover of their 50th birthday issue. It would be such good exposure for the brand, and to the right kind of gadgety people. I quoted a low price that would just cover costs and give me a little margin, way lower that I would normally offer. I recognise that this would help both of us out, so there is no point in being greedy.

I put the Rabbit Mock up as Mock of the Week, as it's Easter. I figure he can pass as an Easter bunny!

I am still getting lots of emails from customers asking questions about Mocks. I have developed standard answers to questions to save time, and if I get the questions more than once I add them to the FAQ page on the website. I need to try to minimise work. But it is great that they are contacting me.

Mocks sold this month: 8,713
Total stores: 245
Original target: 1,000 by the end of 2005
Business bank account balance: $6,392
Mood: ☺ ☺

April 2005

Friday 1st April 2005

I trained this morning with my trainer, Silvia, at Shelly Beach. My God, hard work! I did the steep steps three times in a row and each time had to try to beat my previous time. I did manage it, but it was hard. It's not like I'm running up five stairs; I think there are about 50 … It's funny how I can do it when I don't expect to. If before I started Silvia had told me that I would have to run up the stairs three times in a row getting faster every time, I would have gone really slowly the first time to make it achievable, rather than go all-out the first time. However, I did beat my time each time. Sometimes I think it is pretty amazing what can be achieved when I'm pushed.

I finished the layout plan of the office today, so I know where everything is going to go when we move in. I have almost all the furniture; now I'm just working out the Mocks storage system. At Ikea I have seen some great plastic storage tubs, which are probably what I will go with. They are pretty expensive at $20 each, and I need 20. But, I think they will last; I don't want to be replacing them in six months.

Today Fone Zone paid me $5,393. I know people say you shouldn't be dependent on one customer, so I need to find another large customer to balance sales out.

Jane came in and helped out today. She is so keen, I love it!

Wednesday 6th April 2005
I went to the *E-Myth* book study group held by the Australian Businesswomen's Network tonight. I have already read it, and it was great to discuss it in depth with others. I got a lot more out of it. There weren't that many people there, which was a bit of a shame. I was hoping that they might make this a regular event.

I finished putting together Jane's contract this week. I just adapted one that my bookkeeper Ella gave me, which she uses in her business. I can't really afford to get a proper one done at the moment by lawyers, and this one looks like it has everything covered. I know it's not really the best way to do it, but it will have to do for now.

Friday 8th April 2005
I've been out and about the last two days: coffee yesterday at Blue Water cafe in Manly, talking with a guy about cinema advertising; and lunch today with one of the *Total Girl* magazine team. I love having these kinds of meetings, especially if they are interesting. We get chatting for ages. Melanie from *Total Girl* gave me all the inside gossip on the mag, because she really wants to help Mocks succeed.

I'm still waiting on payment of $11,000 from Cellnet, the distributors I met in New Zealand, which is rather annoying. I asked them to pay up-front and I did expect it by now. I have called and followed up. The business really needs the money.

Saturday 16th April 2005

This week I've been busy organising supplies for the new office. I've been dealing with setting up phones, faxes, signs, fridges, filing cabinets and computers. This is a really expensive undertaking.

I have managed to get the head office buyer at Civic Video to give me some discount vouchers to use with the Mocki Club, my Mocks fan club that is about to launch.

Tuesday 19th April 2005

I started work on the launch of iMocks today. I think they will be the next generation Mock, with two Mocks in one that can be turned inside out for a whole new look! I think that they will appeal to people who want more protection for their phone, or for use on their iPods/MP3 players. I don't think they will be out until the end of the year, but I need to start thinking about them now.

I had to call round the stores that owe money today, which I hate doing. I can't wait until I can employ someone to do it. It's not that the people aren't nice; I just hate the way they fob you off.

I had some good news today – *T3* magazine wants to go ahead with personalised Mocks for their 50th birthday issue. They are going to order 12,000. I won't make much money from this deal, but the publicity will be worth it.

Tuesday 26th April 2005

It was Anzac Day yesterday, which means a public holiday. I went and played two-up at my local pub. It was lots of fun, but now I have a million things to do! The extra stands I ordered finally arrived last week, so I can get out the orders that were waiting on them.

I have arranged to get the keys to the office on Friday. I can't wait – how exciting. It will be great to have a lift to get into the office, rather than carrying Mocks and stands up to our unit on the first floor. It feels further with a heavy box. I am going to need to hire a van for the move on Saturday, just to get everything from my place to the office; otherwise we will be there forever.

Friday 29th April 2005

It's a *big day* today. I'm moving into the new office. The phone guy came and set up all the phone lines and new plug sockets, and the locksmith changed the locks – I thought it best. Meanwhile I was cleaning and sticking up translucent paper on the bottom half of the windows, to give a bit of privacy. I found a very cheap alternative to getting the professional glass people in; it was going to be around $300 to get the bottom of each window done, but I got the paper from the art shop and stuck it on myself for around $30 – what a bargain. Tomorrow I get the van at 8am, Mr Johns and I will have a full day of moving, so exciting.

Mockers (people who work at LaRoo) – Jane an all rounder, Ella bookkeeping
Mocks sold this month: 4,005
Total stores: 264
Original target: 1,000 by the end of 2005
Business bank account balance: $7,278
Mood: ☺ ☺

May 2005

Monday 2nd May 2005

It took all day Saturday to move in, then Sunday I spent sorting and rearranging everything. It actually took less time than I expected. Today I walked in to find it all done! I love my desk. I have windows in front of me, and so I get lots of light, and I can have a stickybeak on what the neighbours are up to. Jane started today. She seemed pretty impressed with the place. Well, it is practically a palace compared to the spare room – we even have a sink.

Saturday 7th May 2005

It has been a crazy, crazy week. No broadband internet access as yet. Luckily we have two phone lines, but I had to disconnect one phone line to use dial-up internet so that we could access emails – what a pain.

I had an office-warming party last night – not just the two of us, I asked about eight of my friends. They are used to me having a party for every event in my business's life – I love to celebrate events. I ended up getting very drunk. Everyone was very impressed with the office. It's much better than they expected. It does look pretty posh from the outside – all glass and metal.

Monday 10th May 2005

I emailed lastminute.co.uk in the UK again. It is so hard to get any answer from them. I just can't understand if they are selling well here why they won't take them there … frustrating. I will just keep onto it.

I have set up a 10am weekly catch-up with Jane, even though it is just us two in the office. I want to have a certain time each week to go through bits, since we are both going to be busy doing our stuff all week.

Still no broadband access. ☹

Friday 13th May 2005

I went to the Telstra Business Women's Awards information night last night; I am thinking about entering this year. They have a young businesswomen's award, for women 30 years and younger, so this is the last year I will qualify. I definitely think it is worth applying, although filling in the application form is going to take ages. If I win it will be fantastic PR for the business.

I met up with Web Wizzes today regarding the new website I want to get built for the iMocks. They are a new small business, but they seemed keen, and were pretty organised. They are going to get back to me with a quote. I have three months in which to get the site done, so it shouldn't be too hard. They came recommended by a designer I know, and I have checked them out through other contacts, and they seem to have done an OK job in the past.

I filled in the duty drawback forms this week, so I can claim the customs duty from Mocks I import to Australia and then export to the UK and New Zealand. It is so time consuming that I absolutely hate doing it, and usually put it off for as long as I possibly can. This time I got $560 rebate, so it was worth the time and hassle.

Friday 20th May 2005

Mr Johns was away this week in Japan, so I have been able to get on with work. I've been working late and going out every night seeing friends – I love it!

I met Alex, my "goals group" buddy, for breakfast on Tuesday, and we discussed my Telstra award application. She is going to help me with it; reading it through and making sure that I have met the entry criteria. It will be good to have another set of eyes going over it and it's really kind of her to offer. It's not as if she doesn't have a million other things of her own to do.

The iMock launch is still an ongoing project. I updated the timelines and it's totally doable, but I need to get the designs going. I am having issues with some stock I sent to New Zealand for a giveaway. The invoice I sent with the Mocks had the wrong price on it, so I got charged around $7,000 in customs duty on the Mocks, instead of less than $1,000. I've since gone back and said that I made a mistake, and done another invoice, but I don't think I am going to get the duty reduced as the customs people think that I am now trying to pull a fast one – I can't believe I could be so stupid ... I will definitely learn from this mistake. I hope I can get it sorted I really don't want to have to spend $7,000 on customs duties for a magazine giveaway. Yuk.

I finally got the list of New Zealand stores that are stocking Mocks. There are 192 in total, and I am hoping that it will increase once the distributor gets going ... I will see. I need to keep up the relationship, which will really help to drive sales.

Web Wizzes presented the quote for the iMocks site today. It seems pretty comprehensive, and they say they can do it in the time allowed. I will think on it and decide. They have some good ideas. I'll also discuss it with Erica, my graphic designer, to see what she thinks, as she will be working with them.

I've been working hard in the gym this week and with my trainer. It's nearly killing me! Well, no pain, no gain, I guess. All my friends commented on how fantastic I looked last week at my birthday party.

Thursday 26th May 2005

I went to the CeBIT technology exhibition at Darling Harbour in the city today, just to check out what is out there and see if there is anything I need to be worried about. There were very few mobile accessory products there, mostly phones and computer companies showing off their latest x or y. It was full of computer geeks. I so didn't fit in … thank goodness.

I briefed Erica, the graphic designer, on the new website yesterday. I think we will end up going with Web Wizzes. We are planning a whole different type of website. It will reflect the iMocks product with two looks to the site, rather than one, and the user can choose which look they want to have. It really fits with the feel of two designs in one.

Wednesday afternoon was spent brainstorming new Mock designs. I love doing this – just getting lots of magazines and ripping out designs, ideas and anything that would appeal to the Mocks target audience. Jane was really struggling to understand it and get into the right groove. I think it is much easier for me because I have been doing this since I was little at home - Mum was an art teacher and really encouraged our creative side. Even if I explain it to people, I can't force them to be creative. It comes from within, or with lots of practice. I find it strange when people find it so amazing that I can do it with reasonable ease.

Friday 27th May 2005

I did those stairs again this morning with my trainer – a total killer.

I had to check the Turtle Mock stock today. I seem to be selling a lot, which is great, but I will need to order more. It is so hard knowing what demand is going to be, since new stores are coming onboard every week. A bra company called this week saying they are interested in doing a branded Mock as a gift with purchase. This is one of the market leaders, which sells in department stores like Myer and David Jones. It would be a great way to increase brand awareness and maybe get an in for Mocks to be sold into the department stores. I have quoted her a great price to reflect this. I just need to get the samples done now.

Mockers – Jane an all rounder, Ella bookkeeping
Mocks sold this month: 18,942
Total stores: 275
Original target: 1,000 by the end of 2005
Business bank account balance: $8,661
Mood: ☺ ☺ 1/2

June 2005
Wednesday 1st June 2005

I spent the whole day today at a workshop for year 10 and 11 schoolgirls called "Girl Savvy", a government initiative to promote women in business, rather than let girls think that they can marry a rich man! It was a lot of fun, and great to talk directly to my target audience, I got to talk to the group about what I do, and there were lots of questions, more than any of the other mentors had … not that I'm counting. I even got my photo in the *Manly Daily*.

Friday 3rd June 2005

I finally finished and posted my Telstra award application today. It took ages; I have been working on it on and off for two weeks, but I think the end result is really good. I put in lots of charts and images, to make it interesting, and included a Mock with my application … ☺ It can't hurt.

The Mocki Club press releases went out today to journalists. Hopefully Mocks will get a few mentions. I will call round next week and see what people think. The press release is definitely quirky enough to get people's attention.

I got the designs from the bra company today for the Mocks that they are looking at, and I sent them on to Jackie in China so he could make some samples.

The Mocks lanyards arrive soon. I've just done one version – I had to order 4,000 per design; I can see how it goes and take it from there. I am not really convinced that they are going to be a huge seller, but they can be used as a promo item if they don't take off, so either way it will be OK.

Thank goodness I have Jane helping me. It has been crazy this week, and it is lovely having someone to delegate anything and everything to, especially someone I know I can trust to get the job done.

Today I've been chasing Crazy John's, a mobile phone retail chain, to get them to take Mocks. I just want to speak to the buyer; is that so hard? The receptionist just won't give out any details, and so I have to send the information to "the buyer" then it means I don't have the name of a person to call up and check they got there and see if they like them ... Grrr!

Tuesday 7th June 2005

I had a great meeting today with the sales manager from the diary company Collins Debden. I am really keen on producing a Mocks diary for 2006 as a promotional item. I figure that if someone looks at it every day it will increase awareness with people, plus I could sell them to customers. I just need to get the quote and see whether it's affordable. I don't really have a budget for marketing materials. I should, I guess, but it is hard to know what I am going to do, I usually see what comes up and how sales are going; not the best business plan, I know.

I got my lawyers to check out my terms and conditions of supply to customers yesterday. Previously I just had generic ones, which the Austrade person gave me. I thought I better get them checked to see if I had missed anything. I'm starting to get proper documents now, rather than cheap and cheerful. I feel so professional!

I went to an Australian Businesswomen's Network networking event last week and met a lovely woman who is starting up a marketing agency and wanted to meet for coffee to catch up. I enjoy the networking side of business, although sometimes I feel that perhaps I spend too much time doing it, and not enough working on other aspects.

Saturday 11th June 2005

I went on a fantastic course on Thursday this week, all about customer service. One thing that really stuck in my mind was a company that advertise on its website that you can choose to pay in cash or chocolate – how cool is that? Apparently since they have been going only one customer has paid them in chocolate, but even so, it is a great way to make your company stick in people's minds and also generate PR. I came back full of lots of ideas that I can implement straight away to improve our customer service. I felt so inspired; I love going on courses like that. Jane in the office thought I was crazy. She was saying that normally people go on courses, come back and nothing changes, whereas I came back and was saying "Right, from now on we will do this like this", and she loved that I was so enthusiastic about it all. That is definitely one of the best things about running my own business. Yes, if I mess up it's all my problem, but also, if I want to change and improve processes there is no waiting around – I just do it!

Sales are up to $6,296 for this month so far, which I think is pretty good considering we have only had 10 days.

I really want to get Mocks into the UK market, so I booked my flights to the UK this week. I fly out on 4th July and will be away until 27th. I really need to focus on the UK market, especially as there has been interest from a distributor there. I want to go over and cement the relationship.

Thursday 16th June 2005

Jane was off sick for two days this week, which was really annoying. I obviously was concerned, but it is just that we have so much to do. I know that she wouldn't be off if she wasn't sick, but still, it is hard,

76

especially as I have to pay her. I know when I was working my boss was awful about me taking a sick day, so I don't want to make her feel bad, there is nothing I can do about it. I have thought about how much easier would it be if I could clone myself, and then just have clones of me running the business, but I am sure even that would go wrong – it always does in the movies.

I finalised the Mocki Club leaflet today. They will be arriving next week from the printer, then I will send them out to stores. Each store will be given a unique number, and if a customer picks up the leaflet and sends in the application the store will receive three free Mocks. I think I have to incentivise the stores to make sure that the leaflets are displayed. I am hoping that this will be a good way to boost the number of members, since otherwise the Mocki Club is only being promoted online, through the e-newsletter and when people order Mocks by mail.

Tuesday 21st June 2005

I have started on my company procedures manual. I want to try to get a procedure written for everything that is done in the business. This will make it easier for when new staff start, plus it apparently adds to the value of the business when I sell. Jane and I are getting there, but there are so many procedures to document that it's hard to find the time. It needs to be done, but obviously it is not super urgent, which usually means it is left and other more urgent or important tasks are done first.

I had a great meeting today with the Australian and UK Austrade representatives, to go through exporting to the UK, and gain more understanding about the market. They have said that they can help me to find distributors, market to buyers and find a fulfillment house to send out the Mocks, as well as give me market research reports, and help and advice in general. I feel that I am getting there. It's important to understand the mobile market over there, and it is fantastic to have people to dig up the research for me.

Friday 24th June 2005

I had a Mocktastic meeting today with the marketing coordinator from Sony Ericsson mobile phones. It would be so cool if they order branded Mocks. She seemed very keen. It fits really well with their promo plans, and obviously with their product. I just need to get back to her with quotes.

The samples for the bra company Mocks still haven't arrived. Jackie has been really slow with this; it is very frustrating! The company has now decided not to go with the idea because it has taken so long ... very, very annoying and frustrating.

Yesterday I briefed Erica on the designs for the new Mocks range and the artwork for the diary that Collins Debden is going to produce for me. She was so excited about the diary idea, and came up with lots of suggestions. It is fantastic; I love her enthusiasm. I love working with people who get excited, probably because I get excited myself, and because I love seeing people react rather than just sitting there.

I went on a PR course this week to get some more ideas to promote Mocks in the media. I met a copywriter, who could be useful, as I am running out of time to write press releases. It's definitely worth keeping in touch with her. I also met a girl whose company makes really gorgeous teddy bears. As part of the course we are supposed to support each other with writing a press release. I am not entirely sure that this will happen, not because I don't want to, but I can already see that the next few weeks are going to fly by. There are so many great free courses out there on all aspects of business run by the government, networking groups and chambers of commerce; it is really easy to gain additional knowledge on areas where I'm not very strong. It still amazes me that more people don't go ...

Mockers – Jane an all rounder, Ella bookkeeping
Mocks sold this month: 5,383
Total stores: 311
Original target: 1,000 by the end of 2005
Bank account balance: −$871 (oops, I wrote a cheque and it got cashed too early)

Mood: ☺ ☺ ☺

July 2005
Friday 1st July 2005

The first day of the new financial year. I had to do lots of paperwork, like workers comp insurance. How fantastic – *not*! They are just bills; I really can't see the point of them. What will happen is what usually happens with insurance: I'll pay out a stack of cash and never make a claim, and so never get my money's worth! It's negative, I know, but I am so against insurance. It just feels like money for nothing. I know that everyone says it's worth it, just in case, but I really don't agree. ☹

I am still trying to follow up Sony Ericsson on the personalised Mocks. Their representative seemed so keen in the meeting, but now it is plain hard to get hold of her … I just don't get it.

I think I've got everything done for my trip to the UK next week. I have put together one page of key contacts for Jane, so that she knows who to contact if she needs to, plus it will be really useful when I get more staff.

Thursday 7th July 2005

I have arrived in London to a balmy hot summer – actually, more like warm. I am staying at my sister Maud's house where she lives with her boyfriend, and my brother Will is also there at the moment. The house is being renovated, so it's all kind of upside down, including there being no sink in the kitchen, so we have to wash up dishes in the bathroom! Luckily I have found a good internet place around the corner, so I can email people and check the bank account. I have been calling the office every day to check Jane is OK. Today I found out that I am a finalist in my local newspaper awards, the Manly Daily Business Achiever Awards. So apparently I have a certificate and there is a ceremony to go to later next month. Very exciting.

Friday 8th July 2005

Today I took the train out to meet a mobile phone distributor that I have been talking to. He absolutely loved the Mocks. I left him samples of all the designs, and talked him through the plans for the future. He has placed an order for 5,000 Mocks for one of their customers – Carphone Warehouse, the largest mobile retailer in the UK. How totally fantastic! This is going to be the way into the UK market. With the exchange rate as it is, I make so much more money on the UK orders; it will really help the Australian business get off the ground. Now the only slight dilemma is going to be getting the Mocks to them in time. They want them for next month, which is a bit of a challenge. I definitely don't have enough in Oz to supply them, plus they want to order more in the lead-up to Christmas … Oooh, so exciting! I so love getting these large orders; it makes me forget about all the chasing I had to do.

Monday 11th July 2005

I had meetings today with the two main teen girl magazines in the UK: *Sugar* and *Bliss*. I took Carla, the friend from university who helped me at Homebake last year, and is doing my PR in the UK. She works for a PR company. Meeting with the magazines should help to get Mocks into them. Both magazines were very interested in Mocks, which might just translate into some free PR. However, judging from speaking to magazine staff, it seems that they are much tighter on what they give you for free compared to Australian magazines. I showed them the *Girlfriend* covermount I did in Australia and they loved the idea, but were saying that I'd have to pay to be on the cover, in that I would have to pay for the bag to be put on the magazine as well as providing the Mock – I can't believe it! I think this is going to be much harder than I thought initially, or much more expensive. The UK magazines are approached by lots more companies to get free product exposure, so I guess that they can be more fussy as to what they feature, and how much they charge. It is £10,000 a page to advertise in these magazines, or $A25,000. There is *no* way I can afford that, so I really need to milk the free PR angle.

Wednesday 13th July 2005

I met the gift buyer for lastminute.co.uk and told her about Mocks. She was really keen, especially when I said that they are the number two best-selling gift on the Australian site. I just need to get images etc. to her when I am back and we will be all systems go – hurray!

Yesterday I met another potential Mocks distributor, someone who targets gift stores. To be honest he seemed rather slimy. I don't feel that I could trust him. The company sells novelty gifts, but they import a lot themselves, so I really don't think the focus would be on Mocks. I left him with some information, but I don't plan to use them. I really can't work with someone who I think is dodgy when I am halfway across the world.

I have still been keeping on top of the Australian business while I have been away, writing the store newsletter for Jane and writing the e-newsletter. I've also been developing a schoolies week Mock and I am striking a deal with Fone Zone to get them to sell it at a discount during schoolies. In addition, I'm working on a branded Mock for the Ninemsn website, they are launching some new mobile content for people to download off the website, and want to send out Ninemsn Mocks to the first 2000 people who join up. Ninemsn saw the Girlfriend covermount that I did earlier in the year and approached me, it will be more good exposure to the target audience.

Jackie, my usual Mocks supplier, is taking ages to give me samples for Ninemsn, so it is going to be delivered late, which obviously they are not happy about. I don't really understand why this is taking so long. Jackie can normally make samples in a week, yet this has taken three weeks already, and it's not as if the design is particularly complex. I seem to be spending the entire time apologising to Ninemsn. I need to start looking for an alternative Mocks manufacturer to have as a backup just in case things go pear-shaped.

Tuesday 19th July 2005

I had a meeting with the Top Shop store fashion accessories buyer on Friday last week, a real last minute meeting, with me phoning up and practically begging to be seen, playing the "I am only here for two more days and I am from Australia" card! She met me in reception at their offices, where we talked for about 10 minutes, and there was an embarrassing moment at the start when I thought she had pen on her nose, and mentioned it to her, but it was a birthmark … Cringe … They have agreed to take the Mocks. *How fantastic is that?* I can't believe that Mocks will be in Top Shop, the place where all teenage girls shop. I just need to get back to them on pricing and when they can be delivered. Woohoo, so so so exciting!

I got the Eurostar over to France on Saturday, and am now staying with Mum and Dad at their house near Rouen where they moved to two years ago. It is about two hours' drive west of Paris. It is great to be staying in a place where I have my own room after nearly two weeks of sleeping on floors, or at friends' houses. I can totally spread out, plus there's no need to make any trips to the internet cafe, as there is broadband in the house – if I can just get Dad off the computer.

I have decided over the time I have been away so far that Jane isn't really working out. She is lovely, but just not really up to the variety of tasks that the role entails. I was really lucky to have her, as I couldn't have gone away otherwise, but I just don't think that she is coping. I'll have to talk to her when I am back.

Monday 25th July 2005

I got some more good news last week from mobile phone retailer Crazy John's. After doing a trial in 25 stores, they have reordered for all their stores, so that's an additional 75 stores. The Mocks empire is growing …

I had an email from Jane yesterday saying that she is going to quit, the role is too busy for her and it is not what she wants to do. I'm relieved I don't have to talk to her about it – phew!

Thursday 28th July 2005

I'm back in the Sydney office … Jane has coped really well, considering, and all is fine between us. She is going to stay until she finds something else or I find someone, which is great. I spent time today putting together ads for the *Manly Daily* and the online job site seek.com.au in the hope that I can find someone reasonably quickly.

Some good news today: the Ninemsn Mocks are on their way to me. They are very late – about four weeks late – but at least they are coming. The delay has totally ruined any chance of a future order from them, which is very annoying.
Mockers – Jane an all rounder, Ella bookkeeping
Mocks sold this month: 13,861
Total stores: 345
Original target: 1,000 by the end of 2005
Business bank account balance: $4,029
Mood: ☺ ☺ ☺ 1/2

August 2005
Thursday 4th August 2005
I had a *big* day today … I interviewed five people for Jane's role, but only one really stood out as being good. I have two more lined up for tomorrow, so I will see. I don't want to rush into getting just anyone; I really want to find the right person. I went on a state-government-run workplace policies course yesterday to learn about more about the rules around awards, pay and employing people. It was interesting, and gave me more of an idea of what I should do as an employer.

I met up with a guy about setting up a service for customers to be able to buy a Mock via SMS, using their mobile credit, rather than cash or credit card. I figure that not many of my target audience of teens have the ability to pay by credit card, so this would be ideal, plus it's instant gratification for them. They see the advert, they SMS and the Mock is mailed to them. I would have to charge $13.20 per Mock rather than $9.95 as there would have to be two $6.60 SMSes sent by the buyer, as there isn't a larger SMS tariff; apparently it is restricted like that. I don't think $13.20 seems unreasonable for a Mock, considering how you are buying it and the ease of it all. The set-up fees are pretty high, around $1,800, but the guy is going to get back to me with all the costs and I can decide.

Monday 8th August 2005

I bought a new car on the weekend. After completing my tax return for 2004/05 financial year I found that I couldn't claim all the business kilometres I'd done on our car, as I went over the 3,000km limit I can claim, so it is logical for me to buy a car and run it through the business. I test drove the Toyota Echo and loved it; I knew I would, as I had one when I lived in the UK. I bought it there and then, and I'm going to get it in black and get Mocks logos stuck all over it. It will be great for brand exposure.

I interviewed another candidate today, Cathy. I really liked her; she was very switched-on. No real experience, but very enthusiastic. I also second interviewed the girl I liked from last week. I still like her, so I am just not sure between the two of them. I will second interview Cathy, I think, and see after that. Mr Johns came in today and gave me his view on the second interview; it's good for me to have another opinion. I know I can be rather too subjective.

Wednesday 10th August 2005

I'm still trying to sort out this mess-up I made with the Mocks I sent to New Zealand for the giveaway which incurred the customs duty bill. I have the guy from the freight company on the case trying to get it reduced, but I'm really not holding my breath – so annoying.

I second interviewed Cathy today. I think that she would be great; I have one more person to see on Friday so I will decide then. Cathy would be cheap, since she is straight out of university, which means I could potentially afford to have another person part-time, if I needed it.

Friday 12th August

The final girl didn't turn up today for her interview, so I will offer the role to Cathy. I really liked her and I can see us working well together. I will need to teach her a lot, from writing a business letter to all aspects of what I need her to do, as she really has very little experience. I have mentioned this to her, and said that it is my main concern, as I will have to invest a lot of time in training, but she is very willing to learn, so I think it will work out. She definitely has the right attitude.

I met up with my dentist's son yesterday for coffee. He wanted to ask me about exporting, as he has a product that he is looking at exporting to Asia. I find it hard when people see me as an expert. I mean, it is nice, but I really don't feel like one. I feel like I am just making it up as I go along, or getting it from a book, and to be honest I don't always think everything through properly. I can get caught up in the passion of the moment – I think passion is good, but it has led me to an expensive learning experience of a $7,000 customs duty bill.

Monday 15th August 2005

Yesterday I walked and ran the City to Surf, a 14km fun run from the city to Bondi Beach. I wanted to jump the whole way in a giant Mock, as if I were in a sack race, but Mr Johns told me it was too dangerous, he thought I might fall over – I can be a bit accident prone at times. Maybe, but think of the publicity … Instead, I wore it as a cape, and people were calling me superMock! I went with some friends, and we all wore Mocks T-shirts, which made a good splash. I just wish there'd had been more than five of us. Next year I need a team of 20 or 30 all running together.

Thursday 18th August 2005

Last night was the Manly Daily Business Achiever Awards ceremony. I didn't win. I wasn't too upset, as it was lovely having the support of my friends there and good from a business point of view to be nominated. I really want to focus on winning the Telstra Business Women's Award now.

Cathy started today, thank goodness, since Jane finished last week, and this week has been hectic. She will pick up the role really quickly, I think. I just need to make sure I take the time to show her things properly, at least that procedures manual that Jane and I slaved over will help.

I got the entries from the *Girlfriend* "design a Mock" competition today. There were over 600 entries, which they said was a good number, especially as some girls sent in 10 designs! I've gone through them all and selected the ones I think would work. Two of the actresses from the TV show *Home and Away* will decide on the final design, so I will wait to hear.

Monday 22nd August 2005
I had my interview for the Telstra Business Women's Award today, which means that I am a finalist. Two women interviewed me, and I wasn't entirely sure what to expect, but they just basically asked me about what I'd put on my application form in a bit more depth. It was still totally nerve-racking. I gave them both a Mock. They said it might be construed as bribery, but they were willing to take the risk. Fingers crossed I impressed them.

I met up with the Australian Businesswomen's Network's communications committee tonight. They all wanted to know about my interview. The chair of our committee has been a finalist before, so it was interesting to get her opinion, plus she helped me with the application. It is great being in such a supportive group – I don't always see my own success and when other people get excited about my story it reminds me of what I have achieved. Having said that, I usually feel as though I haven't done much because I am too busy looking forward to what's coming up.

Friday 26th August 2005
I had a meeting with a guy today in the office; he had said he had an opportunity to discuss with me. In hindsight, I should have got more information about it from him on the phone. He came with his business partner. Basically they have a new product that are going to launch and they came to ask me how to do it. I ended up talking to them for 1.5 hours because I got carried away, as I do, and then afterwards I felt really used. They want me to do the distribution for their product, as it is a kind of mobile accessory. I thought about it afterwards and thought it would be a lot of hard work on my end, as they haven't got a clue, and realistically the return would not be huge. I would prefer to spend my time on Mocks rather than

organising them. I feel that this sounds like I'm being mean, but I also think it was rather unfair of them to expect all the help from me. I'm annoyed at myself for not ending the meeting earlier. I got so passionate and carried away that I forgot to stop.

Tuesday 30th August 2005

I am still following up Jackie in China about the shipment of the Mocks which was supposed to have left about four weeks ago. I am waiting on them for the UK order. The UK distributors have been really understanding about the delay, but it is very late for them and I am starting to panic, as he just isn't getting back to me, I have called, emailed, faxed, SMSed – there isn't anything else I can do – he just isn't returning my calls. I have decided I have to go to China and find a new supplier. It may be rather dramatic, but I really have to get these orders filled. It will be difficult to leave the office as Cathy has only been here for a week, but I really don't have a choice. I booked a flight today - I leave on Friday.

Wednesday 31st August 2005

I had a sudden panic today – do I need a visa for China? The answer was yes, so I had to drive to the city go the Chinese Embassy, apply for the visa and pay the extra fee for it to be ready in 24 hours. I have to go back tomorrow and pick it up.

I went online today and found nine different suppliers of socks on the alibaba.com and globalsourcing.com websites, which I've used before. Most of the contacts I found are manufacturers rather than middlemen. After the experience with Jackie, I don't really want to use a middleman again. I would prefer to deal directly with the factory. This should give me more control over what happens with my orders. I have emailed them all, and I managed to set up meetings with them in the first few days of next week. I will have meetings with them all and then decide which one or two of them to go with, and have another meeting with them. I have booked a hotel online. The hotel reception staff speak English and the hotel is in a central tourist area, so hopefully I can go out at night on my own without any worries. I fly back on Thursday evening; I think I should be able to cover everything in five days. I am going on my own. It hadn't even occurred to me that I might need or want to take anyone. Mr Johns said he would have gone, but he has to be in Japan with work.

Mockers – Cathy an all rounder, Ella bookkeeping
Mocks sold this month: 18,707
Total stores: 345
Original target: 1,000 by the end of 2005
Business bank account balance: $19,530 (lovely $11,000 payment from Fone Zone)
Mood: ☺ ☺ 1/2

September 2005
Thursday 1st September 2005

I picked up my visa today. Thank goodness that was all OK. Knowing how strict they are about visitors into China I was slightly concerned. Now I just need to organise samples and the designs I need made, and I will be ready to go. Unbelievably, I emailed Jackie to say that I was coming and ask if we could meet up, and he said he would pick me up from the airport. I find that very hard to believe. He didn't say anything about the Mocks that I have paid $5,000 for and he hasn't made. He just ignored that point. At the end of the day I am willing to lose the money if I have to. I can't deal with him, he is so unreliable. I think I can probably still get him to get the Mocks made to cover the payment. I'll see when I see him at the airport – although to be honest I don't really want him to pick me up.

Friday 2nd September 2005

The flight was fine. I arrived OK and, surprise, surprise, there was no Jackie at the airport. Awful as it sounds, I have no idea what he looks like, and there were lots and lots of Chinese people; whereas as a westerner, I stood out like a sore thumb, so I figured if he was there he would have spotted me. I showed a taxi driver the hotel address and hoped he understood. My Chinese is nonexistent. The hotel is fine, pretty basic, but the staff are friendly and they understand me, which is a big plus. I have three meetings set up for tomorrow, fingers crossed I will find a good, reliable supplier.

Saturday 3rd September 2005

My first meeting was at the office of the manufacturer. It was highly hilarious: the hotel receptionist had to look up where I was going in Chinese, as opposed to the English address I had, then tell the doorman, who then took me to a taxi and told the driver. Meanwhile I didn't understand a word, and was just relying on them to get me there. Despite the fact I couldn't speak to the driver, he took me to exactly the right place. It took 40 minutes, and thoughts about abduction did briefly pass through my head! At the office the driver got out of the taxi, took me to the building sign and showed me which floor the company was on. Such a nice guy.

At the manufacturers office I met two girls. They were sweet; they said they could make the Mocks, no problem. They quoted me a price and said that they would get samples to me at the hotel before I left. It was a very positive meeting. The girls were very surprised that I was travelling alone, and kept telling me to be careful, which was kind. I will wait and see how they compare with the other manufacturers. The company they work for is big, and they make a wide range of clothing as well as socks. I could find myself as a tiny fish in a huge pond, which isn't the ideal situation.

I got back to the hotel fine, and for my next meeting I was taken to lunch at Pizza Hut! I felt bad about the factory owner and his assistant taking me to lunch, as I wouldn't necessarily be using them, but they were very lovely, and are going to make some Mock samples for me, and get them to me with the price before I leave.

The big meeting of the day was at 3pm with the elusive Jackie. He was 30 minutes late. I didn't think he was going to turn up. Jackie said that he has been sick for the last month and no-one else could do his job. He then came out with lots more excuses –unbelievable. He's just not reliable. I definitely don't want to use him again, which I think he realises, but I do want the Mocks I have paid for. He has agreed to supply them, but I am not really holding my breath.

Monday 5th September 2005

Yesterday I spent the day being a tourist. I thought that while I was in Shanghai I should really see some of it. It feels a bit strange walking around, as there are hardly any westerners here. I might have seen 10 so far …

I had a meeting with an Austrade representative today. It was really just a brief chat to see if there is anything they can do to help me while I am here, and to let me know that they are here if I need them. The office is in a really rich expat part of Shanghai; the shopping centre next to the office is all high-end designer clothes stores like Prada, Gucci and Lacoste. In contrast the parts of the city I have seen from the taxi on my journey across town were so dirty and cramped, with poor people begging on the street and huge apartment blocks about 30 stories high, all with external air conditioning units on the buildings, and washing hanging out from every window. It is unbelievable the huge difference between rich and poor in the city.

At 6pm I met Laura, a sales manager from another factory. She was totally lovely and really seemed to know her stuff. She goes to the factory once a week, every week. She is going tomorrow, and I asked if I could go with her. She was surprised, but said yes. It is three hours on the bus. I think it is important to see how the socks are made; I don't want to be buying from a company with bad staff working conditions. Laura is one of those people that I just hit it off with straight away. I've got a really good feeling about this.

Tuesday 6th September 2005

A *very* eventful day … I took the three-hour bus journey out to the factory. When we arrived they took me for lunch at a traditional Chinese restaurant where I got to choose what we ate. I had no idea, but luckily they had plates of food made up and I had to look at those and choose, while Laura explained to me what they were. Her English is fantastic; she worked in London for a year. The factory manager was there, but he speaks practically no English, so it was an amusing lunch. Even though they all drank beer, they ordered wine, because they thought I'd like it. Aside from rice wine, wine is not really a Chinese drink, and not surprisingly really, it was horrible!

The factory was not really what I expected. A new one is being built and will be ready in a few months, but currently everything is spread out across different buildings, rather than being located all in one building. We had a long chat with the quality control technician. He made me samples while I was there. It was hilarious. As he spoke no English and I speak no Chinese, we were using a kind of sign language with each other and a lot of laughing. The factory conditions were quite depressing, I thought. I said to Laura that I was willing to pay more for the Mocks than the amount she quoted me to ensure that the workers were being looked after, but she said that there was no need and that the workers are well looked after compared to other factories.

While we waited for the Mocks to be completed and the bus departure time, Laura and I had a game of ping pong. Hilariously, they had a table in the office. I expected Laura to be great at ping pong, but she was worse than me! The Mock samples came back looking good, and I was really impressed with the service from them. The price was slightly higher than some of the other manufacturers I have met, but Laura seemed so organised and straightforward that I think we would work well together.

When we got back to Shanghai we went for dinner with Laura's husband to a place where you cook the food yourself in a vat of boiling stock. Laura's favourite is sheep's brains, so I said I'd give it a go. It looked exactly like something from an Indiana Jones movie, and tasted like scrambled eggs – I wasn't a fan, I just couldn't get the image of the raw brains out of my head. Laura thought it was hilarious...

Wednesday 7th September 2005

I met two other potential suppliers today, but I have decided to go with Laura; we just got on really well, and I feel very happy that they can do what I want. However, after the experience with Jackie I know that I should have a backup supplier, hence these meetings.

Both meetings went well. Their English wasn't fantastic, but they were very enthusiastic about their socks and the Mocks.

Tuesday 13th September 2005

I've been back in Oz as of last Friday. The business is still fine. Cathy kept the business going well on her own, considering that she had only been here a week before I left. I think it's amazing what can happen when I have to do something, whereas if I'd planned it more it might not have worked so well.

Saturday 17th September 2005

I entered a Mocks team into the National Breast Cancer City Treasure Hunt today, and we managed to come second out of 20 teams. Five of us ran round Sydney CBD in Mocks T-shirts chasing answers to clues. We got stopped and asked quite a few times what Mocks were – great branding, plus there were Mocks in the goodie bags given out at the end.

Thursday 22nd September 2005

It has been a crazy few days. Tomorrow is the Telstra Business Women's Award lunch, when I find out if I've won. I'm not feeling that confident. We went to a cocktail function tonight for the finalists. It was great meeting the other women, and interesting to see what they had achieved. I didn't get to meet all my competitors, but I do now know who they are. The atmosphere at the event was very supportive; the other attendees were really interested in what I had achieved. It seemed to be pretty high profile.

Saturday 24th September 2005

I didn't win. I can't say that I am not disappointed because I am. My friends from the Australian Businesswomen's Network who came with me said that it was a huge achievement to get to where I had, especially considering I'd only been in business for nine months when I entered. Still, it doesn't feel like an achievement. The organisers really encouraged us to make the most of being a finalist, so I will get the finalist logo added to my business cards. In a way, actually, I felt relieved that I didn't win, because it meant that I didn't have to do a speech. The girl who won had been working for a company for 10 years. She had a lot more experience than I do, so it wasn't really a big surprise that she won rather than me.

I have advertised this weekend for a part-time packer to help send out the Mocks store orders. I'm finding that we really don't have enough time to do that as well as everything else. Hopefully I'll find someone good.

Tuesday 27th September 2005
Julie, the daughter of a lady from the office next door, came in today for an interview for the packer role. She is only 17, but seems pretty switched on, and it is only a part-time role. I checked her references, which came back positive, so she is starting tomorrow. What a relief.

Mocks can now be purchased via SMS! I added it to the website today, it has taken a while to set up, but I really believe that it will work, given my target audience and the fact that Mocks are a mobile accessory.
Mockers – Cathy an all rounder, Julie in dispatch, Ella bookkeeping
Mocks sold this month: 13,224
Total stores: 425
Original target: 1,000 by the end of 2005
Business bank account balance: $13,545
Mood: ☺

October 2005
Friday 7th October
I had a lovely long weekend in Brisbane visiting friends; it was good for me to have a bit of time-out, although what with the China and UK trips this year, it feels like I have been away quite a bit …

My new packer, Julie, is working out well. Orders are increasing, so she is working more hours, which is a great help for me. It means I can get on with the sales bits. Cathy is enjoying her admin role, and fitting in really well. We are going to have a six-week review next week. I can't believe how fast that has gone.

I went speed networking on Tuesday evening. It was a lot of fun. I met 20 people during the night. Having just five minutes to chat to each person meant that I got lots of chances to practise my elevator speech. It was good to force myself to chat to a wide range of people. Often I end up chatting to the same people, or just to people I know, or I get stuck talking to someone and finding it hard to escape.

Tuesday 11th October 2005

Cathy had her review today. It went well. I am really pleased with what she has been doing, and she is enjoying it, which is important to me. I have given her a couple of small projects to run: some promotional cards for the iMocks and some new promotional ideas. I think it is important to have ownership of projects. I'll monitor this first project closely and the next one less, and then less and less each time. Cathy was really excited about it, she really enjoys the creative side of marketing and wants to be involved in the business.

Thursday 13th October 2005

My brother Humbert arrived today from the US where he has been working as a basketball coach, to stay for about a month. It is rather nice to have a visitor.

I went through website training for the new iMocks website today over the phone, some of the site is finished, but much of it isn't. To be honest I am really not impressed with the service I am getting; they are now over a month behind on the project plan. I am starting to hear excuses as to why they can't do something, and not professional excuses, but excuses such as "I have to go to the dentist", "I have to take my mum to the dentist" – it is pathetic. I am not sure how much I will be willing to put up with … I hate it when people give me excuses …

The winning Mock from the *Girlfriend* "design a Mock" competition arrived today: a magic eightball Mock. I think it is going to sell really well. The girl who designed it was very, very excited that it was being made.

Wednesday 19th October 2005

I advertised today at the local TAFE for an accounts data-entry person. The number of invoices we are processing is growing, and it probably takes around 10 hours a week, so I think it is time to get the right person doing the job, rather than me or Cathy trying to fit it in around everything else. However, the office is going to get pretty cramped with four of us working in it – I have roped my brother Humbert into help with Mock packing – we are getting more orders with Christmas coming up.

I got approached this week by Crazy John's asking if I would sell them a competitor's product, a mobile phone pouch. They want me to buy from the pouch company and sell to Crazy John's, because Crazy John's don't want to add another supplier. I spoke to the pouch company, but I am not entirely convinced of it all. They seem pretty disorganised, and to be honest I personally think their products are out and out ugly – well, not all of them, but they appeal to the more mature lady. I got their price list sent to me, and it became very quickly apparent that they haven't dealt with a large company before – there was no barcoding on the products, the information sheet they sent was in Excel and it was just awful, it looked homemade. I think it would be a lot of work on my part, as I would be embarrassed to send what they have put together to the buyer. Maybe I am just far too fussy, or a perfectionist … I have to think what is best for my business, and doing this will take the focus off it – and do I really want to sell something that I don't like? I think I will say no.

Wednesday 26th October 2005

I spoke to Crazy John's about the pouches, and explained that I had decided not to take them on. They were fine with that, and they had another option that they can look at for them. I told the pouch company; they were disappointed. I didn't tell them about what I thought of what they sent me, but explained that I just don't have the time and resources to do it for them at the moment.

It was our packer Julie's 18th birthday today as well, so we had chocolate cake. I love celebrating birthdays, and can't understand when people don't. I have decided that we will always get a cake for birthdays – new policy! I better remember to write it in the procedures manual.

Last night my admin assistant Cathy and I went to the Ultimate Girls Night In party, it was basically lots of drinking, dancing and pole dancing lessons. We had a table selling Mocks along with about 10 other companies, it was a fundraiser for the National Breast Cancer Foundation organised by Polestars, the pole dancing company. A friend of mine invited us, but Mocks didn't really fit in, as the other products were more adult, although we did have some interest in Mocks for vibrators! We sold five Mocks and showed the product to a few people, but it was one of those events where everyone goes to get drunk.

I have found a new bookkeeper, as Ella, my last one, fired me. Well, not quite, but she had too many clients and not enough time and so had to reduce the number. I found Jenny, the new one, through the Australian Businesswomen's Network group I belong to. She lives miles away, but was happy to travel to the office every month to do my BAS.

I made another call to the web company today. Still no website … I have decided to give them to the end of the month and if nothing appears then I will be asking for a refund for the money I have paid so far (and got nothing for). This is ridiculous; they are nearly two months late on delivering a finished website. I probably should have been on their backs earlier. Well, I will know for next time.

We had the weekly team meeting today. We now have to each write our win for the week up on the whiteboard. It doesn't have to be huge, but something, so that we feel that we have achieved something during the week. Then we went through what everyone is up to, and what is coming up. It seems to work well to build the team feeling, even though there are only a few of us.

Friday 28th October 2005

I met Vanessa, the *Girlfriend* magazine marketing manager, for lunch today. I love catching up with her, because we have the same staff issues in common, and she tells me all the celeb gossip, as well as what is coming up that we can get involved in with the magazine. I tell her what is happening in the Mocks world. Plus Vanessa always buys lunch as a business expense, which I love. It is like being back in the corporate realm …

I still have no website. I have asked them for a full refund, and they have said that they don't have the money. I have decided to report them to the Office of Fair Trading, as I don't want this to happen to anyone else.

I heard from Laura in China about the iMocks today. I approved the samples a few weeks ago and they will be with me next week, at last! It is a slight problem that the website isn't ready, but good to know that the product is. I plan to spend time in 2006 advertising and promoting them. It's too close to Christmas to get much done now.

Mockers – Cathy an all rounder, Julie in dispatch, Humbert helping, Jenny bookkeeping
Mocks sold this month: 29,721
Total stores: 425
Original target: 1,000 by the end of 2005
Business bank account balance: $2,046
Mood: Grrrr

November 2005

Friday 4th November 2005

I had lots of meetings this week. I had a follow-up meeting with the SMS company; sales are going well. We had 500 orders from the first advert in *Girlfriend*, so it is looking good for the future. I met the advertising manager from another female teen magazine, *Dolly*, to chat about opportunities. There seems to be lots coming up with them, and our year commitment with *Girlfriend* is nearly up, so it could be a possibility for next year. I will have to see what they propose. I have loved working with the *Girlfriend* team this year, and

I think another year with them would work well, but I will have to see.

I got an order from a UK company for personalised Mocks this week. Laura is now making the sample for them. They want 5,000, which is great news, especially with the exchange rate. It is a really good profit. I really need to push the personalised angle with Mocks more. It doesn't require anywhere near as much work as getting a new store onboard, and it is an effective way to develop the brand and make money that we can use to publicise Mocks further. It does, however, take me a while to contact and recontact people to initially get the deal.

Today I met a potential new freight company to ship Mocks from China, to compare prices and service versus our current company, UTI. They could be good, although I am rather wary after the issues I had before trying a new supplier. I might pay slightly more for UTI, but we have a good relationship with them, and I feel that I can count on them, but I will see what they come back with. I think it is important to be open to new suggestions.

I am still looking for someone to work part-time doing the accounts data-entry role. I have another ad in the *Manly Daily* tomorrow. I can't believe how hard it is to find someone. It really is not that hard a job, but I think that maybe people think that you need special skills, even though I have said that you don't.

Monday 7th November 2005
I had a nightmare start to the day. I had a computer guy in to set up the computers so they are networked properly, and set up a shared drive that we can all access. I briefed the guy last week and he reckoned it would only take two to three hours. Needless to say, it didn't. I'm not entirely sure he knows what he is doing. It seems to be taking ages. It wasn't finished today, even though he had looked at everything beforehand. Grrr, it makes me annoyed when people don't work out properly what they need to do before they start.

I had some bad news today: my admin assistant Cathy has been offered the opportunity to go to Israel travelling for three months. She applied for it before she came to work for me. I can totally see that it is far more exciting to do that than work for me. I have been really supportive about it; she feels bad anyway about letting me down. Luckily she has given me lots of notice, she won't finish up until 3rd December, so there's definitely enough time to find someone and hopefully get her to do some training with them. It is rather annoying that I have spent time and effort training her, and I won't really see much of the benefit, but there is not much I can do now. She has been a great help during the time she has been here, and is lovely to have around. Humbert has offered to cover for her for the three months she is away, and then she would be able to come back to the role, but she thinks she might travel after, so it's best not to do that, but it was nice of Humbert to offer. To be honest, I think he'd find the role quite hard, as attention to detail is not always his strength, but he is great at entertaining people with jokes while Mock packing! His offer may also have something to do with the fact that he is sweet on Cathy and wants her to come back!

Tuesday 8th November 2005

I sent out the Christmas Mock mail-out to stores today: a newsletter and info on the six new Christmas designs. I figured I should get in early to let stores know. We have 3,000 of each design to sell, so hopefully they will be flying out the door. So far Fone Zone has agreed to take three of the designs, so that's a start. I don't really want to get stuck with any of these, as it will be another 12 months before I can sell them again. Laura, the new Mock supplier is turning out to be great, and we have finally got everything organised for the last of the UK orders. They went out from China a few weeks ago, and are apparently selling well. The UK has already reordered – I love it!

I have given up on Sony Ericsson ordering any personalised Mocks. I have followed her up lots of times, but I just haven't heard anything and it has been months.

Wednesday 9th November 2005

I interviewed two people today for the accounts data-entry role. One guy, Ben, seems like he would be good. He has done this before, so I'd need to do minimal training, plus in the interview he seemed to have some interesting ideas for making the business run more smoothly. I will reference-check him and see what happens. He is older, probably in his forties, but that doesn't have to be a problem, as long everyone is happy to be working with him.

Thursday 10th November 2005

I had five interviews today for Cathy's role. It has changed a bit, and is more of a marketing assistant role. I now have Julie in packing and dispatch and will have Ben in accounts, so hopefully this person can focus on the marketing, admin and all the bits I need for sales. It seems to me to be pretty amazing that in six months I have gone from one to three staff members. Good, but also rather crazy.

Of the interviewees I saw today there were two I particularly liked. I will call to arrange second interviews, and try to get Mr Johns to be there, so I can get a more impartial opinion. I am getting to be a bit of an expert at interviews. It does help that I have a book on interview questions; some are pretty hard. It is useful to see how people perform when asked something completely different. One of my questions: if you were a lolly, which lolly would you be and why? When I got asked this years ago when I went for a role as a graduate trainee with a confectionery company, I said I would be a mixed bag of lollies, like Allen's Party Mix, because I have lots of different qualities that come together to make me, qualities like determination, organisation and marketing expertise/skills, and I'm good at planning and executing, hardworking, conscientious, ambitious, friendly and willing to take a risk.

Monday 14th November 2005

Ben's reference checks came back fine, so he starts tomorrow in the accounts data-entry role. I got his contract ready, so we are all set to go. I did the second interviews today for Cathy's role, my favourite was Kate, I knew as soon as I interviewed her that I would get on well with her. Kate doesn't have much experience in marketing, but she has just finished a Tafe course and is really keen. I decided to go for Kate if the references check out. I really liked her in the first interview. We got on well, and I think we would work well together.

I had a positive meeting today with the team at the National Breast Cancer Foundation. I proposed to them that I produce a Breast Cancer Mock, with $1 from each one sold donated to their organisation. They were really keen, and want to sell them at the Mother's Day fun run in May next year, which will really help build Mocks brand awareness and raise cash for a good cause. It is great to be able to align with a charity which appeals to the Mocks target audience. I explained how well the Reach Out! Mock sold. We raised $3,000 for Reach Out! in total; however, they are having a change in focus for next year, so we decided not to produce another design for them.

The computers are still not set up properly, and it has taken the guy about three times longer than he quoted. I think that I will try to find another company. He just doesn't seem to be up to the job. I hope that he doesn't think that I will be paying for all this extra time it has taken. As far as I am concerned I gave him all the details and he saw what had to be done. There have been no surprises, so it shouldn't have taken longer.

I am developing a website in Microsoft Frontpage for Mum and Dad for their French painting holidays. It is coming on well, and my graphic designer Erica is doing a logo for them, so hopefully I can get it up and running by the end of the month.

I have thought that maybe a rewards loyalty scheme that you get in stores like Sanity music and Just Jeans might be a way to go for Mocks. I need to explore it; I'll add it to the list.

Humbert and I have cooked up a plan that perhaps he could launch and run the US office for Mocks when he goes back there in January. There is a trade show on at the beginning of January in New York and it would be the perfect opportunity to launch. I have set up a meeting with Austrade for us on Wednesday. Humbert will have to write a full business plan before he goes, so that we both know exactly what he will be doing, and have our expectations set.

Tuesday 15th November 2005

Ben started today. It wasn't good. He took about three hours to enter four invoices. I am not joking; 45 minutes per invoice, which is ridiculous, considering he said that he has used QuickBooks before. I can understand that you would be slow at the start, but this is unbelievable. Considering sometimes there are 100 invoices per day, and he is only going to work 15 hours per week, there is no way he will get through it all. Plus at $20 per hour, it is so expensive! I really don't think this will work. I will let him come back tomorrow and see if he improves, and if he doesn't I might have to fire him.

Wednesday 16th November 2005

We had a great meeting with Austrade today. The contact from the New York office was there, and Humbert and I had a good chat about the trade show, and how they can help us there. So I just need to get the business plan together now, work out the costs and Humbert can be off and running.

Thursday 17th November 2005

I fired Ben yesterday. I just told him that I didn't think it would work, given the workload that we have and that really I expect entering an invoice to take about five minutes max, so he would have to speed up by nine times his current speed. He didn't really seem to be that upset about it. I can find it hard having people working for me – I pick up things pretty quickly, then I expect that of others, but in reality that isn't how it works. As people who think quickly don't tend to want to do accounts data-entry work.

Friday 18th November 2005

I interviewed another person for the accounts data-entry role today. She wasn't suitable. I am getting rather over interviewing!

Excellent sales so far this month – $45,000 including the UK sales, and we still have nearly two weeks to go.

Thursday 24th November 2005

Kate has accepted the marketing role, and starts on Monday – hurray, that's one dilemma sorted … One of Julie's friends, Elizabeth, started today to help her with the packing. Orders are coming in thick and fast with Christmas coming up. One part-timer isn't really enough, plus there are lots of back orders to be dealt with due to the stock shortages. That whole back order thing was a nightmare. It just caused so much extra work and confused us, the customers and the stores. I need to get a better system in case it ever has to happen again. To improve the business I have been thinking about the whole systemising thing a lot this week. I need to get the team to understand why systems are important and then implement them – it's probably easier said than done. The procedures manual works well, but I need to encourage the team to get it totally up to date, and treat it as a living document.

We had a BBQ today at the beach for Cathy's leaving do. There were six of us. It was fun; sausages and salad and a game of boules. Everyone really enjoyed themselves, plus it was very cheap and within my budget.

Monday 28th November 2005

Wow, sales are now $96,000 for the month – woohoo! The UK sales have really helped drive that number, but still, it means we are on track for this year's target. I love it; I find it really hard to determine sales numbers, and I have been so busy recruiting that I really haven't had much time to do any sales.

It was the first day today for the new marketing girl, Kate. I think that she will fit in well. We all went for lunch to celebrate her starting, just to the cafe downstairs in the building – I am sure that guy must love me, as we seem to have been there lots for lunch of late.

A friend of mine, James, is going to make me a 30-second vox pop on Mocks that we can use at the trade shows next year. I am going to go to Spring Fair in Birmingham in the UK and Humbert is going to a tradeshow in New York. James is going to film some Mocks, with a voice-over, and we can put it on a loop on our laptops. I think it will be great. He is going to interview people on the street to see what they think about Mocks. I can't wait to see their thoughts.

Wednesday 30th November 2005
I interviewed another person for the accounts data-entry role today, still no joy ...

I'm busy trying to get the Christmas Mocks onto lastminute.com.au. Mocks are still selling really well on the site, so I am hope they will add these on as well.

I have registered the Mocks logo as a trademark in the US, and I have been busy helping Humbert with pricing. I feel like we are making ground with the US market ...

I was interviewed for the Australian Businesswomen's Network fastest growing new business award today on the phone. It was pretty straightforward. It would be great to win – another way to raise the profile of Mocks.

Final sales for the month are $100,165 – our best month *ever*. Onwards and upwards ... Once Mocks launch into the US and the UK is more established, sales will be going through the roof!

I am thinking about taking a holiday next year; walking the Inca trail in Peru ... It would be interesting. I haven't been to South America.
Mockers – Kate in marketing, Julie & Elizabeth in dispatch, Humbert working on the USA, Jenny bookkeeping
Mocks sold this month: 46,663
Total stores: 430
Original target: 1,000 by the end of 2005
Business bank account balance: $19,503
Mood: ☺ ☺ ☺ ☺

December 2005
Friday 2nd December 2005

I have been thinking about the account data-entry role and how I could make use of the people I have currently. I thought I could ask Elizabeth, who started packing last week, about it. I know that she is having a year out before uni, so it could work out well. Both Julie and Elizabeth are celebrating the end of year 12 at schoolies on the Gold Coast this week. When I spoke to Elizabeth she agreed to try it. Jenny, my bookkeeper, is going to come in to train her. Elizabeth definitely picks things up quickly. Hopefully this will be the solution to my accounts issues.

I am going to try to block out time every day to work on the business rather than in it. I find that I get distracted so easily with people asking me questions. The office is so small at 55sqm, that I can hear everything that is going on, and do I admit have the tendency to butt in if I hear that someone is not doing it right. I know that I need to stop that; otherwise they will never learn to use their initiative.

Monday 5th December 2005

I went to Homebake music festival last Saturday to sell Mocks. I had a stand with Humbert and Cathy. It was her last day. The event was rather disappointing – we only sold about 100 Mocks, which covered the cost of the stand and Cathy's wages, but not my time or Humbert's. It was good for brand awareness – we gave out free Mocks badges and stickers, and we also carried out market research into the new Mocks range. However, I wouldn't probably go again ... I need to analyse exactly what it cost and what we got out of it and then decide.

Jenny the bookkeeper came in today to teach Elizabeth all about QuickBooks. It seemed to go OK. Jenny said that she picked it up. I will need to keep an eye on her this week.

This week was my marketing assistant Kate's first week without Cathy. We started by going through what Humbert and I need for the two trade shows: Humbert's in New York and mine in the UK. I think she will be able to organise us both, no problem. Kate's really pitching in and helping out with everything, it's great to have her on board.

Tuesday 6th December 2005

Toll couriers came in today to train everyone on the new online system. It is going to save us so much time – no more handwriting the address labels – hurray! I didn't learn how to do it. I decided that if I know then they will be asking me and relying on me. The girls, Elizabeth and Julie, were supposed to be taking notes, but I think that Kate was the only one who did ... I will see what happens when they start actually using it. I have also asked them to write a procedure on how to produce the address labels for the deliveries, it should be interesting. ☺

Considering that dispatch is what Julie is doing and looking after, she didn't seem to really take in the new system – after the Toll people left and she was asking everyone else how to do it, which was disappointing.

Thursday 8th December 2005

It was the Australian Businesswomen's Network Christmas party last night. I was really, really late, as traffic was awful, I think it took me two hours to get into the city, instead of the normal maximum of an hour. It was worth going – I won the award for the fastest growing new business. I did a little speech, which everyone said was great, and I got a lovely trophy. It was a funny event, not really Christmas-party-like. I wore a sparkly top to get into the Christmas spirit, but everyone else was in their normal business attire. I do get excited about parties.

I drove out an hour to Parramatta today to see one of the stores that sells Mocks. I have been selling Mocks to this guy for a year. When I first started he only had one store, now he has four. It is fantastic how his business has grown. He is a really nice guy, but always wants to haggle like crazy over price, which I find difficult. I am getting a bit better, but I still think that I give in too easily. I took Kate with me so that she could see what the Mockists are like, she was surprised to see his entire wall of Mocks up in the store, they looked very impressive.

On the way back, we drove into the undercover car park at the office and one of the girls from the office next door drove into my car – not sure how she couldn't see us, a black Echo covered in bright yellow giant Mocks stickers is pretty hard to miss … I had to call the insurance people and get them to come and tow it away. There was about $3,500 of damage. Luckily, it's all covered, but it's still really annoying. Thank goodness we still have Mr Johns' car, which I can use until mine is fixed. The girl who hit me felt really bad. She had been having a bad day as it was, and was going to get a Boost Juice as a pick-me-up. I was very calm about it all, I think because I knew it would be covered by her insurance and could be fixed – at last benefit from insurance!

We had the team meeting today. I had to talk to everyone about phone message taking. It has been a nightmare lately, with names or numbers not written down properly, or messages written on a tiny piece of paper which gets lost before I get the message. I think that they got the idea, but for how long I don't know. Often I feel that it goes in one ear out the other!

Monday 12th December 2005

I met up with a member of the Australian Businesswomen's Network today for a coffee. I realised after a while she was trying to pitch to me, as she has a small marketing agency. I think I was a bit rude to her, because I basically said to her that marketing is what I enjoy doing and where my expertise is, so why would I outsource it? Wouldn't I rather outsource something I can't do or don't enjoy doing? It just seemed really odd that she thought of me knowing my background. Hopefully I wasn't too rude … I am not really that concerned, I have a bazillion other bits to think about.

It was a good start to sales for the month at $21,000 today, but it is a very short month, since we are shutting for Christmas on 23rd and not opening until the new year.

Tuesday 13th December 2005

Today I had to fire Julie who does the packing. She has been driving me absolutely crazy. Over the last few weeks I have asked her to do jobs and they just don't get done, or I explain exactly what to do and she doesn't listen and just does anything she feels like. A prime example from last week was when I explained what size satchels we have available and the difference between them in terms of price, and which labels to use on which. The labels and bags weren't used properly, which if I hadn't spotted it would have meant we were charged double. It is really not that complex. It has been one event after another, and I just don't feel that I can trust her to do everything the way it should be done – I've been through the role so many times with her. It is just not worth the stress on me. I have become good friends with my ex-bookkeeper Ella, and I've found myself moaning to her about Julie to her every day. It is driving me mad. Julie seemed to take it OK when I explained to her, but then ended up getting very upset and crying, not surprisingly. I gave her the option to leave straight away rather than stay till the end of the day, and she took me up on that. It was a bit awkward with her friend Elizabeth working here as well, but still I have to think about what is best for the business. I am not running a charity here. I hated doing it.

Elizabeth does not really seem to be taking to the accounts bits. I think that she is bored and she's not paying the attention to detail that is needed. I don't think it will work out. I will chat to her tomorrow and see what she thinks.

Friday 16th December 2005
The week has gone OK, since Tuesday. Luckily, Elizabeth has been fine. I spoke to her yesterday regarding her performance. I thought I did a really good job. I broached it with her from the view that she isn't really enjoying the role, rather than the view that she is doing a bad job, and she agreed. I put it to her that if she wasn't enjoying it now, then in six months she would be hating it, which she agreed with. We agreed that she will finish next Friday, the day of the Christmas party.

I have advertised for a dispatch person to look after all the packing and sending of Mocks, to replace Julie, this time full-time. I really need someone who can take responsibility for the whole area, and not make me worry about what they are doing. I interviewed one guy yesterday. He seemed OK; he even had his own safety shoes! However, he would need to be told what to do every step of the way. When I asked how he would prioritise, he said according to what I asked him to do, i.e. he wouldn't. No good. I hope there are some better applicants this week; I really want to get someone to start in January.

Monday 19th December 2005

I had a planning day at home today round the kitchen table with Humbert and Mr Johns. We discussed what had happened over the year and where each country, Australia, New Zealand, UK and US was going. I got a lot out of it, but it was hard, as although I had prepared a lot of information, there was still more that we discussed. It is definitely worth doing again next year. I can turn it into a yearly event; however, before Christmas is not the best time, as it is really busy. After Christmas would be better. I took lots of notes; I decided on the direction for Mocks in 2006, and also looked at budgets. Humbert's launch plan into the US is practically done. I can fund it for six months, but after that it will need to start generating revenue. So there is a definite deadline, which is good for both of us.

Humbert and I have got new business cards which have "Sydney–London–Washington" written on them … it makes LaRoo look really global and impressive, I think. This will be particularly good when we are dealing with large corporations.

I've managed to line up two interviews for tomorrow: one for the accounts data-entry role and one for dispatch. Maybe the end of recruitment is in sight?

Thursday 22nd December 2005

I had the day off yesterday with Mr Johns to celebrate our third wedding anniversary. It was lovely; we went horseriding. I got my car back today, all fixed up after the incident in the car park. It's looking like new with the signage redone.

We are just organising the final bits for the US trade show. Humbert leaves on 6th January. I have decided to offer Anna, whom I interviewed on Tuesday, the role in dispatch. She seems sharp. She has done this kind of role before, her references checked out, and she can start in the new year. She is also going to come to the Christmas party tomorrow so she will get to know people a bit before she starts – good old team bonding ...

Tuesday 27th December 2005

We played lawn bowls at Manly for the team Christmas party. We had Secret Santa presents first, then lunch followed by the bowling. It was great fun, and the bowling got quite competitive, as we were in two teams. No-one drank very much. It was really hot, so people only wanted soft drinks. Afterwards we went for ice-cream at Cold Rock. All in all, a very tame party. I guess there were only six of us, so it was never going to be that rowdy. Everyone is really new in the team as well, so they probably felt that they couldn't let their hair down too much. It was a good end to 2005.

Mockers – Kate in marketing, Elizabeth in accounts, Humbert working on the USA, Jenny bookkeeping

Mocks sold this month: 15,658

Total stores: 447

Original target: 1,000 by the end of 2005 (It was disappointing to not reach the goal, but maybe it was a little bit too ambitious? It isn't as if I have been doing nothing this year.)

Business bank account balance: $55,824

Mood: ☺ ☺

2006
January 2006

The start of a new year, with lots of Mocktastic opportunities, Mocks have been selling now for over a year, I've launched into New Zealand and the UK, plus sold some personalised Mocks for companies. When I look back I feel I actually achieved quite a bit last year, although at the time it didn't feel like much – but there is still so much I want to achieve, I'm not too good at looking back, I tend to look forward all the time. I think that my trip to New Zealand and the 5000 Mock order really stands out for me from last year in terms of sales, although the UK order isn't far behind. New Zealand was just so easy, the product totally sold itself. Meeting Laura and engaging her as our Mock manufacturer is going to be a god send I think, I am so glad I took that trip to China. However this year I really have to sort out the team, if I can't get stability I can't progress with my plans to expand.

Wednesday 4th January 2006

At 9 o'clock every morning this week we've been having a status report on the trade shows for both New York and Birmingham, so that we can be sure that everything is covered before Humbert leaves for New York on the weekend. Anna, the new dispatch girl, started yesterday. She seems to be picking up the role OK, fingers crossed. I interviewed another part-time accounts data-entry person today, a mum called Sam who has previously been working in the UK. I think she'll be fine. I just need to do her reference check. I have noticed that the whole interviewing/finding staff process seems to be getting quicker – hopefully that's for the best.

We've had quite a few orders over the Christmas and New Year break from stores, however we also have lots – around 8,000 of the Christmas Mock designs left. It's rather annoying since I will have to hold onto the stock until next Christmas, a definite lesson on seasonal designs.

Friday 6th January 2006

It has been a busy week. I fly to the UK for the trade show at the end of January. Sales so far this month have been pretty good at $10,000.

Anna has been a bit strange this week, but she will hopefully settle in OK to the dispatch role. I have been through the role with her, but I find her a bit hard to connect with. It's great to have my brother, Humbert in the office – he tells me if I am overreacting to situations, which I often need – my people skills still need work. I feel that I try really hard to treat people well, but I find different personalities tricky to adapt my style to, especially if the person is very different to me. Humbert seems to laugh and joke with the team – I think he finds it easier because he's not in charge and they see him as one of them.

Monday 9th January 2006

I saw a fantastic office today with lots of natural light, and lots of space – 150 square metres versus our current 55. I could fit ten people in the bigger office, if I sign a two year lease, I think we could have ten by then. I think I should keep looking, we don't have to move out of this office until May, by which time we will definitely need more space.

Wednesday 11th January 2006

Sam started yesterday. She is picking up the accounts bits that I've run through with her OK. I think it should work out; the procedures manual is very up to date, which makes my life much easier. Today I drove to Parramatta in western Sydney and presented Mocks to about 50 Civic Video store owners at their quarterly store owners meeting. It went well, and five stores ordered on the spot. I used the vox pops filmed last year as part of it, which caught their attention. The Civic buyer was impressed with the presentation, apparently often the store owners aren't very attentive.

Friday 13th January 2006

I spoke to the Office of Fair Trading today about the web company that owes me money for the website that didn't get built. They have to talk to them to see if they can get anything from them before we go to the Consumer, Trader and Tenancy Tribunal. Hopefully they can; I don't want to have to drag it out any longer.

Today I met up with a friend, Lisa, who runs her own market research company. I wanted to discuss running a series of focus research groups for teenagers, so that we can get more input on new designs etc. I think after speaking to her that the best and cheapest option is going to be talking to research friends I know from my previous marketing roles and asking them to run the groups in our office.

Monday 16th January 2006

I had my catch-up meetings with everyone today, and Anna in dispatch quit. Not the best result. She says she thinks I don't like her, and that she can't do anything right. Much as I denied it, that's what she thought. She couldn't see a way around it, so quit and left on the spot. Afterwards everyone was saying that they thought she was weird. Maybe that had something to do with it? So I am back to the recruitment process. One of my goals this year is to go on a people management course. I know I am not very good at it. My track record of people who have been and gone shows that.

Wednesday 18th January 2006

I had two interviews today for the dispatch role; I'm not sure about either guy. The older one, Chris, had no real experience and I had a bad feeling about him the first time I spoke to him on the phone, but in the interview he seemed quite switched-on. The other was younger and also had no experience, and I'd be concerned he would have a big night out every night and be coming in with a hangover – although the girls thought he was hot!

I met the account manager for Star Track Express couriers to discuss moving our courier business over to them, as we have had a few issues with Toll couriers. I will see what rates they can offer me. We are now sending much more freight than when I first started, and that is only going to increase as we take on more Mockists ...

Friday 19th January 2006

I have decided to offer the dispatch role to Chris, the older guy. He doesn't have the exact work experience, but I think he will pick it up quickly and fit in well in the team. When I called him, he agreed to take the role and starts on Monday. I just hope I have made the right decision. I feel kind of nervous about hiring people, having got it wrong before.

I had a chat with Mr Johns tonight, I don't feel that our relationship is going that well, but he dismissed my concerns, he is perfectly happy and doesn't understand what "my problem" is. Maybe it is me, I don't know.

Wednesday 25th January 2006

I met up with the owner of a bed linen company today for coffee. She wants to get some personalised Mocks made to give away with the bed linen to her teen target audience. It is great to see that the Mocks name has got out there enough to get people contacting me. I am pretty sure that she is going to go ahead with 2,000 – great news. It was an odd meeting. She brought her children with her. OK, we were just meeting for coffee, but still …

I found out today that a competitor has launched into the market – it is one of the distributors that I approached in 2004 to distribute Mocks. Their socks are called Meanies, the designs aren't as good – I think and they don't have a website, but unfortunately for us it does give retailers more choice as to which mobile phone sock they stock.

I got a backpacker in yesterday, just through an advert in the local backpacker hostel. I'm leaving on Friday for the UK and I thought I should get extra help in to cover work while I am gone. Cecile is a lovely French girl who is willing to do pretty much anything. I have to say that I am a bit nervous about leaving with three new people onboard, but it can't be helped. The trade show is all booked. I can't back out now. I remember that when Cathy was here last year I had to leave after she had only been with me for a week and it was all fine – maybe I just need to relax a bit.

Monday 30th January 2006
I arrived safe and sound in London, but talk about cold – there is no way I brought enough clothes! The trouble is that everyone here is used to it, so they don't put the heating on, but when you have come from 30°C to 5°C, it is a major shock! I am staying with my friend Carla on her floor. I still have a lot to organise ready for the trade show, such as the printing of the order forms and info sheets.

I really need to open a UK bank account. If the business is going to run here, we can't expect people to pay into the Australian account all the time, plus if they send us a cheque it costs a fortune every time I bank it in Oz. After going to four banks today, I can already see that this is not going to be easy, due to the fact that the company is based in Australia, and not registered as a company in the UK.

Tuesday 31st January 2006
I had a meeting with my current UK distributors today. Although we had a great four months last year, there are a few issues. Firstly, we didn't end up supplying Top Shop because, despite their promises, the distributor couldn't get it organised for them. Although I had been asking about the situation, I only found this out three months after the event, and by then Top Shop were no longer interested. I have contacted Top Shop, but they feel that the trend for Mocks has passed. Very annoying – especially as had I been told sooner, I could have potentially done something about it. Secondly, there is a new account manager to deal with at the distributors, which will be hard, as it seems his predecessor hasn't really filled him in on much. At least he does seem to be enthusiastic about Mocks; well, he was in the meeting. I just hope that the distributor can continue to order as they have previously. I told them that the goal for 2006 is 1,000 stores in the UK, and that I expected them to help. I don't think I was what the new guy expected. He was also surprised about how much profit they made from the Mocks ... I will have to wait and see.
Mockers: Humbert in the USA, Kate in marketing, Chris in dispatch, Sam in accounts, Cecile in admin, Jenny bookkeeping
Mocks sold this month: 21,417
Total stores: 448
Original target: 1,200 by March 2006

Business bank account balance: $45,952
Mood: ☺ ½ frustrations with the UK distributors

February 2006
Thursday 2nd February 2006

Today I had a good meeting with *Sugar*, a UK teen magazine. When I saw them last year, nothing really happened, but this time they have committed to a free covermount – we just provide the Mocks. It will really help raise the profile of Mocks in the UK. Plus we will run a 'buy one, get one free' offer in the magazine, and hopefully get exposure online on their website. This is a huge win since last time I spoke with them they wanted me to pay for it, I'm not sure what changed their minds.

I have had to get all the order forms printed for the trade show. I really didn't know how many to get done. It is one of the biggest shows in Europe, with tens of thousands of people attending, so I ended up getting 3,000 – maybe too many.

The New York gift show finished yesterday. I don't think it was that fantastic. I haven't had a full debrief from Humbert, but I know that he didn't have all the stock due to a major stuff-up involving a delay at customs.

Sunday 5th February 2006

Today's the first day of the Birmingham trade show in the UK. Mum and Dad have come up with me to help, as there is no way I would have lasted five days on my own. Today it's only from 10am to 4pm, but every other day is 9am to 6pm. It's funny, I am really excited, as it is the first show I have been to. Everyone else on the stands around me is kind of jaded already … I wonder how long my enthusiasm will last.

Monday 6th February 2006

Mum got 'arrested' today for giving out Mocks as samples with a flyer at the door to our hall! Apparently you need a pass, which we don't have, so she was taken to the security offices, where she bribed her way out with Mocks! We have decided on a new plan for

116

tomorrow: we are going to put Mocks on the table in the pub, close to our hall with an information leaflet and our stand number. We have arranged it with the manager and bribed him with free Mocks for his staff.

Wednesday 8th February 2006

The trade show is very tiring. We have to get the train at 8am, then stay chirpy and happy from 9am till 6pm and then stay afterwards for an hour or so to avoid the big queues for the train. It is a huge show, there are 24 halls, and it takes about 20 minutes just to walk from hall 1 to 24 – and that's just going around the outside, not through the halls. We are meeting lots of great potential customers; it's definitely worthwhile. Dad is hilarious. He has been going round with a pocket full of Mocks and a pocket of leaflets, plus a Mocks sticker on each lapel of his suit, and has basically told everyone in the stands around us about Mocks, plus anyone else he meets, including the girl serving coffee in the cafe! Great publicity, but I am trying to get him to be a little bit more discerning. I had to stop him giving a Mock to the waiter at the Indian restaurant tonight. I really only want him to give Mocks to people that could be potential customers - either buy one for themselves or some to sell in their store.

Giving out Mocks in the pub is working well, and we have had a couple of people come to us from it. I'll have to remember this for next year. I have decided to stay on in the UK for another two weeks to pursue the leads from the trade show, plus follow up other big chains, as the five days before the show were not really enough, and the office seems to be running really well without me.

Friday 10th February 2006

I am now back in London after the show. At the show we gave out about 150 packs – rather less than the 3000 leaflets I had printed! Store orders were ten, which I am pleased with, plus there was quite a bit of interest in personalised Mocks.

I met people from the company that will be storing and sending out the Mocks to stores for me. They were lovely, and I think the prices are reasonable. I finally got the bank account set up today. Someone at Lloyds TSB found a kind of loophole for me to use to get around the Australian company issue. I have arranged to fly back to Sydney on 21st Feb, giving me another week or so in London. Luckily I can stay with some friends while I work.

Monday 13th February 2006
Wow, what a busy weekend! I've been emailing and talking to China, Australia and Ireland. I have decided that while I am in the UK I may as well pop over and meet Austrade in Ireland. There were quite a lot of Irish companies visiting the trade show, and the Austrade girl I met at the show raved about the potential there. I'm flying to Dublin for one night next week to meet her again before I leave for Sydney.

The Telstra store buyer in Australia called me today saying that he wants to stock Mocks in his stores – *big win*! It's amazing; I have been chasing them for the past 18 months, but to no avail. He says he saw them in another store recently and wants them for his stores, so we just need to sort out the displays and away we go – that's another 100 stores.

My friend Carla, who I have been staying with, has offered to run the UK Mocks business for me. She has been thinking about leaving her job, which I didn't know, and I had mentioned that I really need to get someone full-time on the ground, as it is so hard to do it from Oz with the time difference and all. Then, after half a bottle of champagne she said that she'd be keen to do it. It seems like the ideal solution ... I need to work out the numbers etc, but I will see if I can make it work. It would be good to have someone I can trust.

Tuesday 14th February 2006
I spent today calling, calling, calling every chain store that I think would potentially stock Mocks. I got the buyer's details and then sent a presentation and a sample to them. It feels like I am back in 2004...

Friday 17th February 2006
I have managed to organise a meeting with Carphone Warehouse in

Ireland for Monday as soon as I land. I am hoping the fact that Carphone Warehouse in the UK took Mocks means that they will. The buyer was really pleasant on the phone, so I will see. I also have a meeting set up with the Irish Austrade contact and she is going to take me to meet a company that organises promotional materials for bands and festivals.

Sunday 19th February 2006

I spent all of the weekend working: researching companies on the Net, putting together presentations and mailing them. When I get back I can just follow up. I have also managed to pay back Mum and Dad all the money I borrowed. I am quite impressed with myself! Turns out that Dad wasn't bothered about getting the money back; they just wanted to see me doing something I really enjoyed. Obviously, they were glad to get the cash and they said that they are really proud of what I have achieved so far.

Monday 20th February 2006

I landed in Ireland today for the meeting with Carphone Warehouse. It went really well. They loved the products and are very eager. They want some more information, but I think they will buy. There aren't really any products like Mocks in the market here, and so it will be a really good opportunity for us. I then met the Austrade person, who took me to meet a promotional products company. The meeting went well. They want me to make a Westlife Mock for the band's tour in April, I need to get prices to them.

I'm staying in Dublin tonight but I fly back to London tomorrow, then on to Australia. It has been a very short trip to Ireland.

Thursday 23rd February 2006

I arrived back in Australia this morning. I went home, showered and then straight into the office. It turns out that there have been a few frustrations I didn't know about within the team while I was away, even though I have been in regular contact with them. The issue is with Sam in accounts not getting invoices to Chris in dispatch on time. I will need to talk to Sam next week. I have a feeling it will not go well. Previously Sam has been a bit difficult, I talked to her a few times when I was in the UK when she was having issues with accounts bits, and I found that she got very defensive very quickly. I know that she has been struggling to keep on top of all the work, but it is a busy role, and I think it is better to give people more rather than less to do. I find I am not always overly tactful when talking to people about issues, which is why I am not feeling too good about having the chat.

Monday 27th February 2006

I spoke to Sam today regarding the accounts, and she left on the spot. Actually, there have been a few other issues with what she has been doing. Her attention to detail was not great and she couldn't seem to get through the work. I told her that I thought I needed to get someone full-time, and she replied that she could have told me from the start that she wouldn't be able to do all the work in 15 hours a week. Sam got so defensive; she blamed me for not training her properly, and not giving her the right information on things. I felt this was an unfair comment, but I just let her rant, and then she left. We are probably better off, but now I am back to finding someone again. YUK!

I spoke to Humbert in the US today. Things are pretty hard going there for him, although while he was at the trade show he did find an agent who is going to start selling Mocks next month. He works on 15% commission, and Humbert has said that he is a nice guy. I just need to sign the paperwork. Other than that, he got an order from a company in Canada for personalised Mocks; only 2,000, but it is a start. When I look at what I had to do here to get going, it is not going to be something that happens in a few months, but a long-term plan. I am really pleased he has found this agent, but I am finding the loss of control hard — Humbert is much more relaxed about the agent agreement than I am. I really hope that this leads to more sales for him.

Mockers: Humbert in USA, Kate in marketing, Chris in dispatch, Cecile in admin, Jenny bookkeeping
Mocks sold this month: 8,841
Total stores: 450
Original target: 1,200 by March 2006

Business bank account balance: $29,593 & £10 (opening balance)
Mood: ☺ ☺ fired up and ready to go

March 2006
Wednesday 1ˢᵗ March 2006

I had two meetings with IT companies today regarding getting a server when we move into a new office. At the moment the internet connection is slow because we are using a peer-to-peer network, so we really need to get a server running. Also, we are not really backing up documents properly, which does concern me slightly. It is going to cost a lot, probably around $10,000, but it's part of growing. Good news, I guess.

I put another ad on the job classified website seek.com.au for the accounts role, as a full-time position covering bookkeeping and data entry ... I should get shares in Seek, the amount I seem to spend with them!

Friday 3ʳᵈ March 2006

We made our sales target in January, and I promised the team we would celebrate. They chose what we would do: we all went for a pedicure – including Chris, although he went with clear nail polish! We did it just before lunch today, so everyone went straight home after (we have a policy of taking just 30 minutes for lunch every day, then finishing the week at 1pm on Fridays). I took some bubbles along. It was fun, although I have to say I didn't feel terribly relaxed; I find it hard doing the boss thing.

Today was the last day that Cecile, the French backpacker, was with us, so it was a good send-off. She was a real help while I was away.

Tuesday 7ᵗʰ March 2006

I took Chris, Kate and Mr Johns round today to look at offices. We saw three in Brookvale, including the one that appealed to me back in January, and one in Manly. Manly would be great for me in that I could walk to work, but parking in Manly is so hard to find and expensive that I am not sure it would be practical for staff. Anyway, the place we saw was a dump – I'd hate to work there. Of the

Brookvale places, the one I liked previously was by far the best.

I chatted to Jenny today about the bookkeeping, it isn't really working out for either of us, with all her travel time – 1.5 hours each way, which she now has to charge me for, as it was just not working for her otherwise. I think I will be able to persuade Ella to come back and help me until I find a new person to employ.

Friday 10th March 2006
It has been a busy week with having to do all the accounts bits as well as my normal role. I interviewed some people earlier in the week for the accounts role, in addition to the two I interviewed last week, but no good. Oh, this is going to be hard, and I am already so *over* recruiting. The big problem with the accounts role is that we send out the invoice with the order, therefore the invoices need to be produced every day; they can't be done weekly. Also, they really have to be done on-site, as we use the accounting package every day, which is limiting who we can get to do the role.

Wednesday 15th March 2006
I have decided to go with the office I liked in Brookvale. It is just round the corner from where we are now. It will allow room for us to expand, and I can sign a two-year lease. Obviously, the rent is higher than we're currently paying, but I have managed to negotiate a reduction on what they were asking, and a month free.

I had a few printer issues today. The black and white laser printer I bought has been a pain from the word go. This week I sent it off to be fixed, but it can't be fixed and the replacement one hasn't arrived yet. Considering we have only had it a month, this really isn't good. I find it so frustrating sorting out all these kinds of things.

Friday 17th March 2006
The replacement printer arrived at last!

Monday 20th March 2006
I had two interviews today for the accounts role; Kim, the last one, could be promising. I will reference-check her before offering her

the role.

I am off to Peru on holiday for three weeks on Saturday, and would really like to get the staffing sorted before I go.

Tuesday 21st March 2006

Great news, I can afford Kim and she is going to take the accounts role. She will start on 18th April when I am back. She has been doing a similar type of role, so she should find this reasonably easy. I'd like to start organising the budget for the next financial year once she has found her feet – I really want to keep track of expenses and sales.

I met my friends who work in market research today. They have agreed to run the focus groups for me. It will mean I can afford to run the groups and I know they will do a good job.

Friday 24th March 2006

Last day of panic before I fly tomorrow. It seems like I have only been back from the UK for five minutes, and I sense that the rest of the team feel the same way. Despite the fact that while I was in the UK I worked the *whole* time, they saw it as a holiday, and I don't know how to get them to understand that it wasn't. This is a whole of set of challenges that I didn't even think that I would have in running my own business. When I was an employee it was completely understood that when you were away with work you were working, not holidaying. I guess that I shouldn't worry about what they think, but if it is going to affect their work, then it does matter. They have to understand that it is my business and they are working for me. We are not all on an equal footing … I think that everything will be fine, and Ella, my friend and ex-bookkeeper, is going to come in and do the accounts for me while I am away and keep an eye on things, as it is very unlikely I will have computer access in Peru or Chile.

Mockers: Humbert in USA, Kate in marketing, Chris in dispatch, Ella in accounts
Mocks sold this month: 9,653
Total stores: 453

Original target: 1,200 by March 2006 (this target was obviously far too ambitious. I've only added a few more stores since December, which is disappointing.)
Business bank account balance: $30,962 & £1,960
Mood: ☺ stressed

April 2006

Tuesday 11th April 2006

I arrived back in Sydney and the office today. The holiday was good, different to what I expected, but I enjoyed seeing another culture.

We had an Easter BBQ today in the park. It was a bit early, but my marketing assistant, Kate, is off on holidays for three weeks tomorrow, so I wanted to have it before she left. Everyone seemed to enjoy themselves, and the new accounts girl, Kim, joined us as well. It was good for everyone to meet her.

Thursday 13th April 2006

Today is the last day before the Easter weekend – such a short week, and it has been crazy. I had a performance review with Chris, the dispatch guy, today; he seems to be running the dispatch department really well, so I gave him a pay rise, which he said he appreciated. I am also looking up Excel courses for him to go on as we identified that as a development need.

Cathy, who left to go to Israel, is coming back after Easter on a part-time basis to do some sales for me. I have explained what needs to be done – basically selling personalised Mocks to companies, and she seems to be happy with that. I'm looking forward to having her back, but I'm a bit concerned that sales might not be her cup of tea.

Wednesday 19th April 2006

Today the office was full of people. Ella was in, training Kim, who started yesterday, in the accounts role. It was rather crowded for six people with all the Mocks. I can't wait to move into the new place at the end of next month.

Wednesday 26th April 2006

Cathy only started a week ago, but she left today. It really wasn't working out with her doing sales. She was happy enough to get all the information on the companies, but not to actually ring people, so we called it a day. Luckily she also realised that she didn't want to do it, so it finished on a good note – which I am glad about, I really like her.

We had the team meeting today. We are organising the office move on 19th May, which is not far away at all, and we are starting to get everything together. I am going to get a PABX phone system for the new office. I have been investigating eBay, and bidding but not winning. ☹ The new office is far too big to have the current set-up; we would spend the whole time running to pick up the phone. We need to be able to transfer calls between desks.

I met the new buyer for Strathfield Car Radio today. He's a nice guy and seems enthusiastic about Mocks. I just need to get back to him once he has shown a few of his salespeople – fingers crossed.

Friday 28th April 2006

I flew up to Brisbane for the day today and met Steve, the Fone Zone buyer. The meeting went well, except for one little problem. They found out that we have sold Mocks to Crazy John's for less than we sell to them. It seems that someone sent them a Crazy John's invoice by mistake. I can't believe it. I have had to promise to refund them $2,000 to make up for it. Grrr … if I knew who it was, heads would be rolling. Unfortunately, with all the staff changes it could have been anyone. I need to review the pricing to different customers, having different prices could cause more issues down the line.

While in Brisbane I also had a meeting with the owner of a company that could potentially distribute Mocks to all the convenience and petrol stores across Australia. I have been speaking to him on the phone, after one of the petrol station buyers referred him to me. He was really helpful and agreed to trial Mocks in 10 stores. I left him with samples and he will get back to me. It would be great if he can get them into all 2,000 stores he supplies. It will be a bit hard to

125

judge the results of the trial, as some stores are going to be better for Mocks than others, due to location and shoppers. Hopefully he will choose the ones where they are most likely to sell.

Mockers: Humbert in USA, Kate in marketing, Chris in dispatch, Kim in accounts

Mocks sold this month: 13,095

Total stores: 460

Original target: I've stopped setting targets for stores now. I'm going to focus on sales figures instead.

Business bank account balance: $26,974 & £1,382

Mood: ☺ ☺

May 2006

Monday 1st May 2006

I had to get all the bits ready for the web company hearing tomorrow at the Consumer, Trader and Tenancy Tribunal, since the Office of Fair Trading couldn't resolve it by talking to them. It has taken ages to get this far. I just hope it isn't too confrontational.

I was contacted last week to ask if I would be the keynote speaker at a conference for teachers. It's very exciting. I don't get paid, but it is a good chance to get out there and explore speaking as an option. The lady that contacted me found out about me through searching on the internet, so all the publicity seems to be working.

I spoke to my brother Humbert today on the phone. He is finding the US market really hard to crack, much harder than he initially thought. Although he really wants Mocks to succeed, he doesn't really have the patience and drive to do it, so he is going to pull out. It's annoying, as I had really hoped that he would do it for me, since I don't have the time at the moment. However, there is not much I can do. I will just have to postpone Mocks domination of the US. I just hope that it isn't for to long.

Wednesday 3rd May 2006

The hearing went OK yesterday. The guy from the web company was very petty; he said I was only doing it to be difficult and that I didn't need the money. I said that was not the point; the point was that he hadn't delivered what he said he would and why should that be OK? Anyway, I ended up getting a ruling saying that he would pay me back $2,000, which is not the full amount, but most of it, and it would be paid in full by the end of the month ... I just hope he delivers on that.

We had the Hot Tables event tonight with the Australian Businesswomen's Network. The membership committee I'm part of thought up the idea and organised the speakers. We had 10 tables with a "guest" at each table. We managed to get some great people, like Siimon Reynolds from the Photon Group. After each course the guest moved to a new table, so over the three courses members got to speak to three very different guests, and with only 10 people per table, they actually got a chance to ask all their questions. I was told this morning that I had to be MC – good practice I guess, but I was very nervous. Afterwards lots of people came and told me what a great job I did, even people I didn't know. It was a big confidence booster, but there is always a bit of me that says "Really, are you sure?"

I have been to a new fitness class three times this week from 9.30am till 10.30am, after starting early in the office. It is working well for me, but I know I need to keep an eye on the team. I do love that I can work to my own timetable for the majority of the time, I think going back into a corporate role would be very hard, if not impossible after working for myself!

Saturday 6th May 2006
I am flying off to Bali today; another holiday, I know – I love it. This one is my birthday present from Mr Johns. It is a complete freebie; he has racked up so many air miles and hotel points from his work travel that it is not costing anything except for food and spa treatments! We are also celebrating his new job, which he starts when we get back. His new role means he won't be travelling to Japan anymore, he will be based in Sydney fulltime – it might be hard for us to adjust to this after him being away every other week for the last 16 months.

Monday 15th May 2006

We had a fantastic week in Bali. It's definitely up there as one of my best holidays ever. It was so relaxing: lots of lying by the pool, reading and drinking cocktails, and a bit of swimming here and there. Now I have four days before we move into the new office. The phones have been set up, and the internet is all connected. Mr Johns and I just have to finish off getting the desks ready. We have managed to get some old desks from a company that does office fit-outs (I say old desks, but they look brand new). We will have 10 desks in total. It is going to be great, all ready for the expansion and explosion of staff.

I started Spanish classes tonight; the course runs for eight weeks. I really enjoyed speaking Spanish when I was in South America and found that I picked it up quite quickly, so I decided to learn it. I'd like to go back to South America and spend some time in Argentina one day. Tonight was good fun. It was a big class of about 30 people and most of the other students were there with someone, which made it a little hard when I had to find a partner to practise with in class.

Friday 19th May 2006

Moving day today. The dispatch guy, Chris, has been very difficult this week, since I got back. I'm not sure if it is to do with the move, or me being on holiday … There was a big order messed up yesterday. Admittedly he got in early today to fix it up while Mr Johns and I were there taking the last bits of desks apart. When I spoke to him about the mistake, he got very uppity and defensive. I really felt like saying "If you are going to be like that, then just go now", but Mr Johns dragged me to one side and said "You need him, just because we are moving today". I just wanted to get rid of him, but I thought maybe I was overreacting and went and apologised. Communication with Chris has been a distinct problem over the past few weeks. He seems to dislike taking direction from me. I have spoken to him about it, but he denies it is a problem. I have given him responsibility for a lot of the move, but not everything has been done properly, so I've had to spend a lot of time following it up. Needless to say, the rest of the day I felt awkward with him. I feel that after his performance review last month he seems to have completely changed – maybe because his three month probational period has finished, I'm not sure.

Everyone pitched in today to help with the move. The IT company set up the server so that we will be all ready to go on Monday, and our account manager even helped move things! We were all done by 2.30pm, when everyone went home, except me. I stayed to sort some things out. I am glad that we are all moved in, with no real issues, but I was disappointed that Kate and Kim didn't say anything about the new office. Nothing. No "Isn't this great?"; nothing at all. I felt like Mr Johns and I have been slaving away all week until late every night and it feels like none of this was appreciated. I really wanted the office to be a nice working environment for the team, a place that they would enjoy being, which is why I would have loved some feedback. The girls hadn't seen any of it since we first looked at it, and even the IT guys commented on how good it looked.

On Monday I need to talk to Chris and find out what is going on with him.

Monday 22nd May 2006

The first day in the new office. I have decided not to try to speak to Chris until I have calmed down a bit, as I am still very annoyed with his behaviour last week. I was polite today, but not much more.

I had the inspection on the old office today. Everything was OK. I just need to pay to get the carpet cleaned, which shouldn't be too expensive.

Tuesday 23rd May 2006

Chris was off sick today – not a huge surprise to me, given his attitude yesterday and last week. However, he was due to start the Excel course last night at the college, which I have already paid for, and he didn't turn up. What a waste of money. If he had told me, at least someone else could have gone. Grrr, another annoyance to add to my list.

The iMocks that we launched back in September last year aren't exactly flying off the shelves. The chain stores we supply haven't really picked them up; they have taken one or two designs, but not the whole range. I am disappointed, as I really think they are a good product, but it seems consumers don't really understand them. We have had advertising out every month this year, and yet people still seem confused. I need to find a way to get more interest for them and drive sales ... Looking back I think that maybe the Mocks brand wasn't established enough to help support a line extension, maybe I rushed into it a bit too much.

Wednesday 24th May 2006
I met the buyer for 3 mobile stores today. He really liked the Mocks, and is going to put them forward to the rest of the buying team. He also mentioned that we could do something with the Australian cricket team, since 3 is their main sponsor. He was quite amusing in the meeting. I gave him the range of Mocks and out of them all he chose the Pink Teddy to put on his phone!

We had a photographer at our flat in Manly yesterday, it goes on the market next week. I can't wait to move somewhere bigger.

Friday 26th May 2006
Chris has been off all week, "sick". He came and gave me a note from his doctor. I'm not sure I believe a word of it, because it seems to be rather convenient after our run-in last week.

I did the talk today at the conference for teachers. It went really well. Lots of people came up to me at the end and said how much they enjoyed it, and how inspirational I was. One guy said that he was asleep for the guy before and woke up for me – a huge compliment!

After the talk I had coffee with a girl I have met through networking. She works in recruitment, and as I am having absolutely no luck in finding a salesperson, I briefed her on finding someone. Because I know her, she has agreed that I will only have to pay the recruitment fee if she finds me someone. All the other recruitment firms I have spoken to want an up-front payment of a percentage of the positions salary. I really hope she can get someone. It doesn't matter if I have to pay; it would be worth it. I just can't physically do it all.

Monday 29th May 2006

The morning started well, with a meeting with Vanessa, the *Girlfriend* marketing manager. We had a lovely catch-up. When I got back to the office I interviewed Belinda, a potential salesperson whom I was introduced to by a member of the Australian Businesswomen's Network. I then had to talk to Chris. By this time it was 11am. I had made a list of what I was going to say, and the plan was to fire him. However, as soon as we started, he quit. He had a resignation letter all ready.

He was really snotty about it all, saying that it was entirely my fault, he didn't feel his work was valued, I was too demanding and other things like that. I have to say it left me pretty confused. When I asked him why he didn't go on the Excel course, he said that he never wanted to – it was too basic for him. So I asked why he agreed to it, and he said he had no choice, which was not true; I had asked him about it every step of the way. I said that I gave him a pay rise after only two months, but apparently the increase wasn't enough. At this point in the conversation he became hostile and threatening. I'd thought he was a nice, easygoing guy, but he turned into a real psycho. I then asked him for his office keys, which was quite reasonable, as he was leaving at the end of the week. He turned that round to a nasty comment about me not trusting him. He aggressively demanded I pay him out for the week rather than him having to work it. I don't want to, but I will have to see what happens. He also told me "You will give me a good reference", as if I had no say in the matter. I thought "like hell". If I get asked I will be completely honest: after three months' probation he turns into a nightmare!

He then went for lunch for two hours, instead of the usual 30 minutes. I called the Office of Industrial Relations and they said I could legally deduct the extra time from his pay. When he got back, I told him that is what I would be doing, and he responded with something like "I would expect nothing less". The atmosphere was horrible. I don't feel that I can trust him to work properly this week, and I can't face the prospect of this kind of abuse every day. I discussed it with Ella and I decided to pay him off.

After he left, I called the locksmiths and had the locks changed. I felt really shaky and upset about the whole incident. Kate and Kim were supportive, although Kim said she knew there was a problem a few weeks ago. Hmm.

Wednesday 31st May 2006

I went to my psychologist yesterday. I had to get the whole Chris incident off my chest. It was useful; I need to make sure that I learn from this so that it doesn't happen again.

The IT system needed a few tweaks today, but everything else in the office now seems to be running well. I spoke to the contact at *Sugar* magazine in the UK, and we are all set for the covermount in October. I have managed to negotiate some advertising and promotion on their website as well.

I hired Belinda, whom I met on Monday, for the sales role. She started yesterday. It feels like it is a revolving door at the moment with staff ...

Mockers: Kate in marketing, Kim in accounts and Belinda in sales
Mocks sold this month: 13,339
Total stores: 559
Business bank account balance: $13,304 & £759
Mood: ☺ shaky

June 2006

Friday 2nd June 2006

I'm back to interviewing, this time for the dispatch role. I put an ad up in the backpacker hostel in Manly this week. I am hoping I can get someone for a few months; I can't face another permanent person. After my traumatic experience with Chris, I am also nervous about getting a guy. I have seen three people today. One girl, Tara, could be good. I decided to take her on and see how it goes. It will be on a casual basis, so if it doesn't work I can easily get rid of her. She starts on Monday.

Wednesday 7th June 2006

Belinda is going well in sales. We had our catch-up yesterday. She only does three days a week, but is very enthusiastic. However, she doesn't seem to remember the information I tell her about stores, but I am hoping that this is just because she is new.

Ella and I have been looking at other options for the accounts role. Although she is great at jumping in to help, she still doesn't have the time to do my bookkeeping ongoing. We are not sure that Kim is working out. I find that she doesn't do what I ask, only what she wants, or only in the order she wants, which I find really frustrating. I don't make unreasonable requests; I only ask for reports like a profit and loss statement … We decided to think outside the box and look at outsourcing - the company we saw today could take on all our accounting, and it would mean that we would only need an admin person to send over the orders every day. It could be ideal; however, after seeing him it seems a bit too good to be true. We do need to do something. In addition to the staffing issue, our current accounting software just can't cope with the volume of orders going through, it is unbelievably slow.

Today I met one of the directors of a mobile phone accessory distribution company, the main company that Fone Zone use for supply of their accessories. When I was at Fone Zone last month they asked if I would consider moving all my business to the distributor, so that Fone Zone has one less supplier to work with. It is a cost-cutting initiative on their part. Initially I wasn't interested, but I then thought maybe I should just look at it. The meeting went well. The guy actually offered me a job designing their range of mobile socks … I'm not too keen on that. My biggest concern with this distributor is that the focus won't be on Mocks, but on their product, because obviously they make a higher margin on those, as they import them directly from China. Plus he made a comment that he could ruin my business, strange comment, but I think he meant that moving Mocks to them for distribution wouldn't guarantee sales. It has given me lots to think about, and lots of numbers to crunch.

Tuesday 13th June 2006

It was a public holiday yesterday. It was wonderful to have a long weekend, but it means this week will be hectic. Tara, the dispatch girl, is working out well, but I am closely monitoring her and what she does. If that aspect of the business isn't done right, it ruins the whole customer experience. I found out this week that before Chris left he had been sending himself bags of Mocks, and that was quite early on in his job, so I definitely did the right thing in getting rid of him. I just should have gone with my intuition. I had a bad feeling from the first call he made when he applied for the role, but thought I was being silly. Well, I know for next time.

The focus groups start this Saturday in the office. We have nearly everything ready; Kate has done most of it. We have three groups of different age groups, and the moderator is all organised and briefed. I hope it gives us some good ideas for the future.

Friday 16th June 2006

I've still had no news from the buyer at 3 mobile; I will keep chasing. I have decided to get a personal assistant/office manager. I have been running the idea past Ella. I just spend so much time running the office that I can't really focus on the sales and marketing, so this seems like the ideal solution. We will split Kate's role so she focuses more on marketing and the new person will take on all the admin that she is doing. I put an ad on seek.com.au – again!

I met up with Sally, an old friend who has started her own PR agency. I think it is time we outsourced PR. I just don't have the time to follow up the magazines or the contacts to hear about what is going on. It should work well with Sally; we will pay a monthly amount for a set number of hours of her time.

Belinda set up a meeting with a guy about distributing Mocks to the souvenir stores he supplies. It wasn't a very good meeting, really, since he still needs info before he can make a decision. Really it was just a "Hello, this is who we are". It felt to me like a waste of time, and Belinda was very disorganised. She didn't even bring a notepad and pen.

We are nearly out of the Mocks lanyards we had made to give away to consumers, so soon we can order the button badges that I want. When I first started I had badges to give away to stores and consumers, and they were really popular – the lanyards haven't been as popular.

Monday 19th June 2006
The focus groups on the weekend were really interesting. I was in the office, not watching, but I could hear what was being said. It was all recorded on video as well. There were some good comments that we can act on now about product ideas and the designs.

Ella and I have practically decided to go with outsourcing the accounts; we are just waiting on a few more facts from the guy. I have had some bad feedback from some of our customers on Kim, so I will give her notice next Monday. I spoke to her about the problems in today's catch-up meeting, but it's apparent that it just isn't working. I think that she is probably just filling time until she gets another role. Sometimes I feel that I make my mind up very quickly about staff, I like to think I am fair, and I do give people a chance. I am also wary that once the three month probation is up it is harder to get rid of them, and I feel that by three months they should be able to perform in the role.

Thursday 22nd June 2006
We had our first competitor review today, organised by Kate. We each researched three competitors and then presented our findings. It was good to see that Mocks are still leading the pack in Australia. It was interesting to look at the packaging from other brands. I want to revamp our packaging to make it look more premium – once I have the people situation sorted. The next competitive review will be in six months.

Friday 23rd June 2006
I've interviewed ten people this week for the office manager role.

No good ones yet.

Monday 26th June 2006

I did another firing today. It feels like I do one every week! Kim wasn't surprised. She seemed to be expecting it, so she was very calm. I found out later from one of the customers I know well that she was planning to leave anyway. She finishes on Friday.

Tonight was my last Spanish class. I have managed to pick up quite a lot; I just need to practise with someone. It used to be great when the Spanish cleaner came at 5pm because we could have a good conversation, but now she comes at 4am. I don't really want to be in the office then.

I have done the analysis on moving the business over to the distributor I met, and it isn't really worth it. In some ways I would be better off, for instance I wouldn't need a dispatch person, but with my remaining overheads I would only break even. One thing he said keeps coming back to me: "I could ruin your business", it makes me feel exceptionally nervous.

I am having a few problems with Kate of late, basically since we moved into the new office. I know that she has another job teaching dance in the evenings, and she has taken to going to get changed at 5pm for that. We don't finish until 5.15pm and I wasn't happy about this, and spoke to her about it. It turns out that she doesn't have enough time to get to her class otherwise, so I offered to change her hours so she starts early and finishes early, and this seemed to work for a while. But now she's switching off her computer at 4.50pm, and it is every day, not just now and again. I have now been finding jobs for her to do at 4.45pm to counteract this, but it isn't really working. She is supposed to be stepping up into this new marketing role, which would be a stretch for her, but she isn't showing any commitment to doing it. When I have tried to speak to her about it, she gets very defensive. I will just keep trying to talk to her. I think that there is obviously something wrong that she won't talk to me about, but I just don't know what it is. I really like her and don't want her to leave. I just wish that she would pick up her game or talk to me.

Wednesday 28th June 2006

I interviewed four more candidates for the office manager role. One from yesterday afternoon might be OK. She is very young, but seems to be on the ball and enthusiastic. A lot of applicants are so expensive – more than $50,000 a year, which I just can't afford. That is one of my biggest problems: not being able to afford who I need or want, so I end up getting a cheaper version, and they don't rise to the challenge and perform. I will reference-check the young girl, and then decide.

Thursday 29th June 2006

Kate was off sick today, the day we had planned to spend doing the stock count, which she knew in advance. It seems convenient. I think she is going to leave; she is obviously not happy. I know that this sounds as if I don't trust her, but she has definitely changed recently, previously she would be happy to get stuck in and help, this is just so unusual for her. Luckily Belinda brought in two friends, so we had enough help. I have decided to offer the office manager role to Lina who I reference checked. She was very excited when I told her. She starts on Monday.

Friday 30th June 2006

It is the last day of the financial year today. This year has been so busy, I can't believe it. Moving to a new office, taking on lots of people, firing lots; it is has become a bit of a standing joke with my friends, they ask "Who did you fire today?" every time I see them.

Luckily Ella could come in and finish off the accounts for the financial year for me as a favour. It seems that Kim was not doing it all properly, so there were a few messes to sort out. Then I found out that she hadn't sent Fone Zone any invoices for a month, which was about 600 invoices, so they weren't happy to get them all at once – oh, the joys!

I sent out an email today to everyone I know from my old days in marketing to see if anyone knows of a marketing assistant. I really don't think that Kate is going to stay. Our chats to date have not been productive; she says that she wants to do it and can do it, but isn't demonstrating that at all. I would love her to stay, but only if she can show me a bit more dedication, leaving early everyday isn't doing it for me.

Mockers: Kate in marketing, Belinda in sales, Tara in dispatch and Ella helping me out
Mocks sold this month: 16,021
Total stores: 560
Business bank account balance: $1,501 & £562
Mood: ☺ 1/2

July 2006
Monday 3rd July 2006
It has been all go today ... Lina started in the office manager role and Carla started in the UK. I have given Carla a list of what to do and we have been through lots on the phone. We are going to have a weekly phone catch-up. I have written an induction plan for both of the newbies. I do it every time someone starts – I am becoming a bit of a pro at it now!

Kate quit today. We just had our normal catch-up, and before we got going she handed me her resignation; no big surprise. She said it wasn't because she didn't feel valued or appreciated, but because she felt she couldn't meet my standards, which was interesting feedback for me. I know I have high standards, because I set myself high standards as well. I do expect a lot from people, but I am paying them to perform a role. In larger companies employees can get away with doing less if there are others to cover for them, but that is just not the case here. There is a lot I want to achieve in a short time span. It is positive that she feels that she is appreciated, so at least I am doing one thing right, but it is confusing. I set high standards and when they are achieved I am appreciative. So is the problem that she doesn't want to have to reach my standards? I feel I am improving slightly as a manager, but I'm not quite there yet. I told her that I was sorry she was going. She finishes Friday, but I don't think it's ever good when someone quits on the day that someone starts. I drafted an ad for the local newspaper, the *Manly Daily*, and

138

for seek.com.au.

Wednesday 5th July 2006

Mr Johns and I signed the contract to buy our new house today. I can't wait to move in … it will be good to have more space, the new place has three bedrooms and a garden. We should move in August.

Friday 7th July 2006

It was Kate's last day today; we had cake. It feels odd that she is leaving, as she has been with me for the longest out of anyone: eight months. Lina is having a few issues. I had a chat to her today. Although she said in the interview that she could use Excel and other programs, she can't. This becomes a problem whenever I ask her to do databases and spreadsheets, as I have to show her how to use the program first, which takes so long and is so frustrating – why do people lie? It's not like I won't find out. I think that the role is really too much for her. She humphs a lot, which drives me mad, and asks me questions every five seconds. When I interview people now I tell them what I am like; I am very candid. I explain I have high standards, I am demanding and a control freak, and tell them what frustrates me. I also give my good points, such as appreciating a job well done. I also explain the role thoroughly, but I think that they just hear what they want to hear, and with Lina this must have been the case. I said that the role was busy, but she is really struggling. I really don't want to have to face hiring another person, this is getting crazy.

Monday 10th July 2006

I was interviewed today by a year 11 student for a school project. He was surprised that the company wasn't bigger, which was pleasing to hear. We obviously give the impression that the brand is big. He is going to send me a copy of his final project – it will be interesting to see his views as a fan.

Friday 14th July 2006

Ella came in today to do the accounts for me. The accounts are a lot of extra work for me, especially as there is no Kate to jump in. Thank goodness Mr Johns and I are off to the Blue Mountains this weekend for a break. I need it after all this firing!

I had a new product development meeting today with Belinda; I discussed when the new ideas will be out so that she can tell stores. She seems to be getting through to people, and she now has surf store City Beach onboard for a trial. They have 48 stores in total and are going to order next month, which will be a boost to distribution, and the first surf stores with Mocks.

Wednesday 19th July 2006
Belinda and I went to RSVP, a promotional products show in Sydney today. I wanted to check it out from the point of view of exhibiting next year. This is the first time it has been run in Sydney, and it could be really useful to promote personalised Mocks to companies. There was a wide variety of products at the show, from promo items and event venues to performance acts. There seemed to be a lot of people visiting. I spoke to one of the exhibitors I know and they said that they have had some good leads. I will look into exhibiting next year.

I have a new range of phone charms that I think would go well, they are made from recycled circuit boards. We put them into the focus groups, and there was a very mixed reaction, so I have put them into an online survey on SurveyMonkey.com today. If they bomb on the survey we won't go ahead, as they are pretty expensive to get made and maybe too geeky ... I thought the whole recycled angle would appeal to Australian consumers.

I worked through the August store newsletter with Belinda today. It can be hard some months to find info to put in. I am planning to run a customer service survey with the September one, but this month I just ended up talking about the current range, which is selling well, and giving some tips for display. I am also trying to get rid of old designs we still have in stock, so I put them in at a reduced price.

Friday 21st July 2006
Ella was in today to help me interview for the accounts data-entry role. We saw a girl who was participating in a government scheme to

get people with disabilities back into the workplace. I would get paid to take her, and she would get work experience. She has short term memory loss, but because the role is written up in the procedures manual, it should be fine. Both Ella and I agreed it would work well, so she is due to start next Wednesday, as long as the paperwork has been signed off.

Monday 24th July 2006

I had to transfer funds from the Australian bank account today to cover Carla's wages in the UK. The Cancer Council in the UK ordered £10,000 of Breast Cancer Mocks earlier in the year, which we have sent, but we are still waiting for payment. I was hoping that they would pay before now, so that I wouldn't have to transfer cash, as the exchange rate kills me.

Disappointingly Tara in dispatch, told me today that she would be finishing up on 4th August, earlier than I expected, but it has been good having her. I have offered to sponsor her to stay in Australia and work for me and she has agreed. The dispatch role is so hard to fill that I think this is a good option. It will only cost me $650, and I spend that in one month on recruitment with ads and my time. She is going to travel and come back in January, so I just need to find someone to fill in for a few months. I think I will just get another backpacker. At last, something is going right on the people front. ☺

Tuesday 25th July 2006

I interviewed two potentials for the fill-in dispatch role and decided to give it to a guy called Ted, who starts on Monday. Tara will be able to train him for a week before she leaves.

Wednesday 26th July 2006

The new data-entry girl didn't turn up today, which was really annoying as Ella came in specially. It turns out that the woman organising it got it totally wrong. We will have to leave it now for a while, as Ella can't come in to train her for two weeks, and see what happens when she is back.

Friday 28th July 2006

I'm trying to organise all the various bits this week for a stand we have at a trade show for newsagents in two weeks. Luckily Ella has agreed to come with me and help on the stand, because Belinda is now on holidays for two weeks.

I am finding it very hard with Belinda. She still doesn't seem to understand everything. Yes, she has done a great job getting City Beach onboard, and she is enthusiastic, but she is also very scatty. I ask her to do something and she forgets, or sends the wrong information to someone, or contacts the same person three times because she didn't write down that she had already spoken to them. Plus I had feedback from a friend of a friend who she contacted about personalised Mocks, saying that she was very pushy, to the extent that she turned them off – not good. I have tried to talk to her about it, but she doesn't seem to get it. I will see how she goes when she gets back.

Monday 31st July 2006

I chatted to Lina today. It turns out that she is having personal problems, which are affecting her work. She is going to finish up at the end of the week. We both agreed that this is not really the right role for her. Apparently since the chat my attitude towards her has completely changed. Mr Johns is in the office "renting" desk space while he finds an office to rent for the company he is working for, so often adds his penny worth. According to Mr Johns I have become less demanding and more relaxed towards her, as well as expecting less from her. He is probably right, now I know that she is going, I feel we are just marking time getting through the week. Also I know now what to expect from her, so can lower my expectations and just give her basic tasks to do.

Having Mr Johns in the office can be so frustrating, at times he often undermines me in front of the team, like the time I'd suggested something and he said in front of everyone "that's not going to work", or "that's awful" – words to that effect. It doesn't really help me.

Mockers: Carla in UK, Belinda in sales, Tara & Ted in dispatch, Lina

142

(leaving next week) and Ella helping out with accounts
Mocks sold this month: 15,310
Total stores: 600
Business bank account balance: $19,123 & £229
Mood: ☺ ☺

August 2006
Tuesday 1st August 2006

I went on a leadership skills course today for the whole day. I figured after all the issues I've had with staff that I needed to do something. It was a good day, but not in-depth enough. I have decided to sign up for another one at the end of August, on people skills. The courses are expensive, but not as expensive as all the recruitment I have been doing, I think I worked out that 20 people joined and left last financial year – from July05 to June06, which is a huge number when there were only three roles.

Friday 4th August 2006

It was the last day for both Lina and Tara, so we had cake. It is kind of strange; now there will only be me and Ted in dispatch until Belinda gets back. I interviewed two women for the office manager role to replace Lina, but neither of them was really right. I have now decided that I rushed into it last time, and I need to take longer and find the right person this time.

I have a big tax bill from the last BAS. I hate paying tax. I will have to call the Tax Office on Monday and see if I can do a payment plan, because I just don't have the $20,000 they want in the bank.

I'm having no luck at finding a marketing person. This is crazy. I am going to have to let so many things fall by the wayside to just keep the business running – it is soooo frustrating.

Tuesday 8th August 2006

I had my weekly catch-up with Carla in the UK last night. She seems to be full of enthusiasm and ideas. She has sent me a list of potentials to target, and has followed up our existing stores. There are no more new stores onboard as yet, but it has only been a

143

month.

The IT guy came in for the monthly check-up. They must find it strange that every time they come in there is someone gone and someone new.

Wednesday 9th August 2006

After interviewing four people this week I think today I might have found our office manager: Lucy. She is older than the rest of us in the office, but that could be good. She has run her own business before, so she would be used to pitching in.

Ella took over interviewing for the data entry person for me after we decided not to hire the girl from the government scheme (the unreliability of the person organising it put us off). Ella has sorted all the resumes and interviewed the candidates this morning. It was a toss-up between two, but we decided to go with Helen, on a casual basis for 15 hours a week. She starts next week. At last the team is coming together – I feel as if I have uttered those words a lot this year, I really hope this time it does. I know I need to believe to make it happen – think positive.

Ella also had some *big* news today – she is pregnant, due in March next year. Fantastic news for her, but now we must get the accounts department sorted out, since she will have even less time to jump in and help me once the baby arrives.

Thursday 10th August 2006

I've had three interviews for the marketing role this week to replace Kate. One was too expensive, the second could be suitable and the third was really super keen, a real keen bean, but he had no experience. I would need to go through everything with him, and I'm not sure if I have the time, energy and patience to do that. I want to mull it over for a bit.

I met a business coach today. I applied to be on the TV show *My Business TV* to talk about staff issues and get advice from expert business coaches – I figured I need it. We didn't really cover much in the two-hour session today; it was mainly to help the business coach understand the issues. He will be back with the TV crew on Tuesday to film in the office. He was amazed at my turnover of 20 people. I guess it is pretty high, but that includes temps, and I didn't fire them all!

Friday 11th August 2006

Lucy starts on Monday. She accepted the office manager role, so that's a weight off my mind. I just need to find the marketing person, then we will be back up and running. Plus I'm still looking for a full-time salesperson; Belinda part-time just isn't enough. I came up with the idea today to do a mail-out to all the NSW gift stores in the Yellow Pages, sending them one of the new Mocks greeting cards (which are a card with a Mock attached) when they launch next month. I will put it on the list for Lucy to do.

Monday 14th August 2006

Both Helen and Lucy started today, so a full-on day with not much achieved by me other than inductions.

Wednesday 15th August 2006

The film crew were in yesterday filming for the *My Business TV*. They were great people and they loved Mocks, so I gave them each one when they left. We filmed for about two hours, and they told me I had a good face for TV – better than having a good face for radio, I guess! I think it was because I was very expressive. In the interview the business coach was talking and I wasn't, which concerned the TV editor – and I felt like an idiot just nodding all the time – so they turned it round a bit so I got to talk. They promised it would look good for me. I will get the DVD in the next few weeks.

I interviewed two girls for the marketing role today. I think that the first one Simone would be a great fit with the team, and will do the job well so time for more reference checks.

We have the Mocks second birthday party next Friday. I am inviting friends and some suppliers, and there is a Mocks cake being made. It should be fun. I can't believe it has been nearly two years …

Thursday 17th August 2006
Belinda, our salesgirl, was supposed to meet me today for an hour to go through everything for the newsagent trade show this weekend, she has been taking holiday at home this week, and forgot to come in. I'm not very impressed. I know she was out, but it was her idea …

Friday 18th August 2006
Ella – my bookkeeper come salesperson, and I set up for the newsagent trade show this afternoon. Our stand looks good; we still have the balloons to blow up tomorrow, but otherwise we are set to go. It is a pretty small event, but this is a whole new audience that we haven't even tried to target before, and I am feeling really positive about it.

Sunday 20th August 2006
The show finished today. It wasn't as busy as I expected, and a lot of the other exhibitors said it was quieter than previous years. There was one amusing incident yesterday. A woman visiting the show stole a Mock Greeting Card off our stand. I noticed it was missing after she left, but it was in range of the camera set up on the security camera stand that just happened to be next to our stand. We rewound the film, saw who it was and spotted her just four stands up. I went and asked her to return the Mock Card, and when she claimed that she didn't take it, I asked her to empty out her bags – and there it was. Then I reported her to security. The security stand people were really chuffed and spent the rest of the show telling everyone who visited their stand all about it!

Belinda came to help today at the show, but I found it very hard to work with her. I kept seeing problems with what she was doing; for example, she was encouraging children to enter the competition to win a stand full of Mocks for themselves, when the idea of the competition was to collect store business cards for leads. I was trying to stay calm, but it wasn't really working for me, and I am sure she knew she was driving me mad.

Tuesday 22nd August 2006
I went on a whole-day workshop today with Tribe Research about

designing market research surveys. I designed our customer service survey and another survey while I was there. It was interesting, fun and definitely worth going to.

Wednesday 23rd August 2006
I had to talk to Belinda today about the iMock pricing. She gave a big store the wrong price, so we are selling them for nearly $2 per item less than we should. I'm not very happy with this. I am having trouble finding positive things to say to her. Last night she was the last person to leave the office and she didn't have her office keys with her, so she called me to say that she had just left it unlocked and gone home. I couldn't believe she would do that. She said that she hadn't put the alarm on or locked the outer door either. There are tens of thousands of dollars worth of stock and computers in there. The call came as I was getting off the ferry in Manly, so I drove up to the office and she was there. She had obviously felt bad and gone back. I didn't know what to say, so I asked had she thought how she would feel if this happened to her. She hadn't. I just don't understand how she could do it.

Friday 25th August 2006
Mocks' second birthday! We had around 25 people at the party and everyone enjoyed themselves. Simone, the new marketing girl, came even though she doesn't start for another few weeks. Mr Johns and I moved house today as well; nothing like doing everything at once.

Monday 28th August 2006
I attended the first day of the people skills course in North Sydney. It was definitely worth the investment; I am learning a lot. We discussed the whole hiring and firing process, the team bonding curve, change in the workplace and how to deal with difficult staff. It was all very useful. When I was on the bus on the way home I got a call from Belinda asking me if I still liked her! I wasn't sure what to say. I was on the bus and couldn't hear that well, so I said that we'd talk about it when I was back in the office – I will have to ask my trainer how to deal with this on the course tomorrow.

Wednesday 30th August 2006

I asked the question on the course about Belinda's behaviour, and was told that she is using emotional blackmail to get her own way. She really wants to be liked and has difficulty distinguishing between work and social relationships. We also talked about what to do if you are talking to people about something they don't want to hear and they start crying – you just have to keep going, as otherwise it won't help either of you. It was a very interesting three days.

Thursday 31st August 2006

I spoke to Belinda today and she cried. I tried to explain what needed to be done to rectify the situation. We agreed to give it a few more weeks, but I said that she had to improve. I don't think she got it, but I have to assume (as I learnt on the course) that she did, as I explained it and she said she understood.

I put in the submission to Telstra for advertising in the Christmas catalogue. They have done a fantastic deal for me on the price. I love them. It never ceases to amaze me the number of people who help me in some way or another. Although obviously in this case if I advertise then it also helps Telstra, as they will sell more Mocks.

Mockers: Carla in UK, Belinda in sales, Ted in dispatch, Lucy in admin, Helen in accounts and Ella bookkeeping
Mocks sold this month: 19,770
Total stores: 660
Business bank account balance: $21,260 & £1,852
Mood: ☺ ☺ 1/2

September 2006

Wednesday 6th September 2006

I met a girl from the Optus mobile marketing department today. She is interested in putting a Mock in a prepaid mobile pack for Christmas. We were talking about volumes of 50,000 units! I need to get costs to her and she says that they are looking at a number of options, but if they don't go with it for Christmas, they will use them next year. It's very exciting.

I am looking at options to display the Mock Cards. Yesterday a

148

supplier showed me a flat-packed pop-up stand, but it only holds about 10 cards, which might be a problem. At the newsagent trade show I talked to all the card distributors to see if they would be interested in taking the cards. The cards would be great for newsagencies who don't have the space for a stand for Mocks, since they could put the cards in their existing racks. I need to follow them all up. One guy was particularly interested and wanted me to get in contact at the end of the month. It would be so much easier if I could get someone to distribute them for me. With only 10 Mock card designs, card stores are proving hard to persuade. They seem to want a wider range, but I don't really want to launch any more designs until these ones are out there and are successful.

We got an order this week from a guy in Sweden after an email last week completely out of the blue asking about prices. Only 300 Mocks, but he seemed very enthusiastic so might reorder if they go well. What I love about customers from overseas is that they pay up-front, so it helps with the business cashflow.

Monday 11th September 2006

The new range of Mocks arrived today from China. They look great, and it is good to have them in early for Christmas, unlike the panicked rush before Christmas last year. Laura is working so well for us, I've been working with her factory for a year now, and she is so easy to work with, she is honest and upfront and always delivers when she says. Plus the quality of the Mocks is good, I did have some comments from stores about the Mocks that Jackie made for us – they said the colours weren't bright enough. Its funny, Laura regularly sends me samples of potential new products we could launch and she still thinks it's really amusing that we sell so many Mocks.

The business TV show aired yesterday. I was only on for two minutes. The Mocks looked great, but I didn't say much. I had about five calls today from recruitment agencies because I talked about staffing issues, so it was good to see that people watch it. However, I would have preferred if it the calls were from people who wanted Mocks.

I have decided that I am going to trial using Skype for all outgoing calls in the office. Our phone bills have been over $400 per month and, more to the point, we are at the stage where we need more than two phone lines. This way we will still have two lines, but everyone will be able to use Skype from their own PC to make calls without tying up a line, so people can still get through to us. Everyone in the office has agreed to give Skype a one-month trial, and then we will evaluate it.

Having Helen doing data entry and Lucy as office manager is working out well; I feel some of the load has been taken off me. I have now created a timetable that shows the team when I am available to be asked questions. That is something that drives me insane, so the idea is that everyone saves up their questions to ask me during the two hours per day I have allocated, rather than their usual trick of catching me on the way to the toilet!

Friday 15th September 2006

I took the day off yesterday to go and see Jamie Oliver cook. He is a real entertainer, and I enjoyed it much more than I expected. Also, while I was out the team made executive decisions – I love it.

I have been having a two-hour weekly coaching session as a result of the TV show, not with the original coach I met, but another from the same company. Although I find them useful, sometimes he just doesn't seem to understand the issues. This week we were discussing a price rise. Although I explained the way the mobile stores worked, he seemed to think their margins were far too high, and it was difficult for him to get his head around it. Mocks haven't had a price rise since I started, so I have decided to implement one from November 1st, which gives all the stores one month's notice. It will be a minimum 10% rise, and at the same time I will try to bring all the accounts into alignment. I think that it will cause problems with some accounts, the ones that like to wheel and deal with me, but it is just not cost-effective to deal with the wheeler-dealer accounts, unless they pay up-front. Ella and I have been reviewing outstanding accounts and are also going to implement a system whereby all the independent stores have to pay prior to shipment unless they are ordering over $500 worth of Mocks, to get around the amount of time we spend chasing accounts. I think that there will be backlash from this as well, but it can't be helped. I really need to improve the bottom line.

Buying Mocks by SMS finished yesterday. I worked out that it was just not profitable, and there were so many problems with the company double-charging people, we seemed to spend all of our time sorting them out. I am rather disappointed that it didn't work out, but I can't run it at a loss. It just doesn't make sense. Maybe we were just ahead of our time.

Monday 18th September 2006

I launched the Mocks online shop last month and sales are starting to pick up. I thought that selling direct to customers might create a backlash from the retailers, but it has been fine. The main purpose of the site is to provide a way for overseas customers to purchase Mocks. Ordering Mocks by mail is hard both for them and us, because if they have to post their order to Australia or the UK it can take 2 weeks to get to us, and then if they pay by cheque in a foreign currency it costs us a fortune to bank it . I am still trying to put systems in place to make sure we capture all the information on customers, plus keep stock levels and sales accurate.

Telstra have signed off on taking the new Polka Dot Mock as an exclusive design until the end of December, Telstra stores will be the only place consumers can buy this design. They have committed to taking 2,000 units. I think it will sell really well for them, and we will drive traffic to their stores through our advertising and the website.

I am really pleased with the way sales are going – $30,000 so far this month, and we still have two weeks left. This is just as well, considering I have so many people to pay now!

Wednesday 20th September 2006

It was Belinda's last day today. It just wasn't working; nothing was improving, so I am back hunting for a salesperson. I think she may have been doing more harm than good in some ways, even if her heart was in the right place.

Friday 22nd September 2006

Ella and I met a representative from a company about a new accounting package. Ella has agreed to help me assess them, as she knows in detail what we need for the business. We didn't end up going with the outsourcing option as the guy just didn't come back to us with the information, which I feel is never a good sign. Our current package just can't handle the volume of invoices, so I think we'll need to upgrade our accounting package at the end of this financial year, but it is going to be pricey.

I have started developing Mocks for special events and occasions, which was an idea of Sally's to help us get more PR. Currently we have a wedding couple Mock, a horse racing one, a soccer design and there is a tennis one coming.

Monday 25th September 2006

I had an interview today for the Sydney Business Review Business Woman of the Year awards, which I entered a month ago. I thought it would be good publicity and there are some cash prizes, which would be very helpful. The interview panel loved Mocks, and I gave them all samples. I got the impression that they rather got sidetracked with wanting to know about them rather than asking the official questions.

Friday 29th September 2006

It has been a very busy week. Simone is settling in well to the marketing role. We went through the whole process of launching a new Mocks range, so we can make a start on the Feb 07 range. As her first range, it will take a bit longer than usual.

In the team meeting we all brainstormed ways to get rid of the remaining iMocks. We still have so many left and they are just not moving. It is just cash sitting on the office floor. I think the designs are the problem – I don't think I did a thorough enough job with the market research into them. I offered a prize of $100 to whomever in the office sold the most by the end of October. We looked at all the ideas, and everyone chose one to run with. There are some good ideas, but the product is just a hard sell.

I seem to have spent a lot of money this month. I am going to have to borrow $30,000 from Mum and Dad. With Christmas coming I have to order a lot of stock to cover sales. I have already sent Laura at the factory in China $15,000 this week alone. I have been working with Laura for a while now, so thank goodness I no longer have to pay a deposit upfront when I order, which makes cashflow easier, I just pay when she sends the invoice which is usually after the Mocks have arrived with us. I love that we have such a good relationship.

A guy from SAP came in today to talk to Ella and I about their accounting system. It is really quite complicated to use compared to what we have currently. I don't think it is right for us.

I have developed a sales plan of action until I find someone. It's basically a list of what I need to achieve each week. It is making up part of my business goals that I reviewed this week with Ella. Ella in her capacity as bookkeeper/friend/general sounding board is going to help me be more accountable for my goals – I sometimes find it hard when it is me trying to motivate myself.
Mockers: Carla in UK, Simone in marketing, Helen in accounts, Lucy in admin, Ted in dispatch and Ella bookkeeping
Mocks sold this month: 15,588
Total stores: 719
Business bank account balance: $11,251 & £1,612
Mood: ☺ stressed

October 2006
Thursday 5th October 2006

Simone and I had lunch with the *Girlfriend* team today. We are reviewing how the communications plan is going for us and for them. The Mocks covermount comes out this month, and this year we have a lot more advertising than last year, because are giving them more Mocks. I am definitely eager to work with them again next year. They want to do a complete covermount run, which will be 180,000 Mocks – a lot. We need to work out the deal. It is good to see that they see enough value in promotion to want to work with us again.

In the team meeting yesterday we reviewed the sales targets and where we are; so far this financial year we are tracking OK. The next few months will be the biggest of the year due to Christmas. I think it is important to tell the team about the targets and sales, but at the same time they don't seem to really understand how they influence sales, even though I have explained it numerous times. I did a chart for the meeting with a sales line and an expense line to demonstrate that even if we sell $60,000 in Mocks then if we spend $50,000 on the office and wages etc, then we only actually get $10,000. I think the numbers side is hard for the team to grasp, when I worked in marketing we were held to numbers so much that I had to learn to understand them, but in small business it is very different – I find that many other business people I meet don't run P&Ls etc monthly like I do.

Laura in China has agreed to find a supplier for the button badges I'd like to produce as giveaways, she will be so much cheaper than an Australian supplier. I had button badges made back in 2004 when I first started and they were really popular, we still have people asking for them. We are so lucky to have Laura – she seems to be able to help us get nearly anything made!

I have now contacted all the retailers regarding the price rise; not too much backlash, thank goodness.

Friday 13th October 2006
Mr Johns finally moved out of the office today, which is good and bad. Good to have my own space back, but the rent was handy!

I seem to have spent all week on the phone. I called all the zoos in Australia to promote the Mock designs with animals on them, plus lots of companies about personalised Mocks. It is such a long process to get new stores onboard; it can really frustrate me.

Joanna the buyer at Telstra told me that they were not overly happy about the price rise, because our competitor, Meanies, has dropped its price to tempt Telstra into buying them. I told her how Mocks have a dedicated website, advertise every month to consumers, regularly promote the product on the pack and in stores, provide point of sale materials and bring out new designs every three months. When I explained the difference between the two brands, Joanna agreed to keep Mocks exclusively at least until the end of December. She will review it at the beginning of next year. Phew!

Monday 16th October 2006
I got an email over the weekend from a successful young Tasmanian entrepreneur – Kirsty Dunphey, who writes a weekly newsletter that goes to 3,500 people. She asked if she could interview me for the newsletter. I found it really flattering...

I am still calling companies about personalised Mocks. No salesperson has turned up yet; the recruitment agency I hired hasn't found anyone, and there are next to no applications from our ad on seek.com.au. I know that unemployment is low in Australia, but I can't believe that there are so few people applying.

Carla has been working in the UK now for over three months. There hasn't been much progress in terms of new stores, but she says that opportunities are arising and there is a positive response from retailers.

Friday 20th October 2006
The end of a busy week. I attended two networking events at the Australian Institute of Management. They are free as part of my membership. One was on "Finding and retaining quality human assets", which I found very relevant. The other event was on marketing, which wasn't quite as interesting, just because it didn't really tell me anything new. I do love going to networking events, but I have to be in the right mood.

We got the results today from the sampling of Mocks we did in the *Girlfriend* show bag at the Brisbane Show. There were three questions on Mocks in the survey included in the bag, and the results from the survey showed that Mocks have 74% brand awareness with teens! To have this kind of recognition in just over two years is huge. I am really impressed. When I worked on Windex in Australia brand awareness with all adults was over 90%, but that was for a brand that has been about for over 50 years and has a huge marketing spend behind it. I think we are doing well.

The awards dinner was on tonight for the Sydney Business Review Business Woman of the Year. I went with Mr Johns. I met some really interesting women in the networking session for the finalists before the awards. In the awards obviously I wanted to win the Business Woman of the Year award, but instead I won the Sydney Business Review Business Woman of the Year MBA Scholarship award from the University of Western Sydney. The scholarship is worth $30,000, so it's a huge prize, and I have always wanted to do an MBA (admittedly at Harvard, but beggars can't be choosers). The course is run from a campus near Parramatta, about a one to two hour drive from home, but worth it I am sure. It was funny, as I was walking back to my chair after getting the award I was stopped by a girl who showed me her Pink Teddy Mock and told me how much she loved it and thanked me. The girl came up later and asked to have her photo with me and her Mock. I wonder if that's how you know when you are successful?

Monday 23rd October 2006

I had to speak to Helen in admin and Ted in dispatch about the orders that have been going out with stock missing. In some cases just an empty bag has been sent. I think we need to develop a better system to keep track of customer queries about orders, to ensure they are followed up. I have given Lucy the office manager responsibility for seeing that it is implemented and giving them ideas on how to manage it.

Today I had everyone in the team give me their feedback on how they have found using Skype for calls this past month. It was positive, and looking at our phone bills we have cut them in half – from $400 per month to $200. Also, we haven't had any more callers say they are having trouble getting through, and I find using a headset is actually much easier when you are typing and chatting.

Friday 27th October 2006
Today I had another unpaid speaking engagement that Ella organised for me – the public just can't get enough of me. ☺ I hope that continues. It was a breakfast for Inspiring Women, a networking group on Sydney's Northern Beaches. The women really enjoyed it; they seemed to be amazed by what I had achieved, especially when I showed them the file of every article of free PR I got last year – the file contains around 100 articles. Ella also sold about $200 worth of Mocks at the door. It was a very good day all round.

Monday 30th October 2006
I finally received an applicant for the sales role, a guy called Jason who studied marketing at university with Simone, she thinks he would be good. The interview this morning went well, he was incredibly nervous, but he had a lot of good ideas and seemed very enthusiastic.

I really need to get key performance indicators finalised for Lucy and Helen today, so that I can see how they are performing.

Tuesday 31st October 2006
I have decided to offer Jason the role. Maybe it is out of desperation, but the enthusiasm and excitement he had were great, so I think it is worth a go, plus his references came back very positive.
Mockers: Carla in UK, Simone in marketing, Lucy in admin, Helen in accounts, Ted in dispatch and Ella bookkeeping - WOW this is the same as last month!
Mocks sold this month: 23,164
Total stores: 705
Business bank account balance: $16,966 & £5,524
Mood:☺ ☺ optimistic

November 2006
Thursday 2nd November 2006
Simone ran her marketing product training session for the team

today on how a new range of Mocks is designed. We wanted the whole team to understand what she actually does, since I think sometimes they are not sure if she working, for example when she's reading magazines for ideas. Simone is really coming on, getting to grips with work and taking on responsibility. I am so glad I have her.

Monday 6th November 2006

At the teachers conference I spoke at in May I got some feedback from the MC - she's a director at Toni & Guy hairdressers. She said that the talk was great, but the photo that I had in the brochure was awful! So today I went to Starshots photo studio with a bag of Mocks and had three professional photos taken. I can use them for all the hundreds of speaking gigs that are going to come my way.

I got some good news today: LaRoo has been approved to sponsor employees. The process was much quicker and easier than I expected. Now I just need to fill in the paperwork to sponsor Tara to be ready for when she returns to the dispatch role in January.

Wednesday 8th November 2006

Yesterday was the Melbourne Cup horse race. Mr Johns invited all my team to his office to celebrate with his team. About 25 of us watched the race on the big screen and had champagne and nibbles. It was a real treat, especially as his office overlooks Darling Harbour.

Today Jason started in the sales role. Lucy, our office manager, organised an induction plan for him, and he rotated around the whole team to find out what each person does. He also did some Mock packing.

My MBA application got approved today by the university. Even though I won a scholarship, I still had to apply and be accepted. I am looking forward to starting in January.

Monday 13th November 2006

Helen, our data entry person, told me today that she will no longer be able to work three days a week after Christmas, as her uni work has increased. It is really annoying. She had organised her sister to cover two of the days for her, which I would have been OK with, but now her sister is pregnant and can't do it either. There are three options: one, she job shares with someone; two, she leaves; or three, she works in the evenings, but that would mean giving up her night job. I think that the best option for us would be to find someone else. Job sharing is hard, especially if there is no overlap, and Helen already feels like she misses out on what goes because she isn't there – like info on new Mocks. However, this does mean that I need to find another admin/data entry person – oh joy!

Finally the Mock Cards arrived today. They are a greeting card and a gift in one, and they look great. I think that they will be really popular, but so close to Christmas it is going to be hard to sell the Christmas designs ... I don't want a repeat of last year where we had to hold onto the Christmas Mock designs for a year.

I spoke to the guy who trialled distributing Mocks into petrol stations for me. They didn't sell well enough for him to keep selling them, so he isn't going to take them on permanently, which is disappointing.

Friday 17th November 2006

I met Erica, our graphic designer, yesterday to discuss the potential of a Christian Mock design. I have been researching the Christian market, and it is huge. More people go to church on Sunday than to Australian rules football games – so there is a huge potential to sell to this audience, although obviously not in churches! There was a big article on it in *Marketing* magazine, and on further investigation I've found there is a definite niche out there that we are not hitting. We are going to go with a design with WWJD (meaning "What would Jesus do?") on it. Apparently WWJD is all the rage in the teen Christian community.

I created a Mocks page on MySpace today, as I think we need to get more 21st century. I am also getting Simone in marketing to check out the Second Life website. There are so many brands getting on Second Life now, it might be an option to have a virtual Mocks store selling virtual Mocks for virtual mobiles ...

Friday 24th November 2006

I had to talk to Jason in sales today about his role. He doesn't seem to want to make phone calls to retailers. We had agreed that he would make 30 calls per day, but it is just not happening, and when I asked why he seemed to have no reply. Also, I have asked him to follow up particular people, and he hasn't. When asked why, he said that he thought the ones he did were more important. This isn't a good attitude in week two, especially as we've already sent info to the stores I asked him to call, so if they aren't followed up it is a waste of time and money. The talk did not really go well. I saw the situation as fixable, but he obviously didn't and quit on the spot. He has a problem working with me and said that I am too demanding. Hmm … or maybe he just didn't want to work at it, or maybe it's a hang-up about working for a woman. I am back to the drawing board on sales staff, again.

I changed the business banking to the ANZ Bank this week as they could offer me an unsecured overdraft, while none of the others would. It is bizarre how the banks say that they are for small business, but they are so not. From next week I will have an extra $30,000 to put my mind at ease on the cashflow front.

I have practically finished the US market entry strategy this week. The plan was for me to go over there next year, but until I have a salesperson in place that just can't happen, as I can see that when I am not actively working on sales in Australia, the sales fall.

Wednesday 29th November 2006

I met the woman who organises the merchandise used to fundraise for Jeans for Genes Day today. She loves the idea of a denim Mock, which would be sold in trays by the tills in supermarkets. I need to get back to her with a proposal, but so far it is looking really positive.

Ella and I met people from two more accounting software companies today. Both look promising. There was one where everything was online, which I loved. I would be able to access it easily from anywhere in the world.

At just $67,000, sales this month have been disappointing, especially considering it is November and supposedly the biggest month of the year because of the run up to Christmas. Unless tomorrow is huge, the month won't be anywhere near as good as I had hoped. With all the staff changes this year, I have spent a vast amount of time training and retraining. People starting and stopping has also meant very little consistency in how things have been done, even if they follow procedures. Any new salespeople I hire will take a few months to get up and running, so they can't be counted on to bring in much additional revenue in the first few months. This financial year I really needed to generate enough profit to finance my expansion into the US.

Mockers: Carla in UK, Simone in marketing, Lucy in admin, Helen in accounts, Ted in dispatch and Ella bookkeeping
Mocks sold this month: 21,146
Total stores: 705
Business bank account balance: $11,020 & £4,897
Mood: ☹

December 2006
Monday 4th December 2006
Mum and Dad arrived from France last week for a six-week holiday. They came into the office today, and were very excited. Last time they were in Australia I hadn't even started the business.

I had an enquiry from Fiji on the weekend about Mocks. I sent them samples and pricing today. I suspect that the pricing will be too high, but I will see.

I decided to kill off the Chocolate Teddy today. Sales are really not very high compared with the other colours. I was surprised, because the initial research we did indicated it would do well. I will sell what we have and not reorder.

Friday 8th December
It was the last day for Ted in dispatch today. He has been filling in for Tara, who will be back at the beginning of January, I had planned for a few weeks with no dispatch person. It shouldn't be a problem.

Mum and Dad are keen to help out.

I decided this week to stop my business coaching sessions. They are $260 per session and I really don't feel that I get that much value from them. Sometimes I feel that we are just talking about things for the sake of it, rather than getting to the bottom of issues. I want more guidance from a coach as to what we need to address, rather than me bringing discussion points every fortnight, as I can't always think of what we need to discuss.

We got the approval from Sesame St to make licensed Sesame St Mocks this week. We have to do the samples and get them approved, but they should launch early next year. I think they will be huge. Well, I hope they will be, since I have had to pay $7,500 up-front in royalties.

Tuesday 12th December 2006
We received a lovely Christmas pressie from Laura in China yesterday, a red tissue paper cutting, it was huge – the length of a desk, it came rolled up, I need to organise a frame for it. We sent her presents as well, even though she doesn't celebrate Christmas, but I think it's a nice gesture, ours were very Australian things like Timtams!

I finally got the merchant facilities for the new bank account sorted today. It means that we can process credit card payments online rather than having to go into the bank, therefore saving time.

I went to an American Chamber of Commerce (AmCham) networking event tonight, a Christmas party. There was a woman there talking about how she sponsored a sheep to help the farmers in the drought. I thought this could be a great competition prize for the launch of the new Shaggy Sheep Mock in February. When you buy the Mock you go into the draw to win a sheep sponsorship. I emailed Simone with the idea when I got home.

When I was chatting to Mum and Dad today, I told them how I was getting frustrated with the business, because it isn't achieving what I wanted in terms of my expansion plans. It feels like it is taking a long time to get the UK going, staffing in Australia has been hard this year, sales haven't been as good as I had hoped, and with the US falling through, I just find it challenging to keep fired up and pushing forward.

Monday 18th December 2006

It is the last week before Christmas and sales are quiet. We are going to have a disappointing month, I think. I bought a present for each of the team over the weekend, and also my Secret Santa present for the Christmas party on Friday.

When I was at the dentist a couple of weeks ago, my dentist ordered some Mocks. I got our designer to do a design with a tooth on one side and his name and number on the other. I am getting 1,000 made for him. He absolutely loves Mocks. He told me that to start with he had to force himself to put a Mock on, but now he gets worried about his phone if it isn't wearing it! I love it.

Tuesday 19th December 2006

Erica, our designer, came in for a meeting today regarding the new Mocks stands that Simone is working on. They are going to be great. They are rotating stands with 18 hooks, rather than the six that our current stand has. We've had a lot of positive feedback from stores, so they should be a big hit.

The new packaging artwork is finally signed off. All Mocks made from now on will be in the new packaging. It means that the backing card is inside the bag rather than outside, so no more labels falling off. It looks so much more professional and makes the Mock look more up market.

I spoke to Carla in the UK yesterday. I was really hoping that we would break even at the six month mark, but we haven't yet. The UK business is costing us $9,000 per month to run. I have told her this, and reinforced that I need to see some sales happening. There have been a few sales, but nowhere near what we need. I have agreed to keep going for a few more months, but I will keep a close eye on it.

163

In February she is exhibiting at the trade show in Birmingham that I did this year. That should give the UK a good kick-start.

The UK covermount we did in October produced lots of responses, around 500 girls applied for the offer of "buy one Mock get one free". We are raising awareness, but I think that it has to be on a more continuous basis – so we keep reminding them.

Friday 22nd December 2006
Today's the last work day of the year. Yesterday was the Christmas party, a BBQ at Shelly Beach with pass the parcel. We had some Mocktastic prizes, donated by some suppliers. Some of the team brought their partners, plus Mum and Dad came and had a ball. It was one of our best staff parties, although I think I drank a little bit much …

Wednesday 27th December 2006
Dad and I drove out to visit a company that sells scales for counting coins. This might be the way to reduce human error in counting Mocks for orders. We tried it out on a few hundred Mocks we took with us, and it looks like it will save a lot of time. The set-up will take a while, since the Mocks designs weigh different amounts, so we will need to spend time over the break doing that. The scales were pretty expensive, $900, but will potentially save us money in the future by reducing the risk of miscounts and the time to count the Mocks. The guy assured me that the scales can do what we want - save labour and increase accuracy.
Mockers: Carla in UK, Simone in marketing, Lucy in admin, Helen in accounts and Ella bookkeeping
Mocks sold this month: 11,528
Total stores: 700
Business bank account balance: $31,088 & £2,621
Mood: ☺ ☺

2007
January 2007

Another new year, last year was rather hectic with all the hiring and firing, but I am positive that this year will be better. I think that the staff frustrations have been getting to me, I am learning more about what I do and don't like in running a business. I much prefer to look at the big picture now rather than the detail, but it's hard when there aren't many people to delegate to. However, even with the staff issues I still launched the Mocks cards and we got Mocks into City Beach and some other stores, so it wasn't all bad. December finished up with me feeling a bit demotivated, I think the holidays were good for me, and having Mum and Dad here has been great. I've been able to chat to Dad about the business and where I am going, both of them have been so impressed with what I have achieved. I feel ready to start 2007.

Tuesday 2nd January 2007

The office went back to work today. It's a new year with lots of new challenges. Since we shut over Christmas, a backlog of orders has been building up, so we started the month with $12,000 in sales – always a winner. Now I just need to keep up the momentum. Over Christmas talking with Mum and Dad gave me lots of new ideas to implement. I plan to do a mail-out of the Mock Cards to card stores to try to create some interest. I need to get these cards off the ground. Everyone says how fantastic they are, and how much they love them, but it's so hard to get them into stores.

Thursday 4th January 2007

I went to uni last night for the new student induction for my MBA. Everyone was very nice and helpful, as I'd expect. I am looking forward to getting started. I hope I learn information that can help me drive and grow the business.

We had champagne at work today for the office manager Lucy's birthday, which she brought in. This was at 9am – kind of early I thought, but it was her 50th. I had a meeting at 10am in the city, so I had just a sip.

The meeting with Village Roadshow Entertainment went really well. Their marketing manager, Penny, was really keen on Mocks and on working with us on some promotions, which could be a way to appeal to that older female target audience that I want to target this year. The idea is to put a Mock inside DVD cases and then sticker the outside to say "free Mock inside" and promote this with point of sale materials, like posters in stores.

Sales doubled today. I love January. It was like this last year too – just as well sales are strong, as December was so awful. I am looking forward to Monday when Tara starts back in dispatch. Mum and Dad are good Mock packers, but aren't exactly speedy!

Monday 8th January 2007

It's my first day at uni today. I am taking two modules this semester: accounting and operations. Today was accounting, which is not my favourite topic, but I know that I need to be able to read the figures a lot better, so I will try to get the most out of it.

Tara started today, full of beans, and she seems to remember almost everything from when she was here last year.

Tuesday 9th January 2007

I had a conference call with Carla in the UK and the whole team this morning. The idea is to keep her more in the loop and let everyone here get to know her, so that they go directly to her, rather than through me all the time. Everyone said their bit. I know that this is good for the team, but for me it feels like a huge waste of my time, as I know what everyone is up to and I have catch-ups with Carla on my own. I need to wean them off me being there; they should be able to do this on their own.

I am finding the accounts side of the business frustrating. As we don't have a full-time person, the monthly reports take forever to be done. Now that Helen's going, I am tossing up the idea of hiring an admin person to do Helen's data entry work and help with other areas. But I really feel that the other areas could and should be managed by Lucy.

I did lots of following up today, although really January is a write-off for sales calls, with so many people on holidays or just not in the right frame of mind. I need to get more organised for next year.

Thursday 11th January 2007

I had the day off yesterday and went to the tennis with Mum and Dad. It was the first time any of us has seen a live match. It was great fun, especially when I gave Kim Clijsters a Tennis Mock! Her bouncers were not too happy. Disappointingly it was hard to get to the other players to give them a Mock. Tennis is such a huge sport; I really need to tap into that.

I had a meeting with a guy who runs a sales rep agency today regarding contracting some sales reps to work for me. He seemed pretty knowledgeable about it. This could be the way to go, as having an in-house sales person hasn't been working out.

We had our fortnightly team meeting today. Everyone really enjoys them, especially the quiz on Mocks and the business, which we have at the end. It's good to get that buzz going.

The Christian market distributor, Gary, is going ahead with supplying Christian stores for me. It will be much easier that me doing it, since I wouldn't know where to go and am not sure how lucrative it will be as yet.

The scales that I bought over the Christmas break are not really working as we expected; they are accurate up to 200 Mocks, but then the inaccuracies start, and it is the 200+ orders where we need to save time in counting. I spoke to the company that sold them to us and they are going to try to sort it out for me. I sent them some Mocks today for testing.

Sales are now up to $30,000. It looks like it is going to be a big month!

Friday 12th January 2007

Friday morning Mock de-fluffing started today. I thought if we spend an hour every Friday morning picking off the loose threads and checking for Mocks with holes in them, we can catch up on tidying up the Mocks, which can then be sold. The secondary benefit is that the team will get to know each other better in a more relaxed atmosphere.

I spoke to the buyer from City Beach, Jemina, today. She suggested that we might want to go with a white or black teddy Mock, as those two colours sell really well in their stores. White is a no-no, I said, just too easy to get grubby, and I know that the white Mocks really don't sell for this reason. But black is a good idea. I've asked Laura in China to make a sample. I think if we can meet Jemina's needs it will improve our relationship with City Beach.

I finished the Jeans for Genes Day proposal today. I think launching the Denim Mock with them would be great for both of us. Telstra have agreed to come onboard, which will increase sales for the charity.

Monday 15th January 2007

I had a busy weekend doing uni work and sorting out the spare room into a home office. We bought a PC, which will make life so much easier, but not a printer. Mr Johns doesn't see the point of a printer; he is so frustrating at times. I know I can print at work, and it's only five minutes' drive away, but it's also inconvenient. I will have to work on him ...

Lucy the office manager was off sick today, so I had a few extra bits to do in the office, but no real dramas. I had my first catch-up with Tara in dispatch. It was good to establish what we will go through each week, and how the sessions will run.

I finalised the agreement with *Girlfriend* for this year's contra deal: Mocks for advertising. It's great that we are going to work with them again. The team is fantastic, and the exposure for Mocks really builds the brand.

I had to leave at 4pm today to get to uni for 6pm. The only downside with the course is that the campus is at Westmead, near Parramatta.

Wednesday 17th January 2007
I've had quite a few applications for the role replacing Helen doing data entry. One girl has had a lot of sales experience in a gym, so I called her in today for an interview for the sales job. Obviously she has very little experience in what I am asking her to do, but she is used to making phone calls, so that is a huge plus. If she has the enthusiasm, I can train her to do the rest. I offered her the job for a one-week trial just ringing around the stores that I sent the card mail-outs to at the start of January, and if she is OK then I'll offer her the role.

I am still following up on the Mock Cards, without much luck. I just don't know what else I can do to get out there. The main problem is that John Sands and Hallmark Cards have the market sewn up. I tried approaching them, but no luck there. Very frustrating. I just need to keep pushing, and keep trying to get the cards out there. Maybe smaller stores are the way in ...

Friday 19th January 2007
I sat down with Ella today to work out what we are going to do about the accounts role when Helen goes. I think that the business accounts/data entry/bookkeeping really needs someone to focus on it, rather than Ella doing the bookkeeping, Helen the data entry and me helping out. It's not long now until Ella's baby is due, so I don't want to leave it to chance. I think that small business is tricky when you only have one person in each role. It means much more planning, because if someone's away someone else has to do some of their role for a bit. For the accounts role or roles, I know that I need to get better at delegating. I keep saying "Don't worry, I'll do that", but really I shouldn't, since I am sure the role can be organised better. I think that my control-freak side is coming out.

I wrote ads for the *Manly Daily* and seek.com.au for an accounts person and ran them past Ella. Hopefully we'll get lots of applicants – that is, good applicants, whom we actually might want to employ!

Erica, our graphic designer, came in yesterday. As always, it was lovely to see her; she was her usual crazy self! We discussed the new projects and Simone led most of the discussions, which was great. She is really coming on. Simone has only been here since September, but already has picked up a lot of the marketing. She was really nervous today with Erica, but with practice I am sure she will get more confident.

Sunday 21st January 2007

The weekend is finished. Not that I really had one; it was all uni work for most of it. It's amazing how I fit it all in. Makes me wonder what I did before to fill up weekends. No time to work on the business, but I am learning things I can apply. I am keeping a note of them, and then I can go back and implement. It seems a shame to be inside on such nice sunny days, but I think it will all be worth it.

I did manage to get out for a walk with Mr Johns today, but that was frustrating; he didn't want to walk as far as we agreed before we left the house. I spoke to him about it, but to no real avail.

Tuesday 23rd January 2007

The new salesgirl, Elise, started yesterday. She seems on the ball and she certainly made a lot of phone calls to stores. I feel a bit nervous about rushing in and giving her the sales role on a full-time permanent basis, because I've been burnt a couple of times now with salespeople; there was Belinda and then Jason. I still can't believe how hard it is to find good people. I know it is not just me recruiting the wrong people, because it's the same whomever I speak to in small business. One guy I know has set up his business so that he doesn't have to employ staff. I wonder if they can clone people yet? That would be the best way to do it ...

I have been trying to catch up with the Australian Geographic store buyer for ages, probably about two weeks. He is so hard to get on the phone. Today he said that he has a window to see me in seven weeks' time! I can't believe it. He suggested that I see him at the gift trade show instead, at the end of February. When Mocks are selling well in the stores it surprises me that I find it hard to get face time with the buyer, but I think it is because Mocks are one of hundreds of products sold and have a low dollar profit margin.

I made a decision today to pull the fulfilment stock out of the US. I have to face it, the US is unlikely to happen in the next six months, I just don't have the time, and it is costing me $500 per month to hold the stock there. In addition, the stock isn't getting sold there, and we are ordering more stock to cover Australian orders, when we could just use what's in the US. It was annoying that my brother Humbert quit the full-time US role after just four months, but at the time I thought it was better that he told me straight away rather than continue to do nothing for ages. I think he stopped because he found it was a lot harder than he expected, and not what he wanted to do. I find it frustrating when events don't work out as planned, but if his heart wasn't in it, then he wasn't going to be able to achieve it anyway. Ever since Humbert left, I have felt that the US market needs to be addressed; there is such huge potential there. If only I could get the Australian staffing sorted ...

When Mocks go back into the US, I need to think more carefully about all this. Money is tight, and I do tend to get carried away. The UK business is sucking cash out – I need to tighten up on expenses. One of the things I hate is not having enough cash.☹

I've been chasing lawyers to sort out trademarking the Mocks logo. I am trying to get them to look at an application under the Madrid Protocol, which would mean the logo was trademarked in something like 147 countries in one hit. I can't understand why it is taking so long. I have even said that I can get it done elsewhere if they are too busy, but still nothing happens. Maybe I'm being getting overlooked in favour of a bigger client. Today I feel *so frustrated*. I know it's not always like this, but grrr.

Wednesday 24th January 2007

I started the accounts role interviews today with Ella. We decided the best way to go was to have one full-time person responsible for all the accounts, which will mean no separate data entry person. We quickly developed a signal to use in the interviews for when the candidate was awful, and oh, some were. One guy said that he'd only done accounting qualifications at night classes to get him out of the house! And that he didn't really enjoy it – I couldn't believe it. He then tried to back-pedal on why he'd be good. No way. I want someone who is passionate about numbers, loves getting into the nitty-gritty and doesn't mind going over things until the right answer comes out. The problem with the candidates we saw today was that they were either clueless or majorly over-qualified and not in our price bracket. Even though they said they'd be happy with $50,000, I could see it would only be a stopgap. We have more lined up for next week; hopefully they will be better. I find it hard to believe that people go for a job they wouldn't be able to do. Do they think I wouldn't find out? I asked very basic accounting questions that even I knew the answer to, and they didn't know; it's very worrying …

I have decided to start studying at home on Tuesday and Thursday mornings. I find that otherwise I am just too tired to absorb the information after work; whereas answering emails and dealing with things in the office often requires less concentration, so I can do that more easily in the evenings. It starts tomorrow. My only concern is people slacking off in the office, but I guess that trust has to start to kick in at some point, and I need to let them get on and do their jobs.

Sunday 28th January 2007

Although I was at uni yesterday, I still managed to spend some time with Mr Johns today. We don't seem to want to do the same things, he really wants to improve the garden, but I am just not really interested. It's strange we used to want to do more or less the same things.

Monday 29th January 2007

I had a lovely long weekend. I had to go to uni one day, but it was good to have one day off either side. I decided to take Elise on full-time in the sales role, and she started today. I went through expectations and so forth, but she didn't take many notes, which is concerning. I will need to push that in the next team meeting. She performed well last week calling stores, so I am feeling positive about her.

I had some good discussions with the team regarding plans for the conference – the inaugural LaRoo conference in February at an exotic beachside location, also known as my house in Manly! We are going to get Laura in China to make some Mocks to celebrate it, and hopefully she will also come out for it; she is keen. I keep thinking of a conference with reference to the ones I've been to in my past corporate life, I think this is going to be slightly different, a bit more homemade, I just need to make sure that everyone understands my expectations in regards to the work side of it.

Mondays are so short now that I leave at 4pm to go to uni. After my catch-up meetings with each person in the team, to see where they are up to, there is hardly time for anything! I really believe that the catch-ups are important; otherwise how would I know what is going on? It gives both me and them a dedicated time to focus on what is happening.

We have been having a few issues with the Didgeridoona Mock getting oily when posted to customers. I think it is probably because this Mock is made from an oilskin fabric rather than yarn. I asked Tara to post one to me at home to see how it travelled. It is apparent the oil in the oilskin material is seeping a bit under heat, or something like that …

Mockers: Carla in UK, Simone in marketing, Lucy in admin, Helen in accounts, Tara in dispatch, Elise in sales and Ella bookkeeping
Mocks sold this month: 15,749
Store total: 744
Business bank account balance: $19,567 & £65
Mood: ☺ worried

February 2007

Friday 2nd February 2007
Ella and I interviewed four people today for the accounts role, we were supposed to interview five, but the 7.30am one didn't turn up. I wasn't really surprised, as he lived miles away and I had

reservations about the amount of travel he would need to do. I find in the interview candidates tend to say the travel to work would be fine, then they actually come, realise it is miles on public transport and it is not so fine. Today's candidates were marginally better than last week's. There were two girls who would be good: Clare and Alison; I will have to make a decision. I preferred Clare, but she is English and would need training on the whole Australian tax system, BAS and so on. It wouldn't be a huge deal, but I need to consider it.

I met Erica, our graphic designer, today to discuss the possibility of a couture range of Mocks to launch at Fashion Exposed trade show. I am contemplating going and having a stand, since unfortunately we got turned down by Australian Fashion Week! It was disappointing; since I really believe that as an accessory Mocks could be up there with brands like Mimco. The panel didn't really give me a reason for the rejection, but I think they thought the product wasn't really fashionable enough. Fashion Exposed could be a good way to get Mocks taken seriously as a fashion item. Erica was very excited about the concept. I need to look into what needs to be done as it isn't far off – March.

Monday 5th February 2007

I had all my catch-ups with the team today, and everything seems to be on track. There is a lot to be done as Lucy, my office manager, is on holidays now for two weeks. It's rather unfortunate, but she booked it in months ago. I still need to finalise the last conference bits as well keep on top of the day-to-day work. I went through the gift trade show bits with Elise in sales; it starts in only three weeks. This is the first time we have exhibited at this trade show, so it will be interesting to see how effective it is in terms of sales.

I have decided on Clare for the accounts role. After weighing things up I think her background in management accounting will be more beneficial for the business, so I emailed her referees in the UK.

I am still following up the Jeans for Genes charity to see if they are going to go with the denim Mock. It has been a few weeks since I sent in the proposal and I have managed to get Telstra to agree to

174

support the initiative, which would be huge for Jeans for Genes. I really can't understand why they aren't keener.

Tuesday 6th February 2007
Clare was keen to start in the accounts role today. I had agreed to the salary she wanted, but I got a call today at 8.15am, just 15 minutes before she was due to start, saying that she thought that maybe she could get more money, and that we should sort that out before she started – I was gobsmacked! She said that she had been looking on seek.com.au and felt she was worth more. I felt like saying "Well you should have done that before and asked for more", but I was so surprised I didn't say anything. I really can't believe some people. I called her back later and said that I was withdrawing the offer. I don't want someone like that working for me. I then reference-checked Alison, the other girl, and offered her the role. Only one small problem: she can't start for four weeks, which is 7th March, so we will just have to make do until then. I just hope Ella doesn't have her baby early!

Saturday 10th February 2007
I gave Elise sales targets yesterday in the hope it might make her focus better and get more excited about achieving goals. She seemed really offhand about them. I find her hard to deal with, as she hardly shows any emotion about anything.

I spent the whole day at uni today in an operations management seminar. It was an interesting topic, all about processes today, and I learnt some methodologies that I could apply in the office. I actually prefer the module that's five days a semester rather than 10 evenings for learning, as it seems to give me more time. I think I am going to ask Mr Johns to come in and do some training with my team on processes, since it is his area of expertise.

Mr Johns has been really supportive of my uni work and has taken on lots of the chores around the house, which is nice.

Monday 12th February 2007
I picked up Carla from the airport this morning. She is over from the

UK for two weeks, including the conference. I will enjoy having someone that is on top of everything around. We all had pizza for lunch in the office to get to know each other. It was a little bit stilted, perhaps because they know that we are friends it is kind of hard for the team to relax with her, but Carla is pretty easy to be around.

I sent out the new February Mocks range to the head office buyers today. I am hoping to get Strathfield mobile stores and Target department store onboard, but it is taking a while – they need some arm twisting …

Wednesday 14th February 2007
Carla and I had a meeting yesterday with a dressmaker. I have decided to have a stand at Fashion Exposed in March. It is only for three days, and so we should be OK for staffing. Plus we can show the 10 new Couture Mocks, which I have designed. The designs are very different to the current Mocks. There is one covered in beading and another is black with black chiffon draped on it. They are all embellished in some way, either with fabric or beads. I checked out the dressmaker's work, and I think she will be fine, but it will take quite a long time to do each Mock as they are so small, and will be quite fiddly. I will send her the beads and fabric later this week and she can start.

It was Valentine's Day today. Carla and I went to the Business Chicks Breakfast. It was a huge event, with about 800 women. From the event we got a fantastic goodie bag – including a lovely pink cupcake, yum.

Sales are going well this month again: $36,000 so far.

Friday 16th February 2007
Carla and I went to a sales training breakfast yesterday morning. We definitely learnt a few things – Carla's favourite idea was to get 10 sales calls done at the start of each day before anything else is done, and to decide on those 10 calls the night before. We networked with the people on our table, and funnily enough one of the women from

176

Wednesday's breakfast was there, small world …

I sent all the decorations to the dressmaker today, so we should start to get samples next week.

Monday 19th February 2007

It was Tara's 23rd birthday today, so we had chocolate cake for her and Simone, who was 24 last week. Seems that everyone who works for me likes chocolate mud cake – lucky really as it's my favourite as well!

I had my catch-ups with the team today, and everything is organised for the conference tomorrow. Disappointingly, Laura can't come from China. Her visa was turned down, so she has sent pictures of the Mock production process for me to show my team. Lucy the office manager came back from holidays today. I felt that we hadn't really been overloaded without her being here, which brings a few questions to mind …

I had an exam at uni tonight, what fun! It was accounting, and was harder than I expected. Fingers crossed, I did OK, but if I didn't I could make it up on the two assignments and next exam. Luckily, the lecturer seems to like me.

Wednesday 21st February 2007

We finished the first official LaRoo conference today. It went really well. The girls enjoyed hearing some of my friends speak on relevant topics. The brainstorming went on for a little bit too long, everyone was rather brain dead after that, but overall it went really well. When I asked about what they got out of the conference, everyone said they benefited most from the organising workshop run by Amy. I think because it had practical application it was easy for them to relate to. I found the review of 2006 marketing and sales that we had on the first day was great. It made us think about what worked and what didn't, and we used those lessons in our planning.

We should definitely do a conference again next year. I know I got a lot out of doing the preparatory work, much as it was hectic to fit it

177

all in. Carla was up at 5am one day doing it, which made me realise how much the others can be slack at times. If they don't have time to do things, they just leave them.

I am having a few issues with Elise in sales; I really don't think she is going to last. She turned up 15 minutes late on the first day of the conference, which wasn't acceptable to me, especially as I'd had a talk with her just last week about the importance of showing enthusiasm, taking part in things more and showing me that she is interested. She told me she thinks I don't like her, for silly reasons, like I don't say hello to her. I do say hello, but a general hello; I don't say it individually to each person when I arrive, nor does anyone else. It is not looking good for her. Carla has agreed to stay on and help me with the trade show, instead of me taking Elise. This will make it her second trade show for this month, after the UK one at the start of February! I don't feel that I can trust Elise to be on the stand and give out the right info. I told the team that Carla's flight had been delayed and therefore she will stay and help with the show over the weekend, and Elise can do next week.

Monday 26th February 2007
I called the office today to see how things were going, only to have Lucy tell me that Elise is basically spending all her time surfing the Net, emailing her friends, on MySpace, and applying for jobs. That is it. I will fire her. I spoke to her on the phone and told her not to worry about coming into the trade show this afternoon as planned.

The trade show is going well. It has been pretty busy. It is definitely helpful to have two of us here.

Tuesday 27th February 2007
I fired Elise today. I went into the office last night and went onto her computer to find that yes, she has been spending all her time on MySpace and other sites, as evident from her internet history. She had also written her résumé and saved it onto the server – unbelievable that she could be so stupid. When I spoke to her today before I fired her, she claimed that she had been working really hard. When I mentioned her résumé she said that she was just

updating it, so I told her that it was against company policy to save personal files onto the work server. I told her that I didn't think it was working, and that I'd like her to leave. It didn't go well, I went and stood over her while she packed – which she hated. Tough! I didn't want her a) taking anything and b) getting any files off the server, like her résumé!

Wednesday 28th February 2007

It was the last day of the gift trade show today. We've had 20 orders from new stores, which looks promising for covering all the show costs. Simone in marketing came and helped today since Carla had to fly back to the UK. In terms of orders, the last day was a complete waste of time. It was just stand holders rushing around buying things for themselves from other stand holders. As soon as we realised this, we joined in! Simone told me while we were working that Elise had been playing up for the past two weeks, while Lucy was on holiday. If Elise knew I wasn't in then she wouldn't do any work. Simone said that she hadn't wanted to say anything; however, I think it is good that she has, even if it is late. I feel that I can really trust her. I understand that it is hard in a small office, and you don't want to dob people in, but it does make me wonder what else goes on.

Mockers: Carla in UK, Simone in marketing, Lucy in admin, Tara in dispatch and Ella bookkeeping
Mocks sold this month: 15,485
Store total: 765
Business bank account balance: $7,829 & £654
Mood: ☺ ☺ ☺

March 2007

Monday 3rd March 2007

This is my last week of doing the accounts, thank goodness. The new girl, Alison, starts next week.

Telstra want an exclusive Mock Card for Mother's Day in May, so I briefed the designer last week. Time is tight, so I am hoping Laura can work her magic in China as usual.

Laura sent us some Moon cakes today, they are celebrating the festival of the Moon in China. The cakes were unusual flavours such as bean curd, but the box that they came in was fantastic, really elaborate with each cake in its own little tin – Laura is such a sweetie.

Tuesday 6th March 2007

Simone and I went to a Teen Forum today organised by *Girlfriend* mag. It was really interesting, with lots of good facts about what teens do. We sat next to the marketing manager for the Hey Sister lingerie brand – she could be interested in personalised Mocks and prizes for competitions. I will have to keep in touch with her. I thought afterwards that I need to get Simone to go to more of these events; she hasn't had much experience in networking.

Mr Johns and I talked about holidays today; once again I want to lose weight, so he said if I achieve a three month weight loss goal then he will take us on holiday for a week as a reward. I said that I wanted to go somewhere hot, since it will be May when I finish, and autumn here. However, he wants to go snowboarding, so that I can learn and he can have a snowboarding buddy, I don't really think it is me, but he is so keen I don't really want to kick up too much fuss. But I do feel sometimes that we only spend money on what he wants to do in terms of holidays and going out. It can be hard for me as I am not paying myself at the moment, but that is an agreed joint decision, so I can put the money back into the business.

Friday 9th March 2007

I had a great meeting yesterday with the company that supplies Big W department store with all its products that hang from shelves on a plastic strip. They were really keen on Mocks, and requested pricing for an initial order of 3,000 units. They loved the designs and the ideas, so hopefully they will commit.

The new accounts girl, Alison, started yesterday. I think that she will fit in well. We had the team meeting, with the quiz – everyone always does really badly at the quiz their first week, and as usual Simone won! Ella came in and trained Alison today and said she picked things up quickly, so fingers crossed this will work. I can't believe the issues I have had trying to get the right person in that role.

After a lot of deliberation, I have decided to get rid of Lucy's role as office manager. To be honest, I just don't feel that she is worth the $50,000 I am paying her, and she has been difficult of late. When I ask her to do things, such as record a new message on the answering machine, contact the Office of Fair Trading about the scales, or contact a competitor for information, she says no; plus there are things which have been on her to do list for months and she just keeps putting them off. It makes me wonder what she is actually doing, as I seem to be rushing about, plus there seems to be an issue with Tara in dispatch as well, which may be related, I have noticed that Lucy is rude to her. I told her that I was giving her a week's notice because I couldn't afford to keep her. It came as a massive shock to her, as I suppose it would, but as always, I tell myself I am not a charity and I have to do the best for the business.

I set up our stand at Fashion Exposed today, but I'm not overly enthusiastic at the thought of another three days of trade show. I just hate standing around. I really hope it will be busy. At least at this expo there are the runway fashion shows to promote Mocks – the models will be carrying mobiles with Mocks on them as an accessory. However, the organisation of the show seems awful. The show starts on Sunday and I still don't know which parades Mocks will be shown in. I really wanted to invite some of the buyers to come along. I'll still send out invitations to all the buyers in Sydney, so hopefully they will want a day out of the office and pop along.

Monday 12th March 2007
The new buyer for Dick Smith, Grant, visited me today on the stand, which was very surprising. He has only been in the role two months, but loves Mocks – great news for me! I need to follow him up when I am back in the office to set up a meeting.

Tuesday 13th March 2007
We finished up at Fashion Exposed today. It wasn't worth going; we

had a lot of the same people as came to the gift show in February, and there just wasn't the number of visitors. I spent a lot of time standing around, but at least Simone came along yesterday and today, so I could have a break. Simone is getting much better at talking to people about the Mocks. Her confidence is definitely building. The Couture Mocks had their inaugural outing at the show this weekend. We had a lot of positive comments, with people loving the designs and the idea, but no-one buying; actually one of the other stand holders bought one, but none of the retailers were interested at the price. But I didn't make them really to sell, more to show that Mocks can be fashionable …

The runway fashion shows were good, when they finally worked out which ones the Mocks were featured in; however, we went to some which we were supposed to be in, only to find that we weren't. I have complained big-time to event organisers about the lack of communication regarding Mocks in the fashion shows, plus the fact that they were not featured when they said they would be, and I had actually paid for this. It would be different if the shows were free. The organisers asked us for the Mocks three weeks ago, and yet couldn't tell me until the first day of the show when they would be featured. It meant that I couldn't let my buyers know in time and so we basically lost out on an opportunity to promote Mocks to existing buyers and potential new buyers, as there wasn't enough time to send them tickets.

Ella had her baby yesterday, a girl - lovely news. Fortunately, she finished training Alison last week.

Friday 16th March 2007
Lucy has been off sick all week, but was in today for her last day. I got her some flowers. It was awful; she was still really upset. There was nothing more I could do about it, and I feel really bad, but it couldn't be avoided. If she had performed better and been indispensable, it would have been a whole new story, or if I felt that she could have turned her hand to something else …

Sunday 18th March 2007

I had my final accounting exam at uni today. Strangely it was easy compared to the previous one. I was done in an hour, and felt like I had missed something huge, but I triple-checked and I definitely answered all the questions.

Tuesday 20th March 2007

Sales are going well this month: $65,000. The Mother's Day order from Telstra really bumped things up, which was a help, as cashflow is unbelievably tight – we have no cash at all. Alison keeps giving me grief for not paying myself, but to be honest I don't see the point. If I have to go into the overdraft to pay myself and incur 13% interest, I might as well save the interest and just wait until the business has more cash. At home we can live on Mr Johns' salary, and he is happy to do this for now, so it is not a problem.

I spoke to undergraduate students at the University of New South Wales yesterday. One of the lecturers just called me out of the blue and asked if I would talk to her class on marketing distribution, so I went along for an hour. It was really good fun. They asked lots of questions and seemed genuinely interested, plus it spread the Mocks word to a target audience that is notoriously hard to reach. I've already had two calls from students who heard me; they were asking questions about starting your own business.

I really enjoyed speaking at uni, I think it is something I would like to do more of. I said to Mr Johns that I'd like to get onto the speaker circuit; his reply was "Who'd listen to you speak?" Not awfully encouraging ... It annoys me when he doesn't have any faith in me – I would have thought that after I have proven to him that I can make my business successful he would have been more enthusiastic about new ideas, or at least consider them. I think it's great that in running my business I can choose the direction that I and it take, that is not something I could have done as easily, if at all in the corporate world.

I have had to set myself targets every day to call the stores from the trade shows, because I really don't enjoy it. I tell myself that I will call 40 stores, and will be doing it from 3pm till it's done. I find that starting is the hardest part; once I am going I usually get into the swing of it. I am quite surprised that a lot of stores I have called have said that no-one else has called them; I am the first person to contact them from the show. At Fashion Exposed one of the other stand holders said she doesn't bother to follow up anyone from shows. Her opinion was that if people are interested then they will order, which I can see, but sometimes I feel that they need prompting, especially when they see literally hundreds of products over the days they are there.

I talked to Tara in dispatch about her performance. It has been awful lately. Sometimes there have been 10 mistakes or more per week with store orders that she sends out. It turns out that there was a big problem between her and Lucy. They just didn't get on. She didn't tell me about it, and I am not really sure why. Perhaps she thought that she could solve it herself, but obviously with Lucy now gone it will be solved. The situation has been affecting her work. Her attention to detail and concentration have been hopeless. I have been asking her for the past few weeks if everything is OK, so it is annoying she didn't say anything earlier. She has agreed that if there is another problem, she will talk to me about it.

Wednesday 21st March 2007
I got interviewed today for the Small Business Mentor Club. Class One Productions produces a monthly CD with interesting interviews and topics, and sends the CD to the club's members. The theme was "an interview with an entrepreneur". It was very short, but all good publicity to raise my profile and that of the Mocks brand.

I also heard back from the company that supplies Big W today; they were very hard to get hold of. Basically the price that they are willing to pay is not one I'm willing to accept, especially as they only want to commit to a one-off order. It is a shame, but I did also have concerns about selling Mocks in a discount chain.

Friday 23rd March 2007
Ella, my ex-bookkeeper, came in with her baby for a few hours today

184

to go through accounts with Alison. It was lovely to see her. I can chat to her about how the business is going and she understands. I find it gets pretty lonely sometimes and that I really need to talk stuff through to make decisions.

An interesting opportunity came up yesterday during a conversation with my dentist's son. He has a new mobile accessory product and would like me to distribute it for him. I know that he approached me because my dentist is such a fan, and thinks that I have done an amazing job with Mocks. It sounds very interesting, and it would give me something challenging to do. I don't feel very challenged at the moment. Things are ticking along, but I am not really that interested. Even though we have new products coming out – like the Photo Mocks, which is a Mock with a photo of your choice on it – I just can't seem to get very excited about them. I kind of feel like I have been there and done that. I am still passionate about the brand, but the challenge of new products doesn't excite me to want to get involved in a hands-on way. I think I want to take a step back from the day to day, and focus more on strategic direction. But it's hard, as I have no-one at the moment to hand things to ...

Monday 26th March 2007
I went through the possibility of changing accounting packages with Alison today. We had so many problems last financial year that I really think we need to change for July 1, but it will be so expensive – we are looking at around $20,000, plus all the time ... I have asked Alison to give me a recommendation as to which one she thinks we should go with. It could be good to have another opinion, since Ella and I have already been through them all.

I have signed up with a US company to do an infomercial. Well, I signed up a few weeks ago, and I am now thinking maybe I rushed into it and it wasn't such a good idea. I have already paid out $16,000, so I don't really want to lose that, but it is better than losing $32,000, which is the full amount. At the time I did look into it carefully and spoke to the company and saw what they had produced before. However, now I am working with them it has not been as promised. The US company seems to be completely disorganised and clueless as to what they are doing, which makes me nervous.

I am also hesitant about the US infomercial because I am contemplating selling the Mocks business. To be honest, there are other things I want to look at. I have been thinking about writing a book about my journey in the business, and I have really enjoyed speaking engagements and would love to spend more time on developing that as a career. I've been thinking about selling since Christmas, when Mum and Dad were out. I was feeling bored then, but they talked me out of it at the time. It keeps coming back to me: I don't want to do Mocks forever; I know that there are other things that I want to do. I can't seem to find the right person to look after things, so maybe selling is the best option. Then I will have the money to invest in a new venture. It's a hard decision, as I've always said that I wanted to sell it for $5 million, just a number I like the sound of! I am not going to get $5 million at the moment, since last year we only made a $20,000 profit. I just feel like I want a new challenge, and this doesn't challenge me enough in the way I want at the moment, plus I am tired of doing all the nitty-gritty bits. I want the freedom to focus more on strategy and to think of the big picture.

Wednesday 28th March 2007
I had to go to the Office of Fair Trading's Consumer, Trade and Tenancy Tribunal in the city today about the scales I bought at Christmas to help count the Mocks. The company wouldn't take them back because they were used, even though they didn't do what I bought them for. It was not fun. They agreed to give me some of the money back, so it was not a completely lost cause. I should have done more testing rather than trusting that they knew what they were doing when they said the variation in Mocks weight would not be a problem. It was a problem. Well, that was my second Tribunal visit, and hopefully my last.

Friday 30th March 2007
I flew to Perth last night with Mr Johns for a long weekend. I met Living Digital today, one of the mobile store accounts I have in Perth.

The marketing girl was very nice, and she was very keen on running an in-store promotion with Mocks to get them going again. I'll get a proposal to her next week.

I had another call from a student who was at the lecture I did. She works in one of the student charity organisations and wants to give Mocks away at one of their events. It could be really good for us, so I have handed it on to Simone in marketing to work with her on. I am trying to give Simone more responsibility with marketing, so that she can really take ownership of it.

Mockers: Carla in UK, Simone in marketing, Tara in dispatch and Alison in accounts
Mocks sold this month: 24,715
Store total: 767
Business bank account balance: $2,044 & £334
Mood: ☺ ☺ ☺

April 2007
Tuesday 3rd April 2007

I arrived back from Perth this morning, rather tired. The weekend was good, although we didn't have time to go everywhere we wanted. We took the midnight red eye flight back from Perth so I missed the presentation meeting I was due to go to, but I knew that Simone was going. I couldn't bear to go straight there without a shower! I had another meeting today with my dentist's son and his business partner; they seem to be keen on me working with them, but are also rather vague as to when anything will be ready. They say they will get back to me at the end of the month.

Thursday 5th April 2007

It's a very short week, as we close today for the Easter long weekend. It has been busy. In the team meeting yesterday I went through our targets for the next three months, and discussed budgeting. I want to have everyone's budgets for the next financial year in this month. I am getting everyone to do their own area, which they will then be held accountable for as part of their key performance indicators.

I got the results back from my two uni modules from last semester. I got a high distinction for both, which I was pleased with. This semester I am going to take another two modules: a weekend one and an evening one. I start next week.

Monday 9th April 2007

We got back today from an Easter weekend away with friends, I organised the whole weekend, it was really good fun. Except because of my weight loss challenge I wasn't drinking much, which was hard on the first day, as everyone else had a liquid lunch. Mr Johns got cross with me because I didn't want to do what he wanted, but I think when you are away with friends you should hang out with them, not as a couple.

Thursday 12th April 2007

I drove two hours up to Newcastle today to meet a potential distributor, which supplies toy and gift stores. They agreed to take Mocks. It was a good meeting, and their margin is not too massive to work for me. It's exciting, but I feel kind of wary as I don't really know the full potential until they start ordering from us.

I gave Tara in dispatch two movie tickets today for completing one month without a single mistake on any order sent out – a major improvement on previous months! I developed the accounts budget template with Alison, and am looking forward to not having to do it all myself this year.

The whole team had a conference call with Carla in the UK. I am still trying to get them to interact with her more. It is proving difficult, but I hope this regular chat every month will soon show results.

I have decided to get in an admin/general helper one day per week, because the monthly store newsletter and other very basic admin jobs are taking up a lot of time and distracting the team from their day to day tasks. I have put an ad in the *Manly Daily*.

Tuesday 17th April 2007

Wow, it was a full-on day today! I interviewed 13 people at half-hour intervals for the part-time admin role, which I advertised on the weekend. If they were any good, I had the rest of the team come round to ask them a question each and we then debriefed after each candidate left. We managed to narrow it down to just three, but it was really hard. There were lots of good people. After much deliberation, we decided on a girl called Zena, who seemed promising. I just need to do the reference check now.

I heard from Gary, the Christian distributor today. He sold Mocks over Easter at a show, but not a huge number – about 40. The whole Christian market hasn't really taken off as well as I had hoped; perhaps it is the designs. We have had feedback asking for a fish design. Gary has got the Mocks into a chain of seven Christian bookshops, however there haven't really been any other sales as yet.

Thursday 19th April 2007

I seem to have spent every morning and evening over the last few days just doing uni work. The modules this semester involve quite a lot of reading, which makes preparing for classes pretty time consuming.

I interviewed a woman today for the sales role. I'm still after the holy grail of good salespeople. I am making a bit more of a concerted effort now, as I really am getting fed up with doing it all. She was good. I will offer her the role if her references are OK.

I met a new trademark lawyer today, the other one just wouldn't get back to me, which was driving me mad. She seemed pretty switched-on, so I left her with a list of things to investigate for me.

Tonight I went to an MBA workshop for MGSM (Macquarie Graduate School of Management). I would like to change to MGSM because attending my current uni, although free, involves a huge amount of travel. Some days it can take two hours to get there for a 6pm class. It makes the day so long when I don't get home after class until 11pm. Also, the quality of teaching staff and students is not fantastic there. There are a lot of people who are just doing it for the piece of paper, which isn't why I am there. The workshop at MGSM tonight was good. The other potential students seemed to be interested and genuinely wanted to learn. I am keen to swap. In the paperwork I got tonight there was information on a scholarship for one module; I'm going to apply for it. I also need to check that they will accept my credits from my current uni.

Monday 23rd April 2007

I had a whole weekend of uni work, which was not terribly relaxing, but at least I got it done. Zena's references checked out fine, so she started today in the admin role. She is going to work all day on Mondays and then a couple of other half days, depending on how busy we are.

Sales are not going so well this month. I know we have had Easter, and the Anzac Day public holiday is coming up, but we are only on $14,000 so far this month – way, way off target. I need to pick things up. I followed up the big accounts to see what was happening with them, but not much joy there.

The references for the saleswoman I interviewed last week were fine, so I offered her the role. I had to leave a message, though, so hopefully she will get back to me soon.

Friday 27th April 2007

There is still no word from the saleswoman about the role, which is very unusual. I am guessing she won't take it – how frustrating.

I bought a new mobile this week, after I finally got fed up with mine. I can access my emails on it, which will be great. It should be much easier for when I am out of the office. I love gadgets.

There is still no word from Living Digital regarding the proposal I sent to them after my trip to Perth. I really don't think they are interested. This isn't too surprising since they often take a while to get back to me, but why meet me and discuss things if you don't want to do them? It was even their suggestion ...

Surprisingly, I had an order from a company in Bulgaria today for some personalised Mocks. They found out about us through Austrade. The order was for 2,000 personalised ones for HP (Hewlett-Packard). It seems odd that they are ordering from us, but it is fantastic that Austrade have been so proactive in promoting Mocks. Things like this coming out of the blue really give me a high!
Mockers: Carla in UK, Simone in marketing, Tara in dispatch, Alison in accounts and Zena in admin
Mocks sold this month: 5,292
Store total: 767
Business bank account balance: $9,107 & £860
Mood: ☺ ☺ ☹ frustrated

May 2007
Tuesday 1st May 2007
Today I had a good meeting with a Sydney company that distributes mobile phone recharge cards and accessories to newsagents. They are going to add Mocks to their range of products. It is a great fit for them. Finally, after a bad April, sales are starting to look up.

Tonight I went to the new members' night for the AmCham (American Chamber of Commerce) network. I have been trying to get there for ages, but something has always come up. I ended up joining; I think it could be great for personalised Mocks, as there are a lot of big companies to target. I am going to start with a mail-out to their database of 300 companies.

I have finally decided to pull the plug on the USA infomercial. It just wasn't what was promised – they wrote the script, but then expected me to basically re-write it, which was odd, as they are supposed to be the experts in what works and what doesn't for infomercials. There was a lot of delay in the script and I just didn't have the confidence in them to do a good job. I have lost $16,000 by pulling out, but it is better than investing the full $32,000 and losing that. I am annoyed with myself because I didn't make the right decision. I did talk to the company on the phone and reference check them, but nothing turned out the way they promised. I tried to take legal action and get my money back, but the letter from my lawyer achieved nothing, and it is hard when I am not in the USA to chase them.

Friday 4th May 2007

I went to a local business breakfast this morning. It wasn't as good as I expected. The information was very basic; it only covered what I already knew. Disappointing. I met a few people, and there is still a lot of education on Mocks to be done. It made me think if I give it up, what will I say for my elevator speech? After three years I have got it down pat. It is hard, because I am not clear on my new direction. I don't want to be one of those waffly people who spend five minutes telling you about what they do but still leave you without a clue!

Today I chatted to Kirsty, my friend from Tasmania who owns a real estate business. It was lovely to catch up – I suggested we do a business swap since I need a change. This could be a whole new idea, rather like *Wife Swap* on TV. It could be called *Get the Experts In*, where the expert shows the business owner what can be done.

Tuesday 8th May 2007

Today's my birthday, 32 ... I don't feel that old. Yesterday, I went and saw a career counsellor about deciding on whether to sell the brand or not. It has cemented in my mind that I am not really doing what I enjoy in running the business; yes, there are lots of things that I do love, but it just isn't fast-moving enough. I think the issue is that I don't have the patience to consolidate at the moment and wait to build up the funds, but then again I also don't have the funds in the business to be able to expand as quickly as I want to. I still think that there is a huge opportunity in the UK and US, but I need the funds to do it. I am just impatient, and I feel like I have been going a long time.

Wednesday 9th May

Our first Couture Mock was sold today online. We added them to the online store back in March, but with the prices starting at $90 we haven't sold any until today. Someone bought the $270 Ocean Jewels design – the top of the range, very exciting news! I flew down to Melbourne today for an events trade show where I had a stand. I really want to target companies to use Mocks as a promotional item, and this should be the ideal venue to do that. The show goes for one-and-a-half days. It is the first time it has run in Melbourne, but I went and looked round the Sydney one in February, a few people I know exhibited there and said it was good for sales for them.

Friday 11th May 2007

I finished the events trade show in Melbourne yesterday. There were lots of very positive comments from people about Mocks; they loved them. People commented about how different and unusual they are, and how they'd never seen them before, which was annoying. I kept telling people that they've been out for nearly three years, but to them they are still pretty new. It made me realise while for me it seems like ages, for others it is nothing. The guy on the stand next to me asked if my business now supports me. I replied "Yes, and five others." He was surprised. I keep thinking back to an article I read about how long it takes products to gain mass brand awareness: sometimes up to five years. The brand in the article had a huge marketing budget compared to mine. Maybe I am just too impatient. But why should it take that long? I guess I have to change people's minds and educate them, which takes time, but still ... I thought I'd be further along by now. I really thought that in three years I would have the UK market running profitably and the US market going, so that we would be moving into brand extensions.

I popped in to meet with the buyers from Crazy John's today. It was good to finally meet them face to face. They are really pleased with the way sales are going, and said that we are good to deal with as a supplier. It is nice to get positive feedback from a customer.

Tuesday 15th May 2007

I got into the office today feeling tired, I have to say, after the weekend, even though we did next to nothing yesterday. I was on a real sugar-high all day today – cakes for my birthday and lots of lollies and chocolate – which is probably why at about 4pm I hit a wall! It was hard to get focused, so I reviewed where the team are up to. I am trying hard to keep up the Mocks enthusiasm, but it is difficult. Most of the team are working hard, but I want to push them harder to achieve the goals I have set. Perhaps it is not realistic, but if we are to stay ahead of the competition it is needed. I think that when I feel demotivated, I find it very hard to motivate others – much as I try.

I need to concentrate on what to do this week. There are still lots of stores that haven't ordered the Sesame St Mocks, so I need to follow them up. They said they would, but people get busy and then don't get around to it, and I know that the Fone Zone head office is short-staffed. It just means that I need to remember, rather than assuming it has been done.

I have started to look for business brokers today, I am really not feeling motivated and keen about running the business, my enthusiasm goes up and down, but the thought of doing something else excites me. Mr Johns thinks I should stick with it, or become a marketing consultant – which there is no way I am going to do. I don't see the point in doing something that I don't enjoy 100%, that was the whole point of me starting this business.

I looked at the profit and loss report today. It seems to be going backwards, with a loss of $69,000 this financial year to date. I really need to focus on turning it around, but it's hard, as the UK business is busy sucking out the blood as I speak. I think I have pretty much decided to pull the plug on the UK on June 30. There was only $700 in sales revenue last month, which just doesn't support the UK business. It's taking longer than expected, probably partly due to the fact that it is not Carla's business and so her dedication is not as strong as mine and partly to the fact that the UK market is harder to crack than Australia. It is very frustrating. I just feel that after 10 months things should be further along. I only initially budgeted to support the UK for the initial six months. After that I expected it to break even.

194

I had a lovely letter today saying that I have been nominated for the Telstra Business Women's Awards by Kirsty Dunphey, who interviewed me last year for her newsletter, a lovely surprise and huge compliment from Kirsty.

Wednesday 16th May 2007

I chatted to Alison regarding the accounts today, after looking at the P&Ls yesterday they just didn't seem right, I checked a bit further and found that the bank accounts haven't been reconciled since she joined over two months ago. She didn't seem overly bothered by it, I asked her if she knew why I was concerned, which she did, and I stressed the importance of having information up to date. She did stay late to get them done today, and I think she has understood about the importance of accuracy.

Thursday 31st May 2007

A big day today – I met Grant, the buyer for Dick Smith. They have 370 stores, and want to put Mocks in all stores, with a first order of 18,000! Wooohoo! He is so excited by Mocks that it is just great to deal with him.

Disappointingly I still hadn't heard from my dentist's son about the new mobile accessory, so I called him today. He has moved to Hong Kong due to a new role, and so it is on hold for a while. I was sort of looking forward to a new challenge ...

Mockers: Carla in UK, Simone in marketing, Tara in dispatch, Alison in accounts and Zena in Admin

Mocks sold this month: 17,853

Store total: 768

Business bank account balance: $17,435 & £142

Mood: ☺ ☺

June 2007

Friday 1st June 2007

Firing day for Alison in accounts. It's been a while since I fired someone: three months, to be precise. It definitely gets easier with practice. I think it is best to do it first thing, so I get it off my chest; otherwise I just can't act normal.

I really thought that she was going to work out, then recently I found that she wasn't doing simple things like reconciling the bank accounts, which meant the reports she did for me were wrong. She gave me the revised reports yesterday, but when I checked, they still weren't right. They weren't just a few dollars out, either – it was more like $20,000. I asked her if the report was right, and if she was happy with it, to which she said "Yes". I then pointed out the bits that were wrong and she said "Yes, of course, apart from those bits". Really for me this was the straw that broke the camel's back. I'd had a big talk to her about giving me reliable information last week, since I have had a few issues with incorrect reports over the last month. I am not sure whether she just doesn't understand accounts, or can't be bothered and is lying, but either way it just won't work. Luckily she decided to leave today, rather than work out the week, which is better for me.

I had a meeting with a business broker, Ethel, today regarding selling the Mocks brand. She seemed very positive about it all, and seemed to think we would get a good price. I have had a real problem finding a good broker. I have contacted many, but they haven't got back to me, which I don't think is a good sign. There is a contract to sign regarding fees and to agree to her terms and conditions, and there is an up-front fee of $990 for evaluating the business. I liked the fact that she was an accountant in a past life. I have really lost enthusiasm for the business. The staffing issues really get to me. I can't achieve what I want to due to lack of resources and I just see other challenges that I want to take up and I can't see how if I have to run Mocks.

Monday 4th June 2007

I had my regular catch up with Carla today on the phone. I gave her a months notice, in that if we don't have 100 stores on board by the end of June then I will be pulling out of the UK market. It's unfortunate as I really believe it will work, but the Australian business is suffering because of it, so I have to do this. Carla understood, and still believes it will make it by June 30.

Wednesday 6th June 2007

Zena finished the AmCham mail-out today to the Australian companies in the networking group; 335 will get a US flag Mock. I think that should attract some interest. Hopefully at least one or two large companies will want personalised Mocks with their logo on them. I really need to get some cash in for the end of the financial year! The UK is really not doing well. I can see now that without the UK we would have made a profit this year – OK, not a huge profit, but about $50,000, which is about $30,000 more than last year.

Thursday 7th June 2007

It was an odd day today. Only Tara and I were in the office, Simone is on holiday visiting her mum in Greece, Alison has gone and Zena wasn't in. It was quiet, but I seemed to get lots done on the accounts. They are nearly all up to date now. I am just waiting on the bank to get back to me regarding getting the overdraft increased from $30,000 to $50,000. Ella and I have decided to hold off on the new accounting package for now. We just don't have the human resources to implement a new system, and with the business about to go on the market, it probably isn't worth it.

My broker has told me that I should carry on running the business as if I wasn't selling it. I am finding it really hard to think like that – it means that I need to keep up enthusiasm.

I sent out Mock G'Day Cards to the people I met at the networking lunch yesterday; they seemed genuinely interested in Mocks, so I thought a card would be a nice touch.

Friday 15th June 2007

I flew up to the Gold Coast today for a long weekend. Mr Johns has a conference next week, so we're having a few days to relax before it starts, then while he's at the conference I will work and catch up on my reading, as well as seeing customers. It will be nice to have a change of scenery. I don't feel that I organised myself very well for this trip. I should have brought samples with me, but didn't. Sometimes I can be such a muppet-head. I just get too excited about what is going on around me, and forget to plan. Big mistake. I am normally such a good planner, but I think since I've finished uni for a while I am rather up in the air – no homework for a few weeks!

Tuesday 19th June 2007

It's rather nice sitting here in the hotel room typing, during another relaxing day before I go and see buyers tomorrow. It's a good time to reflect, I think. We are staying at the Hyatt, which is always a winner with me, and I love the fact that it is sunny when I hear that it is raining cats and dogs in Sydney. I went to the hotel gym this morning and did a boxing class. It was a pretty hard workout, and I will go back tonight with Mr Johns to burn a few more calories. I am on a fruit and vegetable detox diet for a week. It is hard. I went out and had a fancy bowl of steamed veggies and a mineral water at lunch. I can imagine what being a lady of leisure would be like. But I'm not sure I'd last long!

I emailed more info to Ethel, the business broker, today, so she can send the mail-out to her client base and I can start seeing some results. I'd like to have it sold by September so that I can get on with the other things I want to look into. I know that September is only a few months away, but it means that I can finish this year and start on a new project in 2008. I have said that as part of the sale I would consult for three months back to the business. I really think that selling is the right thing for me. I am sure that the brand can be grown and a lot more can be achieved, but I just want to try something different. One thing that came out of my meeting with the career counsellor was that it was surprising I'd stuck with my business for so long, given I have the personality type that gets bored quickly and moves on within two years.

I read *The Secret* yesterday and afterwards I was visualising having sold the business in September. Now there's a book that has sold millions. I have to say that I find it hard to believe some of the stories about people making their millions, but I guess I can't knock it until I've tried it.

I don't feel stressed out about the fact that I am away. I have a tiny niggle at the back of my mind about the office – are they doing everything OK? – but I am trying not to think about it. I had a call today from a company responding to the AmCham mail-out we sent last week. That is the third one; it's great to see that it's working. I plan to start calling round later this week and following up, but so far I have had a 1% response rate, which is pretty good for a mail-out.

Monday 25th June 2007

Back in the office today Simone and Tara debriefed the team today on the Mocks they sold at the Education Expo over the weekend and it sounds like they really enjoyed themselves. They are so much more confident now than when they started, especially Tara. It is great to see that they have grown while being with me. That's one lovely plus side to having staff! Simone is turning out to be good at leading and organising a team, she just takes it in her stride.

Sales are not looking that great for this month, only $20,000 so far, and I can't see it really increasing much over the next four days. This is what I find so frustrating. I do want to increase sales, and I do follow up people, but to be honest I do find the whole sales thing hard, especially now I am selling the brand. The motivation is just not there. I am contemplating getting a telesales person in part-time to take some of the pressure off me, maybe someone who can work from home. I think it is worth paying for it.

I have just spent the weekend at MGSM, as an induction to the MBA course. It is an exciting learning environment. The people there were very different to those I met at my previous uni. I got the one-module scholarship, which is fantastic; it will save the business $3,000. Also, my credits from the other uni have been approved and transferred. I am really looking forward to starting – I love learning.

Today I got the Dick Smith Mock sample for a Dick Smith conference in July – it looks fantastic. I think Grant, the buyer, will be thrilled. When he saw the photo of it he said it was "gold", so the actual sample will have him even more excited! I sent it off to him by Express Post.

I really need to get stricter with Zena, the problem is that she is working as many hours as she wants, rather than what I have agreed with her, so she just stays as late as possible. I need to address the issue as soon as possible, as it is only going to get worse. I just can't afford for her to go over what I have agreed, as I just don't have the money – although it's great that she is keen to stay.

Wednesday 27th June 2007

I went out to Parramatta this morning with my friend Louise, who also runs her own business, for a training session on telemarketing. We got there to find it had been cancelled and they had forgotten to tell us – how annoying! But the good part was that we sat down for hot chocolate and came up with a new great non-Mocks business idea. We just need to work out now how to implement it. We are going to have a planning meeting on Sunday. I know Mr Johns will get cross – another thing that I am doing, when he thinks I am already doing too much – but I just love taking on new projects. It is exciting working out how you are going to do it.

We had feedback today from the Mocks giveaway we did with the uni student. They gave them away at an event in a goodie bag, apparently the audience loved them. We put a voucher in with the Mocks, we have had five redemptions so far, so hopefully there will be more to come. Five is OK, we only gave away 200 Mocks, and the voucher doesn't expire for another month.

Friday 29th June 2007

The last working day of this financial year. It was a rather a disappointing month for sales. We didn't make the target; in fact we didn't even break even this month, which really is not good. Next month I need to focus more and bring in the sales. Overall this year, the Australian business only performed at the same level as the 2005/2006 financial year. Maybe I was trying to do too much? Or maybe it was the lack of staff, the staff turnover, the trouble finding the right people or hiring too quickly ... or maybe I am just procrastinating and trying to find an excuse, when in reality I don't think there is one. I just didn't try hard enough; that's the bottom line.

I spoke to Carla in the UK earlier this week regarding sales. They haven't reached our expectations, and therefore I explained that we would have to close the UK office and operate the UK from Australia to cut costs. She really believes that it will work, and so offered to work without pay for six weeks to try it, while I just pay for expenses. I agreed to this, since expenses are quite minimal and she seems to think that we are on the verge of getting a distributor onboard, or a major retailer or both.

Mockers: Carla in UK, Simone in marketing, Tara in dispatch, Zena in admin and Ella bookkeeping temporarily

Mocks sold this month: 2,489

Store total: 768

Business bank account balance: $1,204 & £563

Mood: ☹

July 2007

Monday 2nd July 2007

The first day of the new financial year. Today was the nine-month review for Simone in marketing. She is going really well, showing unbelievable improvement since she first started. However, it was a stressful day for me, since Tara in dispatch was off sick. Zena was in, but I had to oversee her packing the orders. I can't wait to get to the stage where I don't have to oversee the day-to-day operations.

An exciting meeting with Grant at Dick Smith today. He definitely wants to stock the range of Mocks, and will kick the competitor out to do so. Great news for Mocks, but the small catch is that we have to buy all the competitor's stock, about $15,000 worth, from Dick Smith, as they can't return it. The initial order from Dick Smith is going to be around $80,000, so I think in the long term it will be worth it. I can probably sell the competitor's product on eBay, so the loss won't even be that big. Grant has agreed to mark down the price in stores to get rid of more of it before I have to buy it, so I won't need to spend as much.

Tonight at MGSM, Naomi Simson was speaking about how she set up her business RedBalloon. It was interesting to hear her, and there were only about 30 people there, so I got to chat to her afterwards.

She seems to use the same philosophy of trial and error, and learning from mistakes, as I do. It was good to know I am not the only one out there!

Wednesday 4th July 2007
I had a lovely day today. I worked from home all day, and a friend came over for lunch, which turned into a rather alcoholic affair, but fun. My friend is a schoolteacher, and it was nice to have someone to hang out with during the day. Apart from drinking wine, we discussed the book I want to write, and how I can use it to promote the business while I travel. I am planning a trip overseas next year and it would be great to incorporate some speaking dates and sell the book at those events.

Yesterday Simone and I met Sally from the PR agency at a cafe for a catch-up. Sally is really helping us to get the Mocks name out there. I like to meet with her face to face every few months – it gets me focused on PR and gives it more direction.

I have decided that we need to hire someone to do telesales/marketing on a part-time basis. I just cannot follow up all the small stores; it is crazy. I have been thinking about this for a while, but I've now worked out the figures and it makes sense. I think we could hire a mum, who could work from home and use Skype for calls – like we do in the office – and she could just come in once a fortnight for our team meetings. I definitely think it is worth a shot, since so far none of the other salespeople have worked out.

Thursday 5th July 2007
Sales are up to $6,019 today, which is a pretty good start to the financial year.

Monday 9th July 2007
I interviewed someone for the accounts role today, but she was no good, just not the right person. I'm now especially wary of hiring just anyone, after the number of staff changes we have had. I really want to get the right person. This girl just didn't seem to be au fait enough with the processes and procedures involved.

I had my weekly catch-up with Carla today. Things in the UK seem to be progressing slowly, but I get so frustrated because she doesn't always give me the information I need, such as updates on how many of the stores she has called were interested. I have to chase for it quite a few times before I get it. I think it is great that she really believes the UK will work, but I am still doubtful that we can make enough money to cover her salary at the moment.

I wrote the job description for the telesales/marketer role last week and posted it on careermums.com.au, which specialises in mums looking for part-time work. I've already had about 10 applicants over the weekend, and I have one lined up for an interview tomorrow.

I was supposed to start at the new uni the weekend just gone, but they didn't get me enrolled until Thursday, so there wasn't time for me to register for the course I wanted and do all the preparatory work required. So I will have to wait and start next semester, in September. It is probably a good thing, as without an accounts person things are pretty hectic in the office.

Tuesday 10th July 2007

Today, I interviewed a telesales/marketing lady, Kylie, and she was great. I think she will be perfect, so I have offered her the role. She is going to invoice me, which will make the bookkeeping so much easier: no taxes or superannuation to pay. Kylie can't start for a few weeks as she'll be on holiday, but that's fine. It gives me a chance to organise everything she is going to need.

I had a great meeting with Supre, the teen clothing store chain, today. They love Mocks, and hopefully we can work with them later in the year to make a Supre-branded design to be sold in stores or used as a giveaway. I'm not feeling 100% today. I seem to have come down with a bad cold. It doesn't look too good when you are sneezing over people in meetings.

Thursday 12th July 2007

Tara in dispatch sent me home yesterday because I was sick. She didn't want to catch anything. So I have had two days lying around chilling, catching up on reading and answering a few emails from home. I can't believe this is the first time since I started the business nearly three years ago that I have had a sick day. Wow. Usually I just battle through, but I really feel that I can't this time, and it was actually nice for someone else to tell me I had to go home.

No news yet from my business broker. She has all the information now, but is not awfully good at giving me updates. She has agreed that the asking price will be $500,000, which is the same as the figure that I suggested and would be happy with.

Friday 13th July 2007
I feel much more full of beans today, and back to normal. I'm still sniffling, but not as much. I managed to get all the business bills paid, so that will keep suppliers happy for a little while.

Tonight I had a meeting with my friend Louise about our new business idea. The whole concept hangs around service-based businesses swapping time with one another. We've started to develop the concept and now need to start the research to determine if other people think it's a good idea. We should be able to write the survey on Sunday, and get things moving. At the moment I am leading the way to some extent, but once we are going it should be more of an even split.

Monday 16th July 2007
Louise and I met my friend Lisa, who has a market research business, to get her advice. It was lovely of her to give up the time and she had some good suggestions for the survey, and indeed the whole concept. Now that I have to explain the concept to people, I really need to know exactly what we are offering. The idea has started to form, but we still need to work out the details. The more people we talk to, the more questions we get, making it easier to flesh out.

Louise and I then had lunch with Kirsty Dunphey, who was in town from Tasmania to give a talk. It was the first time I've met her in person. She was totally lovely; very enthusiastic and passionate. She had lots of suggestions for our concept, and recommended website designers and other people we could contact.

Today a company that supplies McDonalds inquired about ordering 10,000 personalised Mocks. I'm not sure if will come to anything; I seem to do quite a lot of quotes that I don't hear back about until I follow up the inquiries with calls. I think it is quite rude really, considering that it does take me time to do the quote.

Wednesday 18th July 2007

I followed up Grant at Dick Smith yesterday. He is keen on Mocks, but it seems that the wheels move slowly over there ... I should get the contract this week, then once we have a supplier number we will be rolling.

Louise and I had lunch with a guy from Bartercard today, basically to suss out the competition for our new idea. What they are doing is very different to our plan. Bartercard is all about selling goods and services for barter credits, which can then be spent with companies that accept the credits. Often it is used as a way to get rid of excess stock. He was a very pushy salesman, not my type of person at all. He is obviously in it to make money, rather than to help people, which is more my motivation. Maybe this is the reason that I have had issues finding sales staff myself – that I am not looking for the usual type of salesperson?

We had another order from Bulgaria today; that's their third. It is great to see that Mocks, both standard and personalised ones, are going so well over there. I think it's mostly due to Austrade helping out. I hope it continues.

Monday 23rd July 2007

I had a very full-on day today, including catch-ups with my team and a meeting regarding a new freight company that might help us out. It is a slower way of shipping overseas; the only problem is that most of the time customers want the Mocks yesterday!

I interviewed a guy for the accounts role today. He is at university where he has to complete eight weeks work experience working in a company, unpaid, for 20 hours per week. I think it sounds like a great idea, but the guy I interviewed had absolutely no idea about accounts, which is a bit worrying when that's what he is studying. I told the placement organiser that he wasn't the right fit for us. He hadn't prepared at all for the interview, so really struggled to answer the most basic of questions, such as what are your strengths – disappointing.

Tonight Louise, Mr Johns and I ran a focus group for the new business time-swap idea. Four friends who run their own businesses came along; they were very honest and up-front about it all, which gave us more ideas and clues as to what we should be doing. They have all been in business for between three and 10 years, and one key point that came out of it was that the idea will appeal more to people just starting a business, rather than those already established. The reason for this was that those established would have the money to pay for the services and would not have the time to give away, whereas start-ups wouldn't have the money but would have the time.

Wednesday 25th July 2007

I had a meeting with Nick from Civic Video today. They want to put Mocks into all stores; however, the stores are all franchises, so the head office can't force stores to take the stock. We are going to trial selling stock on a consignment basis for the 200 stores. I think it might be rather messy, but it will get the product out there and potentially sell more than if it was sitting on the floor in the office. I think it is worth a go and I can evaluate it in three months. We will start in October.

Grant at Dick Smith has asked for a special stand to be built for their stores, so we will need to supply 350 stands. I know from previous experience that the stands help sell the Mocks, because they make them more prominent, and usually the stands are located in a good position in store, like the counter. It is going to be expensive –

$2,000 to provide the stands – but I feel we need to show we're willing to help the product sell.

Yesterday my marketing manager Simone and I went to a workshop run by the NSW Department of State and Regional Development's Women in Business program. It was about improving your website and traffic to the site to increase sales. There were quite a few tips that we can use both on the Mocks site and on the new business time-swap idea, such as offering freebies to sign up to the e-newsletter. I thought one idea we could implement was offering a discount voucher for mockstore.com for anyone who registers for the e-newsletter.

I am enjoying not having to study for uni this semester, and it is probably lucky that there wasn't time to enrol, since the new business time-swap idea is taking up a lot of time.

Monday 30th July 2007

I had a lovely weekend away with friends in the Hunter Valley, wine-tasting and enjoying an Aussie Christmas in July. Erica, my graphic designer, and her husband came along. I appreciated the chance to get to know them a bit more. Everyone really enjoyed the weekend, I feel I really should spend more time with friends.

I finally finished the website brief for the business time-swap idea today. We don't have a name yet, and the brief is a wish list of everything I think we need. Now I need to see how much it will cost. Simone and I are off to Melbourne this week for a gift trade show for Mocks, so it is busy, busy in the office. We are taking Mocks in our suitcases, but I had to repack after finding I only had enough room left for about two pairs of knickers ... and no other clothes!

Mockers: Carla in UK, Simone in marketing, Tara in dispatch, Zena in admin and Ella bookkeeping temporarily

Mocks sold this month: 11,117

Store total: 770

Business bank account balance: $1,994 & £984

Mood: ☺ ☺

August 2007

Wednesday 1st August 2007

I popped into the mobile shop in Manly and topped up their Mocks stand today. They had sold a lot, and they filled me in on other accessory products and what is and isn't going well. They are always a mine of information.

We have decided to bring out a birthday Mock this month to celebrate Mocks' third birthday. It has "Happy Birthday" on one side and a cake with candles on the other. We will send it out to the media and to all our stores to celebrate.

Wednesday 8th August 2007

The trade show was really tiring. It ran from 9am until 6pm for five days, and we also had to stay on top of day-to-day inquiries from the office. Also, staying in a hotel is not exactly easy, especially when it is like the one we had, similar to Fawlty Towers! However, the hotel location was great for going out in the evening.

Simone and I got back tonight from Melbourne, from the trade show. It was not a good one. There were two venues, one in the city and one out at the racecourse, and we were at the racecourse. It just didn't have the volume of visitors. None of the stands in our aisle did much business, and we didn't need two people there for most of the time – a real contrast to the Sydney trade show. At Sydney we gained 20 new stores, and here we gained about five! However, we did spot a competitor selling the Spanish Bagmovil mobile socks (their stand was next to that of some friends of mine), apparently they were pleased with the way things were going ... They had socks for reading glasses and sunglasses, which was interesting. It is a concept I have thought about previously, but I haven't had enough interest from consumers. I find it worrying that they are at the show. The Australian market is getting flooded; we need to make sure we keep innovating with Mocks.

I had a funny conversation with Simone over dinner one night, it might have been to do with the wine we had drunk, as she still seems a bit nervous with me. She told me that I have become a lot more relaxed since February. I think I was a bit too much of a control freak before. It made me think back to what may have happened in February to bring it on, but I can't find anything. Maybe I had subconsciously made the decision to sell then …

Friday August 10th 2007

I'm back in the office and there is a real backlog of accounts bits to do, so much so that I can only really get through the immediate essentials. This situation really needs to be sorted out, but I am now wondering if there is much point getting someone in, since the business might sell soon … I hope I can get Ella to help me out again on a more permanent basis now her baby is a bit bigger.

I had to make a call on deleting the Princess Mock design today. When stock gets low, I decide whether to reorder or kill it off. Sales on this design were less than 10 a week, so it got killed! It's a shame, as I really like this design, but if it can't pull its weight, it has to go.

I went to another Business Chicks networking breakfast this morning, and met a completely new set of people. The girl I sat next to was especially nice, and we are going to arrange to have coffee soon. She works for a large corporate travel company, and was very keen on the personalised Mocks concept.

Monday 13th August 2007

I am feeling a little stiff today after completing the 14km City to Surf fun run yesterday, from the city to Bondi Beach, wearing my Mocks T-shirt, of course. It was a great atmosphere, Mr Johns and I went with a big group of people.

We sent out the customer service survey to all the independently owned stores that we supply today. This is our annual survey to measure satisfaction in a number of aspects of the business, and this year includes some questions around the designs, as well as about whether we can finally email their monthly newsletters to them rather than mail them.

We have had one order from the AmCham mail-out. One company is definitely going ahead with 2,000 personalised Mocks with their logo on it, which means that we have broken even with just the one order – the order covered the cost of the mail out and the Mocks. Good news.

I booked a table for the Mocks third birthday lunch for the team for 26th August. We are going to a nice seafood restaurant in Manly. It has been a good year. There were a few ups and downs, but overall it was good.

Wednesday 15th August 2007
Kylie started today in the part-time sales role. She came into the office for an induction, I ran over the role, and she will start from home tomorrow. I have started her on 10 hours a week working from home, to see how it goes, and she will come in once a fortnight for our team meeting. I think I will be able to measure results well.

Yesterday I had a good meeting with the buying team at Telstra. I showed them the Mocks range, and the Happy Birthday design. They loved the new products we have coming up, and overall it was very positive. I hope that this will push them into ordering more, but at least they know what is going on with us, and hopefully it will keep our competitor out of the picture.

I went to a very interesting networking event last night. It was speed networking, so I had five minutes with each person to talk about what each of us do and swap business cards. Over the night I met around 20 people. It was a lot of fun. If they have another one, I will definitely go. I really enjoyed meeting a wide range of people and I think it opens my mind.

I am going snowboarding for the week in New Zealand next week – I made my weight loss challenge.

I had to do some training with Tara in dispatch on invoicing. It is pretty straightforward and we have a procedure for it; however, her attention to detail isn't always fantastic, which worries me slightly.

Simone is going to be in charge while I am away, I am sure she will keep an eye on everything.

Monday 27th August 2007

I got back into the office today after a very bruised week away! I got run over twice by the chairlift, and I can't say that snowboarding is really my thing, after two days on the slopes I switched to skiing, which I found much easier. Mr Johns was very disappointed; he was really hoping that I would be a snowboarding buddy for him. It wasn't a very good holiday really. We didn't get on very well. I felt that we were both on edge and couldn't agree on things. I talked to him about it yesterday.

At the birthday lunch I felt was quite stilted, probably because Mr Johns was there and I haven't been getting on with him, and I could feel his disapproval at my behaviour, knowing for instance he thought I drank more than a boss should at work functions. Sometimes at these events I feel like I am split between my team and him. I think that everyone in the team enjoyed themselves. We all went for ice-cream and more drinks after, plus everyone got the afternoon off.

Wednesday 29th August 2007

This has been a very busy couple of days, as it always is after a holiday. Simone and the team coped really well; no dramas at all while I was away. It was really good to have someone I trust to look after the business. I have quite a few follow-ups to do for personalised Mocks. It is hard to get companies to commit once they have made an inquiry.

I went out for a bike ride this morning with my friend Louise. Exercise usually makes me feel better about the day. Things at home are still rather difficult, and will be until I can work out what is going on in my head. I have made an appointment to see a relationship counsellor tomorrow on my own, in the hope that talking it through will help. I am just not happy at the moment in my marriage; I really don't feel that it is working, although Mr Johns doesn't think that there is a problem – he thinks it is all in my head.

Friday 31st August 2007

It was good to talk to my counsellor yesterday to get things off my chest. I still don't know what to do. I really like things to be cut and dried, so I can make a decision. I don't like waiting to see. I have very little patience. I like to plan things out and move on, which makes this situation very hard for me.

Yesterday I went to a great seminar about building up my business. There were a lot of useful tips that I can incorporate, such as making sure your whole team is your brand ambassador.

If I am seriously thinking about leaving Mr Johns, do I really still want to sell the business? My business broker hasn't found anyone yet. There have been a few inquiries and one guy seems very interested, but until I have a solid offer I won't count my chickens.

I went to a boxing class last night and walking this morning, trying to get the endorphins flowing. Then I had a good meeting with Grant at Dick Smith this afternoon. We have finally signed off the paperwork, which means Mocks will hit their stores next month! I can't wait to see them in there, a total of 350 additional stores to sell Mocks. Sales should start to go through the roof.

I've booked in some activities to do with Mr Johns to try and get things more on track. We are going to go to a chocolate-tasting session at the Lindt Chocolate Café next month. Now that will be good, and will give us something different to talk about, instead of me explaining what isn't working and him trying to make me like him.

Mockers: Carla in UK, Simone in marketing, Tara in dispatch, Zena in admin, Kylie in sales and Ella bookkeeping temporarily

Mocks sold this month: 112,426

Store total: 772

Business bank account balance: $9,666 & £310

Mood: ☺ ☹ hard to concentrate on work

September 2007

Monday 3rd September 2007

I just spent the weekend away on my own in a hotel trying to work out what I want from my marriage. It is so hard. I came to the decision that the relationship isn't working for me, not because Mr Johns is awful, but I am just not getting what I want from it, and it is very unlikely that that will change. I really want better communication and emotional support from him. When I look back over the last few years I can kind of see this coming, I've had concerns before, but they were never really addressed. I think that now it has become make or break for me. He is fantastic in every other way, but these two areas are a big deal for me. We discussed our relationship tonight after work. Mr Johns has now moved out into the spare room.

I am finding it very hard to concentrate and focus at work. I had a meeting with a divorce lawyer and saw my counsellor today, just so that I know what could happen.

Simone had her one-year performance review today. Everything is going really well. Her attention to detail has improved, she uses her initiative and often goes above and beyond – it is fantastic. And everyone she works with loves her. I asked our designer Erica and Sally in PR, and both gave me glowing feedback. I actually gave her a pay rise in July, after nine months, so this was just a verbal review. We talked about the next steps and me pulling away more, so I am going to think about what else she can take on to give her more responsibility.

I had a long chat with Carla in the UK today. She now has a new UK distributor onboard; they ordered 9,100 Mocks in August and look set to order again. This is great news, but sales need to be higher than that each month to be able to cover all UK costs. I have put her back on a salary, the same as before, and I said that we will have to monitor sales. It is really hard having someone working remotely for me. Carla has got this account; however, she still hasn't delivered any new mobile stores from the list of 1,200 we gave her. I find it very hard to believe that out of 1,200, none of them were interested

... not even one? When I rang all those mobile phone stores in Australia when I first started, I would say that at least one in four wanted some information sent.

Thursday 6th September 2007

The results of the customer satisfaction survey were in today. There was 95% satisfaction with orders, which is the same as last year, and about 20% opted to receive the newsletter by email. There was a lot of positive feedback on designs. It is good to see that even after all the ups and downs and changes, customer satisfaction has remained high.

Kylie's sales are going well with the stores we met at the gift trade show in Melbourne. She seems to be getting some positive feedback, and we have had a few orders; however, we are still not going to break even on the trip with the accommodation and other costs we had to cover. It's not a show I would do again unless we were in the exhibition hall in the city centre.

I am going to get rid of our part-time admin girl, Zena. Simone said that while I was on holidays she didn't do much at all. She was picking and choosing the jobs she did, out of what Tara and Simone asked her to do – just doing what she felt like. That really can't work. Neither of the girls had many positive things to say about her, so I will do it when she comes in on Monday. I have spoken to her about this previously, but it obviously hasn't sunk in. It might mean we are stuck for a few weeks. I rang Helen who left in January when she couldn't fit work in with her uni class timetable, but I had to leave a message. I didn't want her to leave before, so hopefully she can come back.

Tuesday 11th September 2007

I think I will look for another business broker to sell the business. Ethel seems to be hopeless at letting me know what is happening. She said initially that she would keep me up-to-date every week, but that hasn't happened once.

I am currently doing a bit of a juggling act on the UK bank account, so that I have enough to pay the fulfilment house that stores the Mocks and sends them out to the UK stores. We have the big order in, but we won't get any payment until the end of September.

Simone gave me her monthly website analysis and a proposal for a scratch card competition today. The web analysis is really interesting; it shows that the mockstore.com shopping site is now performing better than the mocks.com.au information site in terms of visitors and hits. From this, Simone concluded we should merge the two, which would mean a whole new site. It's definitely worth looking at, but I am a bit reluctant to spend money on that at the moment with the sale uncertain and the UK still wobbly. The scratch card promotion would really help drive sales on certain designs, as we would put an instant win card inside these packs. The last time we did something like this it worked well, except that Australia Post didn't forward our mail properly and most of the responses got lost in the mail! It takes a while to organise, so won't happen until next year now, but sales should be good in the run-up to Christmas anyway.

Thursday 13th September 2007

The team meeting today was followed up with my friend Louise, who is also a personal trainer, taking us all for a stretch class in the office. We have been doing these for a while, but I am not sure exactly how much everyone enjoys them. Sometimes I get the impression that they find the class inconvenient to attend as it takes too much time out of their day. At the next team meeting I will sound them out, as there isn't a lot of point in having Louise in and paying her if the team aren't enjoying it or getting any benefit from it.

I am finding that taking on the Civic Video stores on a consignment basis is a lot of data-entry work, entering orders and details for 200 stores; then we will send out the Mocks in a couple of weeks. I really hope that the stores take them onboard and they sell well, as this is going to be a lot of work.

I got some good news today: Helen called to say she can come back to help me out with the data entry/admin work from 2nd October. It will work well. Since she knows how to do everything, there will be minimal training for me to do. We have agreed on 20 hours a week, which will take all the invoicing off me, and hopefully some of the other accounts bits. I am lucky that Ella can still do some accounting for me.

Sunday 16th September 2007

I met Erica, our graphic designer, regarding the website for the business time-swap idea today. I have called a number of web designers, and the quotes have all been pretty much the same. I would prefer to use someone I know and trust, so I think that this is a good option. Erica has someone she can use to do all the programming and her husband is going to project manage the whole set-up. The cost is about $30,000, which is a lot of money, probably the most I've spent on anything apart from a huge Mocks order. Louise, the friend I started planning it with, has decided that she will no longer be involved in the idea, due to the financial investment required, which is a shame, but it is better if she pulls out now rather than later. Today Erica and I discussed the whole concept and the brand. I feel confident that this will work. The research is very positive.

I have decided that the new business time-swapping website will be called GrowCo, as in 'Grow your Company'. I registered growco.com.au and growco.org today.

Monday 17th September 2007

I had a meeting with Jeremy, another business broker, this morning. He thinks that the business is really worth only $70,000 plus stock – nowhere near the $500,000 that the other broker, Ethel, told me. I don't really understand how there can be such a huge difference in the value; maybe Ethel was just agreeing with me to keep me happy? Surprisingly, Ethel called today to say that she has a buyer for me. She told me he will pay $200,000, much higher than the amount Jeremy suggested. It doesn't seem like much for three years' work. I really don't want to sell for that. Jeremy today said that he thought that the business looked like it was about to turn a corner, and that I would be better holding on to it until the end of December at the earliest and really until the end of the financial year in June. It is going to be hard to keep up my motivation until December, let alone June, but it seems to be sound advice, as I think he is right; it is about to turn a corner. I chatted to Dad about it, and he agreed that I should wait.

Mr Johns and I officially separated today. It was horrible, but I think it is the right thing for both of us, as I am really not happy. It is still very hard, but in some ways I feel like I am freer.

I was supposed to enrol for the next semester at uni this week, but I think I will wait until 2008 to go back; there is just too much going on at the moment. I don't think I could concentrate. I think I might go to France and stay with Mum and Dad for a bit to clear my head, but it kind of feels like running away ...

Tuesday 18th September 2007
I had a catch-up with Carla tonight. The UK distributor has placed another order, this time for only 1,600, which is not as good as expected. They definitely seem to be trying to get Mocks into stores there, but they have very unrealistic expectations of delivery times, like wanting the stock yesterday.

We still have no accounts person, so I printed and sent off all the statements to customers who owe us money. I need to get some more cash into the business. I am not paying myself at the moment, but I will have to start now with the separation, and this quarter's sales are not looking like they will cover expenses, so we will be well into the overdraft. The bank has now approved the $50,000 overdraft, and I think we are going to need it with Christmas coming. At least I have repaid Mum and Dad some of the money I owe them now.

Friday 21st September 2007
I got feedback from the team on the stretch classes this week; no-one was really that fussed, so I have decided to stop them. I thought

it was a nice thing to do, but if the enthusiasm isn't there it's a bit pointless.

Life at home is very strained at the moment. Mr Johns and I have decided that he will keep the house, as I can't afford the repayments on the mortgage, but we still have to work out everything else eventually. I started paying myself again today, and set up another personal account for me in just my name, so we can start to live separately.

I met another divorce lawyer yesterday morning. She was lovely, and advised me to try to work out as much as possible between us to save on costs. She thinks that it should be a 50:50 split of the assets. The only thing is that my business is counted as one of the assets, which should be split. I really do not want to have to pay Mr Johns any money from the business; I simply cannot afford to. I know that I could make the business look like it is worth less by increasing my liabilities, so that if it did come to splitting it up I wouldn't have to give him as much. I don't think I want to take this path, but I think I should consider it; Mr Johns can be very difficult when it comes to money. I have pretty much decided not to sell the Mocks business now. I am concerned that if I sell I wouldn't have any income. I would have a cash injection, but realistically I would like to have an ongoing income. It will take me a while to get GrowCo going.

Wednesday 26th September 2007

The office has been very busy, as we are short-staffed until Helen starts next week in the admin role. I have managed to get out of the house every night. It is hard to be there at the moment, I have decided that I am going to go over and visit Mum and Dad in France for a few weeks. I leave on 5th October. I just need some time out and a change of scenery. Then, when I get back, I will move out.

Mocks went into the Dick Smith stores this week. There were great reports from Grant, he is such a huge fan of them! The stands we produced for them have worked really well. I just hope that the store staff persuade lots of people to buy.

I am having a few issues with stock. The reports I look at every week seem to be out, and it is really affecting the ordering I do. We all did a big stock count one day at the end of June, but now I doubt it was right. I have found 1,000 additional Gelato Mocks and 1,000 additional Camouflage Cards. That's a whole box of each – a lot to miss. I have asked Tara to do another count to double-check all this for me.

Friday 28th September 2007
I went out last night to the Last Thursday Club networking event in the city. The speaker was talking about his project management of disaster situations, which was really interesting but also rather depressing, as he showed us images of all the body bags they collected. I bumped into about five people whom I haven't seen for ages, so it was great to catch up. It always amazes me that you seem to meet more or less the same people at networking events, regardless of who puts them on.

Working with the Civic Video stores is taking a lot of time, and we are going to need to hire another mum to work from home. Part of the agreement with Civic is that we will call each store every month. There is no way that Kylie can call 220 stores a month all on her own. I put another ad on careermums.com.au to try to find someone.
Mockers: Carla in UK, Simone in marketing, Tara in dispatch, Kylie in sales and Ella bookkeeping temporarily
Mocks sold this month: 51,483
Store total: 1,322
Business bank account balance: $11,146 & £9,712
Mood: ☺ ☺ optimistic, new challenges ahead

October 2007
Wednesday 3rd October 2007
I went to the chocolate appreciation night at the Lindt Chocolate Café tonight with Mr Johns, and it was awesome! Even for a hardened chocoholic like me it was extreme chocolate overload. We both really enjoyed it, and it was nice to do something together that didn't relate to us as a couple. I was initially feeling apprehensive,

but we both love chocolate, so we started to relax after a while, and conversation was easier in the car on the way home.

I have found a new mum to work from home. Her name is Liz, and she is going to start while I am away. Kylie, my current salesperson, is going to train her for me. She will be working on the Civic Video stores, calling them to make sure that they have enough stock and whatever else they might need. I am sure Kylie will do a good job training her. She is very switched-on about Mocks, and has picked up things really quickly. I think that things are finally starting to look up on the staffing front for the business!

GrowCo is starting to form. I am spending a lot of time trying to work out how to get it launched. I am aiming for 10th November as a launch day, as there is an expo organised by the Australian Businesswomen's Network on that day. Around 400 businesswomen will attend, so it would be the perfect place to gain interest. Erica says that this date is doable, and that I will have a fully functioning website by then.

Friday 5th October 2007
I am waiting at the airport for my flight to Paris. This morning was very hectic, there were a million last-minute things to be organised.

I registered the GrowCo logo as a trademark today, all ready for when it takes off. My plan is to have 500 members on GrowCo by the end of May 2008, a big target, but I think it will be achievable. I've managed to find a lot of events that I can go to to promote it.

Tuesday 9th October 2007
I am in France with Mum, Dad and my brother Humbert. It is always kind of strange staying here, because I didn't grow up here, but the house is lovely. It is a very slow-paced environment with Mum painting, Dad pottering and Humbert working on his functional art projects.

I spoke to the office yesterday on Skype. They are all fine; it is all under control and there are no dramas at all, which is good to hear. I can check all my emails remotely, so the time delay if there is something urgent isn't too bad. I have left Simone in charge again, and Ella has offered to help her if she needs it. Ella knows so much about my business, we have known each other practically since I first started and are now good friends.

Today I spoke to Carla in the UK. Orders are still coming in from the distributor, but they are still expecting stock delivered within days, which is very difficult when we have no idea in advance how much they will be ordering. We don't hold that much stock in the UK, since until now there hasn't been a huge number of Mocks sold. I asked Carla to push back on the distributor to try to get forecasts; most of the stores I work with in Australia carry a certain number of weeks of stock on hand, and therefore can produce forecasts. Carla is planning to exhibit Mocks at the Clothes Show in Birmingham in December. We will be able to sell Mocks there as well as promote them; it sounds like a good opportunity, but I am still waiting on the final recommendation from her with the breakdown of costs.

Carla is still following up stores from the trade show that she exhibited at in February. I am not sure if this is a good use of time. It seems to me if they haven't expressed any interest by now then it is unlikely that they are going to. However, she doesn't agree. I need to monitor this, I am concerned that she is not getting any good results from the work she is doing there. Carla contacted gift stores in Bristol last week, so we are hoping that some of those will come through. I am still surprised that there haven't been more Mockists added to the UK list. As far as I am aware, she has only gained us an additional five stores on top of the ones that I got at the trade show last year ... Obviously the distributor is a big win, but now we have them, the contact will only require maybe an hour a day ... it's puzzling.

Sales so far this month for Australia are $9,767, which is a good start, but we have a long way to go to reach the $80,000 target.

221

Friday 12th October 2007

The GrowCo logo and promotional flyers have been finalised now. Erica can now get on with the website graphics. I think that this is going to look really professional.

We received another order from Telstra yesterday, so sales are going to be good this month. I had a report back from Kylie about Liz, the new salesgirl, who started earlier in the week. Apparently she picked things up well, and thought that there would be no problem with her doing the role. The first calls to Civic Video stores start at the end of this month, so in the meantime Liz is going to help Kylie call around the rest of the existing Mockists, to check that all is OK with them.

I really enjoy the fact that I have the ability to work anywhere in the world running my business, although I really feel that I need someone in the office running that for me, as there are day to day issues that arise.

Monday 15th October 2007

I had more catch-ups again today with the Australian and UK offices. Carla in the UK really doesn't seem to have moved on much since last week. I do know what it is like following up stores, but she has now been working for me for well over a year. I am really not sure it is worthwhile. I will do some analysis of the UK market and profits this week and bounce ideas off Dad.

Sales are now at $65,000 for Australia, which is very good news. The business seems to be doing better without me there!

Thursday 18th October 2007

I am supposed to be flying back to Australia on Monday 22nd October, but I have decided to stay a bit longer. I now will leave on the 29th. I have had a few accidents while I have been here ... I fell off my bike in the first week and grazed my arm, which wasn't so bad, apart from the fact that I had to cycle back for 30 minutes with blood dripping out of my arm, and I nearly gave Mum a heart attack when I got back! Then when I was just getting better and the wound was finally healing, I walked into a park bench last Friday. I thought that the scab was just knocked off the previous bike wound, but no, I gashed a hole in my knee and had to go to hospital for three stitches. So I am staying longer to get the stitches taken out before I go. This has been a bit of an accident-prone trip.

Dad and I have been doing a lot of analysis this week on the UK market. Basically the only part of the business really bringing in any money is the distributor we have working for us. I could easily liaise with them from Australia, since most of it is via email anyway, which would save Carla's salary. At the moment we are making a maximum of £1,000 profit a month, and that is in a good month. I can't justify having her there; she is just not adding enough value. All the online orders she sends for us could be done by the fulfilment house, and I could hire another mum in Australia to look after the UK stores we have.

This is a really hard decision, since Carla is a friend of mine, but the Australian business is still supporting the UK and by doing so is limiting what we can do there. I am still waiting for her to give me an update on the 1,200 mobile stores that she was supposed to send me weeks ago. I will ask for that again today and then see what comes through, but it is not looking good. I trusted her to do a good job because I know her, and yet I feel like she has let me down. I received her expense report today. She has claimed for tube tickets to go to the bank and the time on the tickets is 8pm, when obviously the bank isn't open. I feel that she might be taking advantage of the fact that we are, or were, friends. To be fair, everyone had told me not to hire friends, but I really thought it would work.

Australian sales are now up to $86,212. This is going to be a good month.

Monday 22nd October 2007
Carla sent me through the report I'd requested. Of the 1,200 stores, she claimed she had called 1,000 but only had time to fill in the details for 600, and that all the comments were on paper. This seems exceptionally strange to me. We had laid out the information

in an Excel spreadsheet so she could type straight in to save time. When I looked at the comments she had added, they were things like "called three times no answer". Really not useful. I doubt that she actually did call them. When I asked her if she could send through her phone records, so I could get more detail of when she called for someone to follow up, she said that there were none: all 1,000 calls were made for free on her home internet phone.

The situation is obviously not working. I find it hard to trust her, and can't rely on her. Today she sent me her recommendation for the Clothes Show stand we were looking at, and I've worked out that she would have to sell one Mock every minute to break even. It is just so unlikely, given that when I have done similar events in Australia we have sold around 100 per day maximum.

I told her that I would have to call it quits, since it is just not profitable, and that it was stressing me out, which with the break-up of my marriage I didn't need. I didn't make it personal at all. I said that I would pay her out three months as per her contract, rather than make her work it, and I needed her to return everything to me this week in France. I feel that the situation was partly my fault. I should have kept on at her more to give me the information I needed and not just left her to do it. I have learnt a huge lesson from this about supervising staff who work remotely. It made me panic about what was happening with Kylie and Liz in Australia, so I emailed them and asked them to send me a fortnightly update on what they have been doing.

I spent the rest of today emailing the contacts in the UK and letting them know what has happened and that they need to talk to me for now. No-one had a problem with it.

Wednesday 24th October 2007

There was another order today from the UK distributor for 6,000 Mocks. They have managed to get Mocks into another mobile chain in the UK. This is fantastic, and it happened without Carla. I had to arrange to get Mocks sent from Australia. I also followed them up about future sales forecasts, and they have promised to send them.

It has been good having Dad here to chat to about business issues. Normally I am on the phone to him, but face to face is easier. The whole family love to join in and give me their viewpoints, which can get annoying at times! I am finding that I actually know the answer to problems and I do know what to do, but chatting to Dad somehow gives me the confidence to believe in it.

Friday 26th October 2007
The laptop, printer, samples, store information and records from the UK haven't arrived, which is annoying. If they don't arrive on Monday I will have to leave Mum and Dad to sort them out, which isn't ideal.

Australian sales have now reached $90,018. This month could be our biggest month ever in the history of Mocks!

Monday 29th October 2007
I am flying back to Sydney tonight, and am glad to be going. I have enjoyed being with Mum, Dad and Humbert, but I am ready to go home.
Mockers: Simone in marketing, Tara in dispatch, Helen in admin, Kylie in sales, Liz in sales and Ella bookkeeping temporarily
Mocks sold this month: 52,565
Store total: 1,325
Business bank account balance: $37,701 & £5,321
Mood: ☺ ☺ business is picking up

November 2007
Thursday 1st November 2007
I spoke to Mum and Dad yesterday, and the packages from the UK finally got to them on Tuesday; there was a delay at customs.

Yesterday I was supposed to have a meeting with Derek from Optus, a large mobile phone chain, regarding potentially stocking Mocks, but I just couldn't face it. When I arrived back on Tuesday the separation from Mr Johns really hit me hard. I called him and blamed it on jetlag. Luckily he agreed to reschedule to next week.

It has been hard being back in Sydney the past two days; I now realise that the marriage split is final. I arrived back to find that Mr Johns had moved all my stuff into the spare room. It was a huge shock and it made me realise what my decision means. I think before I went to France I wasn't really thinking about the reality of the situation, just that the marriage wasn't working. I still think the split is best for both of us, but it is scary. I am going apartment hunting on Saturday to find somewhere to live.

Monday 5th November 2007

I found a place to live, also in Manly, and I move in on Friday, so that is one thing off my mind. I also had a good meeting yesterday with my designer Erica at her house. The website for GrowCo is really coming on well, but we only have five days left until the expo. This worries me slightly, but she tells me it will be done. It's hard to focus on the business at the moment; I can only really do the jobs that require very little concentration. Hopefully this will improve as I get more used to the split. My team are being very supportive.

I met Derek from Optus today, and he has agreed to stock the Mocks range! This will add another 100 stores to our total. The only slight problem is that he wants us to sell to them through a distributor, Cellnet. I am usually not really keen to do that, but in this case it is the only option. Derek gave me their distributor's details, so I called and left a message with them. Hopefully we can arrange a meeting for later this week, or early next week. I have worked with the New Zealand branch of Cellnet since 2005, so it could work well.

Friday 9th November 2007

I moved into my new place today. I think I will be happy here.

I am still doing the accounts at work. It is slightly less work having Helen here, but I am pretty busy at the moment. There has been a lot of admin to do with the GrowCo website in terms of getting everything up and running for this week. I have sent out a few flyers already this week to my friend Lisa, who runs her own market research business. She is going to promote GrowCo for me at some networking events. I have decided to offer everyone at the expo three months' free membership if they join before the end of November. I have signed up about 10 friends who run their own businesses so far, and given them a free membership so I can say that we already have members.

My business cards for GrowCo arrived yesterday, as did the promotional flyers, so I have been rushing around all week making sure that I have everything for tomorrow. My friend Louise is coming with me to help on the stand, even though she isn't involved in the business, just for moral support. I checked the GrowCo site tonight before I went to bed. It is not quite finished as yet, which worries me slightly, as the expo is tomorrow. I just hope that they are working on it now!

After tomorrow I want to spend Sunday organising my place.

Saturday 10th November 2007

Launch day for the GrowCo website. The Australian Businesswomen's Network expo went well today, although there were not as many women attending as I was told to expect, probably around 250 rather than 400. We had a lot of interest in GrowCo and people seemed very keen on joining. We ran a competition to win a year's free membership if you put your business card in a box. I collected around 60 cards. No-one actually joined on the day, which was slightly disappointing. The positive feedback was really good to hear, although people were a bit confused about me. Since I attend a lot of Australian Businesswomen's Network functions, people associate me with Mocks, and they really struggled to see why I was doing something new that was so different. However, I felt that the expo was a very supportive environment to launch into, with people very open to new ideas. The only technical glitch was that the site is not fully functioning yet. That is annoying. I don't want people to go home tonight and try to look at it, only to see that it wasn't working properly. I don't think they would go back a second time. Erica said they were working all night on the site, and that they will get the rest finished for Monday or Tuesday.

Tuesday 13th November 2007

I went to a Business Network International breakfast this morning with Louise. She has joined and thought it might be a good place for me to promote GrowCo. I wouldn't join the network. It is one of those groups where only there can only be one member from each profession and you refer each other's business. For Mocks I don't think it would be worth it, and for GrowCo I think that I need to meet large groups of people at a time, rather than get ones or twos from referrals.

Mocks sales this month are at $46,000 for Australia. November is usually a big month, with Christmas just around the corner. October ended up at $110,000 for Australia alone, and was our biggest month ever!

I need to start looking for someone to replace my part-time salesgirl, Kylie. She is pregnant with twins. She isn't due until February, but if I start looking now then I can get Kylie to train them.

Simone is taking on more and more of the Mocks marketing. I have worked the budget she developed into her key performance indicators. She is now totally responsible for Australian PR, and I am very impressed with how conscious she is of the budget, and not going over it. It is fantastic!

Thursday 15th November 2007

I went to an "exercise and healthy eating for busy people" seminar this morning, run by AmCham. I am being told by so many people that I am doing too much and need to look after myself, it is getting annoying! The seminar was really good. I learnt a lot, and there were some lovely people there. When I got back I emailed them, saying how good it was to meet them. I do this after every networking event, but very few people actually reply to me. I find this strange, since they presumably go to meet new people …

After the breakfast in the city I drove 30 minutes over to Alexandria for a meeting with Civic Video. Unfortunately the person I needed to see was off sick, and no-one had told me – a totally wasted journey.

The GrowCo website isn't finished; there are still a lot of admin things to be done on it. I also need to follow up everyone from the expo. I just feel that I don't have the energy to do it. Maybe I am procrastinating … I am trying to juggle so many things at the moment, as well as trying to adapt to living on my own after seven years of living with someone. I don't really know what keeps me going. I think it is the fact that I feel I have to, because if I don't then I really have nothing.

Monday 19th November 2007

Simone and I had a great meeting with Fran from the marketing team from Fox Entertainment. She is launching a new *Family Guy* DVD and wants to give away a Family Guy Mock to everyone who preorders the DVD in stores. She will need 10,000 Mocks, and they want to do a contra deal with us, advertising and promoting Mocks in return for the actual Mocks. It sounds like it would be a good opportunity for us. We haven't managed to get Mocks into the music stores, and this might make them sit up and take notice. The Family Guy Mock will also bring Mocks to the attention of the male target audience, which we find really hard to reach.

The Sesame St characters have been going really well for Mocks, so Simone and I discussed licensing another character next year. We made a list of sources for possible characters, such as *Mr Men*, *The Simpsons* etc. Simone will do some market research online to see which characters our consumers respond well to. I have handed this over to Simone to work on, she basically managed all the Sesame St licensing which went well. I love having someone who I feel I can give responsibility to.

It is getting close to Christmas party time, and the invitations are starting to roll in. A publisher friend of mine is going to give a Mock to each of her guests; Mocks will reach a whole new audience. I have started to work on our Christmas card and gift list. I think we will use the Mock Christmas Cards again; they were really well received last year and it helps promote the cards. I will only send gifts to the buyers for the large chain stores.

This week GrowCo will be featured again with free offers in the e-newsletters of two more friends, so hopefully I will get more members from it. I had two responses from the one Lisa in marketing did for me. I am still not feeling that enthusiastic about it, even though I feel I should. Mocks are still taking up a lot of my time, and it is hard to fit everything in.

I put another ad on careermums.com.au today for the part-time salesperson to replace Kylie. I am hoping that we will be able to get Kylie back after she has her babies and get her to work on GrowCo, but I think it will depend on how she feels.

Wednesday 21st November 2007

I went to a government-run networking event for women in manufacturing last night. I sold some Mocks, probably around $120 worth, and promoted GrowCo to a few people. It was a free event, but there were only around 60 people there. Again there was a lot of interest in GrowCo and a lot of comments about what a good idea it was. I talked to one of the women I met last year at the Sydney Business Women's Awards, and she said she would promote GrowCo at her local chamber of Commerce in Bondi. I hope that she does. I made a note in my diary to follow her up on it in a few weeks.

The presenter at the networking event last night was talking about using packaging as a unique selling proposition. I wonder if we can change the Mocks bags to recycled plastic, to help the environment and make Mocks a more environmentally friendly product?

Matilda, a representative from a sampling company, came in today to present the results from the show bags – we put coupons for a free Mock in the Girlfriend show bags at the Brisbane Show and Sydney Royal Easter Show this year. The research found that Mocks still have strong brand awareness, at 74%, and over 50% of people had heard of the Mocks online store. The coupon redemption was very low, at around 0.05%. Simone is going to look into it further before we decide whether to participate again next year. I have left the decision up to her.

Friday 23rd November 2007

Simone and I attended the lunch to announce the winner of the *Girlfriend* magazine "search for a model" competition. There were around 100 people there. It was lovely to be invited, and we were on a table with the modelling agency that sponsored the competition. The whole reception lasted about three hours, we met the whole *Girlfriend* team and had a good chat with the editor, Sarah. I felt rather out of place at the event, probably because I didn't make much of an effort to dress up, while almost everyone else looked like they were dressed for a cocktail function.

I spent yesterday reviewing the sales budget for the rest of the year. With the UK distributor bringing in sales and the deletion of Carla's salary, we should be a lot better off, especially after the huge October we had. I am increasing the sales targets and cutting down on some of the expenses that we had in the UK. I gave myself a pay rise today. I am now on a huge $50,000! The $40,000 I was on just wasn't working out for me.

Carla asked me for a written reference today. I found it very hard to write, because I wasn't that happy with what she'd done in the last few months, so I ended up just putting in the facts: how long she worked for me and what she did.

The GrowCo website still isn't finished. Some bits have been completed, but others like the online store and forums aren't done. I really don't like going live with something half done. I have chased Erica's team again.

Wednesday 28th November 2007

We sent off Christmas cards to our buyers in the UK this week. We ordered presents for them online to be delivered next week. I am still writing the Australian ones, to give them all a personal touch, but when there are 200 it takes a while!

My friend Ella has agreed to come back and assist me with the accounts for the end of the BAS period. This will be a big help. I am really struggling to keep the accounts up-to-date.

I organised Christmas presents for my team today. I'm going to give each of them a Flatout bear; they are made from lamb's wool and are really soft and cuddly. I'll attach a $50 voucher to each one. I chose an individual present for each person last year, but I just don't have the time or energy this year.

Yesterday Simone and I went to an all-day event on branding. It was a great reminder about ways to promote brands, both online and in the traditional channels. One message that really stood out for me is to look at the actual reason behind why consumers need your brand, and by dissecting that you can use the insights in your promotion. It is something that I haven't looked at in a lot of detail for probably two years. There was also a lot of discussion around enticing people to your website by offering free resources such as articles written by other business owners on aspects such as marketing, networking etc. I could offer free articles on the GrowCo site ... In the new year I want both of us to try to implement some of the things we have learnt from the event. We agreed that Simone would focus on Mocks and I would focus on GrowCo.

This month's sales are about to go over the $100,000 mark for Australia for the second month in a row! Fantastic! It seems amazing that since I split up with Mr Johns, the business is booming. A friend expressed the view that perhaps all my hard work is now paying off. Who knows? I think it is because I have a solid customer base, the Mocks brand is much better known and I have a good team behind me. Or maybe subconsciously I felt he was undermining my confidence, and so I was stopping myself from reaching my full potential ...

Friday 30th November 2007

I met up with Erica yesterday to go through the GrowCo site and where we are up to. There are still quite a few bugs to be sorted; it is not 100% as yet. She and her husband are going to Europe for six weeks next week, and it will be harder for them to fix them once they have left. The database still needs to be tidied up so that I can use it to the max. It feels to me that every time I go on to the website to do something I find another little problem. It is really frustrating me, which I explained to Erica. The first GrowCo newsletter went out today. It was two weeks late due to technical glitches, but nevertheless it looked great, and went out to around 150 people, due to the networking I have been doing.

Today I went to another networking event. I am aiming to get to at least one per week to promote GrowCo. Today's was a lunch organised by the Women's Network, and the people there were ideal GrowCo members. I got there early and put a flyer on each seat – as did about 30 other people. I gave away a one-year free GrowCo membership in the raffle, but there wasn't much opportunity to promote it to people. It was a sit-down lunch, so I didn't get to meet that many people. There were tables there with members showing their products or services, but unfortunately when I had inquired about them they were already full, as that would have been perfect. At the lunch I sat next to a divorce life coach, which I felt was fate, so I took her card.

Mockers: Simone in marketing, Tara in dispatch, Helen in admin, Kylie in sales, Liz in sales and Ella bookkeeping temporarily
Mocks sold this month: 35,144
Store total: 1,327
Business bank account balance: $12,912 & £7,164
Mood: ☺ ☺ ☺ fate is intervening

December 2007
Monday 3rd December 2007
Today I had the meeting with Peter, the sales manager from Optus' distributor Cellnet. It went very well. He was really impressed by what I have achieved with Mocks, and even went so far to say that the product that they brought out was only in competition to Mocks, and hasn't sold at all. They are definitely going to take Mocks on and were very excited about the prospect, so all in all a great meeting.

I am starting to look at the option of outsourcing our dispatch department, which is currently all in-house. At the end of May 2008 our office lease expires, and by outsourcing we could potentially move into a smaller office. The only reason I chose such a huge office was that I anticipated needing more staff, which has happened, but since two of them work from home I don't need all the space. Outsourcing would also alleviate the problem of having to take other members of the team off their roles to help out when we have a huge order to get out in a short time.

Christian Mock sales are still pretty slow. I would like to look at new designs next year to give sales a boost, and also other outlets to sell them into. I still think the market has huge potential, we just haven't tapped into it properly yet.

Friday 7th December 2007

The weeks leading up to Christmas are just flying by. It is unbelievable. Simone and I met Sally from our PR agency yesterday. I ran my book idea past her, and she thought it was one she could definitely publicise. I also mentioned that I wanted her to start doing PR on GrowCo to try and get that kicking, so from January she will be working on that. Mocks PR has definitely picked up over the past few months, and we are beginning to get more and more of the media interested, especially now we are bringing out things such as the Couture Mocks and Sesame St designs.

Leading on from the Cellnet meeting with Peter on Monday, I have put together a proposal with pricing, which I sent off today. We agreed on the pricing in the meeting, so Cellnet will accept the proposal and start to order. The whole process has been pretty easy considering what it can sometimes be like.

I have found a potential fulfilment company to which we could outsource dispatch of the Mocks. They gave me some referees to contact regarding the service they offer, and they came back very positive. On Wednesday my bookkeeper Ella and I went and saw their premises, about one-and-a-half hours' drive from our offices. They appeared to know what they were doing, and had a good set-up. I still need to finish crunching all the numbers before we make a decision.

Thursday 13th December 2007

There is only the rest of this week and then next week until we finish for Christmas. I am still trying to get the GrowCo website completed, as well as contact people I have met, plus get my book written and keep Mocks going. The UK distributor is very demanding, and is taking up a lot of my time, as are the accounts and the overall day-to-day running of the business.

The Crazy John's account we have is not proving to be very profitable for us. I ran the numbers this week and after the cost of delivery, which we have to give them free, we are only making around $200 per month, and then we still have to cover the staff costs relating to the many inquiries we get from them. I emailed the buyer and suggested that we either have to introduce a minimum order per store, to make it worthwhile, or consider that it isn't really working for us. I am waiting to hear.

Tonight was my publisher friend's Christmas party, and I met a few authors. It was interesting to get their take on publishing and why they wrote their books. I met a book distributor; he was really direct in terms of giving me advice. He thought that my book would sell well in the UK, and said he would email me contacts. It has definitely got me thinking about potential global demand for the book.

Christmas has been a bit of a whirl on the social front, with an event on nearly every night, but I like the fact that it gets me out. I am finding living on my own hard. Just being in the flat alone makes it hard to sleep, and silly things are upsetting me, like coming home and there being no answering machine to check, just because I used to do it every day.

Friday 14th December 2007

I heard from Crazy John's today. They agree that the account is not worth it from their viewpoint either, so we are going to call it quits. At least we ended up on good terms.

I met a guy from another potential fulfilment house today, but he seemed very vague. He kept asking me how I organised the dispatch.

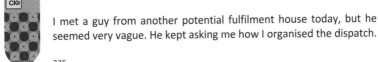

He seemed to have no idea about how he would run it, which worries me.

Tuesday 18th December 2007

Today I had very positive feedback regarding sales from Grant at Dick Smith's: they are much higher than expected. I have been surprised as well, since they have already reordered three times since their first initial huge order.

This week I finally feel like I am getting some energy back, just as we are about to finish for Christmas. That's OK, I will catch up on work over the break.

Friday 21st December 2007

Today is the last day in the office before Christmas. Sales this month only reached $50,000, but at least it covered our outgoings. To be honest, it is not that bad for December, but seems very small compared to the huge November and October sales we had!

I took the Telstra buyer, Joanna, out for lunch on Wednesday for Christmas. We get on very well and had a very frank off-the-record conversation. She told me that I should put in a price increase, as they are taking advantage of me, and that I need to improve my negotiation skills — I have noted that down for next year. It was surprising that she told me that, but I am so glad she is so up-front with me.

We had our Christmas party today at noon at Shelly Beach near Manly. It was organised by Tara and Helen. They volunteered to organise it and did a great job. Apart from us four in the office, my friend Louise came, as did Kylie in sales, but Liz couldn't make it. This is the first work Christmas party I've had without Mr Johns there, and I found it felt very different. I was much more relaxed than usual, probably because the girls know what I have been through in the past few months. We had my favourite champagne, and both Simone and I proceeded to get very drunk, which I don't normally do at my work things, being the boss.

Everyone had a good time and at about 6pm we finished up, Simone and I went back to my place, got changed and went out to a bar to meet a friend of hers whom I also know. The night then took a whole new turn. Simone told me after a few more drinks that she didn't want to do marketing anymore. I asked her why and what she wanted to do instead, she told me that she just didn't enjoy marketing that much; she'd prefer to be a general manager and she wanted to run the business! I said OK. This is the answer to my prayers. I didn't think that she was ready to step up, but she does. She wanted a pay rise, which I gave her, and I also gave her a bonus. We agreed that yes, it would be hard work, but she was prepared to do that. It turned out that her dad made the suggestion, and said that she should stay with me for longer, as there is a lot she can learn, particularly when she enjoys it so much. Simone and I agreed that we would hire a marketing assistant to take over some of her role and then we could transition work from me.

Saturday 22nd December 2007

I woke up with a very bad headache today. I remembered the conversation I'd had with Simone last night, and I still feel really pleased. I think that she will do a great job, and it will free me up to get on with other ideas without having to sell. I thought that maybe the alcohol had made me a little over-generous on the bonus, but never mind, I am sure she will be worth it. I emailed her to confirm it all in writing so that she knew I remembered. I think 2008 is going to be great!

Mockers: Simone in marketing, Tara in dispatch, Helen in admin, Kylie in sales, Liz in sales and Ella bookkeeping temporarily

Mocks sold this month: 21,013

Store total: 1,227

Business bank account balance: $7,975 & £7,975

Mood: ☺ ☺ ☺ ☺ ☺ Great end to the year

Where am I now?

It is now the beginning of August 2008, and the book is about to go to print. It turns out that the drunken decision made at Christmas was a very good one. Simone has gone from strength to strength as General Manager. We have hired two marketing assistants – one for Australian marketing and one for the UK, as well as a full time office junior, Helen left due to not being able to work the hours we needed. We now have two part-time mums working from home: one solely on personalised Mocks for Australia, the other on GrowCo and UK Mocks sales. Ella is now back working with us one day a fortnight doing all our bookkeeping. We have dispensed with the data entry role; our office junior does it. Simone is managing her team really well, and I sometimes think that she is harsher than I ever was! Meanwhile I am looking after the UK Mocks business and I plan on getting Mocks into the US market this year. Once Simone is comfortable with it, she will take on the UK and US as well.

In July we decided after much deliberation to move to a distributor model for Mocks, which means no more sales to stores and no more dispatching of Mocks. We did try outsourcing just the dispatch of the orders, but it just didn't work. However, we are still keeping up our relationships with our customers through the store newsletter and regular visits to buyers.

Our next licensed Mock range will be launched in October – SpongeBob SquarePants Mocks, which I hope will be as successful as the Sesame St ones. Plus we have lots of other new projects on the horizon.

My company, LaRoo has been featured in *BRW* magazine's top 100 Fast Start-up companies for 2008, which has got people talking in the business world, and made quite a few people sit up a take notice. In July 2008 we heard that we are finalists in the Telstra business awards – the business has really turned around in the last twelve months, financial year 0708 we turned over more than $1million in sales… ☺

I realised in January this year that my strengths lie in strategy and planning, rather than the more routine day-to-day tasks, so I hired people to help me. It was the best decision I've made yet. I have had time this year to work as a casual tutor and lecturer at a university in Sydney – just for a month – as well as to speak at other events and finish my book. I also hired a personal assistant part-time in March to help me manage not only my work life, but also my home life.

My MBA is still on hold. I am unsure as to whether I will take it up again. At the moment, there are lots of other exciting projects I want to do. I still attend a lot of networking events and read business books, I will see how I feel towards the end of this year.

GrowCo is still quite slow to take off, but I am pushing it along. I think that the decision I made to launch it back in September 2007 was a very emotional one, and had I not been so emotional I would have looked into it more rather than just going ahead at that time. In some ways I feel I should have launched GrowCo later, partly because of the expense; however, I have learnt a lot about myself, and how I would do it differently next time. I just wish that my learning experiences weren't quite so expensive! I still believe that GrowCo can be a huge global success, it just needs time.

My life is hectic and I love it; I have learnt so much from launching my Mocks business, and I would definitely do it all again!

My personal life after the break-up of my marriage is now getting back on track. Mr Johns and I are friends and see each other socially. We agreed that I would keep my business while he kept the house; it ended fairly. I am now back on the dating circuit, going speed dating and to singles parties - generally enjoying meeting lots of new people.

My plans for the future are very full, I feel that I am kind of out of a job in the Australian business, since Simone has practically got it covered, so I am free to concentrate on the USA market and beyond. Plus I am sure that I have a few more books in me ... I have an idea for a TV show, a new website business and I have speaking engagements lined up in October in New Zealand.

I hope that you enjoyed reading my story, it has been a busy four years, with more to come I am sure. Writing this book has been a challenge in itself, a huge learning experience and has been a good way to reflect on what happened – hindsight is an amazing thing, I just wish it came earlier, ie before I make the decision!

If you have a question please email me at Lara@Larasolomon.com or check out the website LaRoo.com.au. Don't forget to turn to the last page where I've put a special voucher so that you can go to our website and buy a Mock for $1.

Some Useful resources
www.surveymonkey.com Online market research surveys
www.alibaba.com Sourcing website
www.globalsourcing.com Sourcing website
www.ozforex.com.au Foreign exchange website
www.gs1au.org Barcodes
www.business.gov.au General website on all aspects of running a
business, including networking events
www.reachout.com.au Youth charity that Mocks donated to
www.ofw.fahcsia.gov.au Office for Women, government site which
has information on a range of events, training, mentoring and other
information
www.smallbiz.nsw.gov.au Good resource for events and general
business information, plus they organise small business month in
September each year with fantastic free events
www.seek.com.au Recruitment website
www.careermums.com.au Recruitment website for mums looking
for work
www.ncbf.org.au National Breast Cancer Foundation that Mocks
donated to
www.austrade.com.au Australian Government export assistance
www.myspace.com social networking site
www.facebook.com social networking site
www.secondlife.com gaming site
Book: The E-myth by Michael Gerber

Networking Groups
www.abn.org.au Australian Business Women's Network
www.amcham.com.au American Chamber of Commerce
www.businesschicks.com.au Business Chicks
www.lastthursdayclub.com.au Last Thursday Club
www.inspirewomen.com.au Inspiring Women
www.womensnetwork.com.au Women's Network Australia
www.connectmarketing.com.au Runs seminars and breakfast
networking events

<u>Order Form</u>

<u>Order Details</u>

I would like to order ………… copies of *Brand New Day*
by Lara Solomon, at AU $24.95 each.

<u>Payment Details</u>

Name on Credit Card:	……………………………………………………..
Credit Card Type: (Visa/Mastercard)	……………………………………………………
Credit Card Number:	
Credit Card Expiry:	…………/…………
Postage Cost:	AU $6.65 within Australia AU $18.00 Worldwide
For the total amount of:	……… x AU $24.95 per book = $………….. Australian or World postage = $………….. Grand Total to be charged = $…………..

<u>Delivery Details</u>

Name:	
Postal Address:	
State/Postcode:	
Country:	
Telephone:	

<u>SPECIAL MOCK OFFER – Buy a MOCK for AU $1.00!!!!</u>

Go to the website www.mockstore.com to purchase a Mock of your choice for ONLY AU $1.00, but hurry, offer is for a limited time only (expires 30 June 2009).

Enter code to redeem special offer: BNDBOOK

To order please email: book@larasolomon.com.au
or send this page to PO Box 61, Brookvale NSW 2100 Australia.